CONTEMPORARY GROUP WORK

CHARLES D. GARVIN

The University of Michigan

PRENTICE-HALL, INC., Englewood Cliffs, New Jersey 07632

Library of Congress Cataloging in Publication Data

Garvin, Charles D
   Contemporary group work.

   Includes index.
   1. Social group work.   I. Title.
HV45.G37   361.4   80-22347
ISBN 0-13-170233-5

Printed in the United States of America

10 9 8 7 6 5 4 3 2 1

PRENTICE-HALL INTERNATIONAL, INC., *London*
PRENTICE-HALL OF AUSTRALIA PTY. LIMITED, *Sydney*
PRENTICE-HALL OF CANADA, LTD., *Toronto*
PRENTICE-HALL OF INDIA PRIVATE LIMITED, *New Delhi*
PRENTICE-HALL OF JAPAN, INC., *Tokyo*
PRENTICE-HALL OF SOUTHEAST ASIA PTE. LTD., *Singapore*
WHITEHALL BOOKS LIMITED, *Wellington, New Zealand*

DEDICATED TO

Janet, David, Amy, and Tony
and to the memory of Janet's mother,
Carlyn Manasses Tuft,
who provided so much encouragement
for this project.

CONTENTS

PREFACE

THIS BOOK is intended as an introductory text on group work in social welfare settings. As such its purpose is to help the reader to understand how to select members for groups, facilitate the development of groups through beginning, middle, and ending phases, and evaluate with the members the impact of the group experience. Groups are used for many different reasons in such settings and no one book can convey the range of approaches required for all of these. We, therefore, focus our attention on groups established primarily to enhance the individual functioning of members. However, a broad, rather than a narrow, conception of enhancing functioning is intended, so as not to preclude this book's application to work with a variety of groups. Thus interest groups, committess, educational groups, and representative groups can all have this as a major thrust. We have, consequently, included content that is applicable to all of these situation.

   The selection of content for this book has also been guided by several of the author's convictions. First, the actions of the group worker should be to help the group and its members attain mutually agreed on goals. The first major task of the worker and the members is to determine such goals and then to guide subsequent events by these goals or to revise them accordingly. This premise leads to the second proposition that movement toward goals should be monitored and that the worker and the group should acquire the means to do this. Third, the worker's actions should be based on an understanding of research and theory from the social sciences, and throughout this book we have included content on monitoring changes and on relevant social science material. Fourth, we believe that social workers with groups should use any effective means that are consistent with social work values and purposes. We, therefore, have incorporated many ideas from other disciplines and professions.

   An important approach taken in this book is that learning requires an experiential element that includes carefully structured observations. To assist with this, many chapters conclude with a structured exercise or an observational guide. Throughout the book, we present many practice illustrations; the chapters in Part Three devoted to applications of group methods in groups formed for different purposes, in addition, each contain detailed practice examples.

While extensive discussions of concepts are presented later, it should be noted that the author utilizes many systemic notions. Thus the idea of the worker as a mediator among members, between members, and the group-as-a-whole, and between the group and external institutions is a view that is maintained throughout the book. Also relevant is a group dynamics approach that views group changes in terms of interactions of forces within as well as outside of the group. Finally, we hold a sociobehavioral view that individual behavior is a consequence of social forces and interactions. Cognitive factors are not overlooked, however, as the author is committed to an approach in which group members determine their own destinies through being helped to an awareness of group forces as they affect individual behavior.

The organizing principles of the book are twofold: first, a group developmental approach is taken that views worker and member tasks as occurring differently at each stage of group development. Second, a "functional" approach is taken that sees group development as affected by group purposes and agency functions. For this reason, a typology of such purposes is presented early in the book and forms the major basis for the final chapters.

The book is divided into three parts: Part One is devoted to background material that will help the reader to understand the historical as well as current forces out of which contemporary approaches to group work emerged. Part Two presents the group phenomena that occur at different phases of the development of the group and the tasks of workers and members in these phases. These include actions prior to the first group meeting, during the "formation" period, the subsequent sessions when members and workers act to attain member goals, and the termination of the group. The chapters on the worker's actions are divided into those devoted to changing group, individual, and environmental situations. In a separate chapter ways of evaluating these efforts are presented.

Part Three presents the ways group services differ when purposes differ. The chapters in this part utilize the frameworks developed earlier in the book as a way of presenting variations in group development as related to group purpose.

In the Epilogue the future of group services in social work is forecast.

ACKNOWLEDGMENTS

Throughout my years as a practicing group worker, supervisor of this practice, and trainer of social work students, the ideas of a number of people have been of great benefit to me. First, I wish to acknowledge the debt I owe to my first supervisors of group work practice, Edna Hansen and Rose Cohn; second, to such writers as Robert Vinter and William Schwartz, who on many occasions encouraged and supported my development and who will undoubtedly find places where they will see that I benefitted as well as strayed from their quite contrasting inputs.

Next, I owe much to my colleagues at the University of Michigan and particularly to such fellow group work teachers as Harvey Bertcher, Sallie Churchill, Charles Wolfson, and Frank Maple. A special word of appreciation should be expressed to Paul Glasser with whom I collaborated on so many group work publications that it is hard for me to tell which of the ideas in this book were mine and which were his. Of great importance to this work is its typology of group purpose, developed jointly with Dean Glasser.

I wish to thank Dean Philip Fellin of the School of Social Work, University of Michigan, for all the facilities of the school that were available to me to complete this work. Cheryl Dunny and Pauline Bush gave invaluable assistance in preparation of the manuscript. The latter in her capacity as my secretary was also a source of much additional support. Finally, all of the ideas here have been expressed, critiqued, and often changed in interaction with social work students. They and their experiences have been the major stimuli for everything I have written.

PART ONE
The Background of Group Services

INTRODUCTION

SOCIAL GROUP WORK is a social work method aimed at helping individuals to enhance their functioning as social beings through face-to-face interactions in small groups. Members of social work groups seek either to change their own behavior, the behavior of other people, or both. The social worker in the group facilitates the way members pursue these goals by interacting with individuals in the context of the group, with the whole group, and with people outside of the group on behalf of the group and its members.

Social group work uses the group approach to accomplish the goals common to all social work activities: (1) to prevent members from developing dysfunctional ways of coping with their situations; (2) to enhance members' engagement in and creative use of artistic, social, intellectual, and other endeavors; and (3) to rehabilitate members who have developed handicaps in their social and personal functioning.

As shall be detailed in Chapter 2, group work services were originally conducted in a variety of settings, such as schools, settlement houses, and community service institutions, by staff members. Eventually these people recognized their common commitment to group development and sought to create a professional identity. Because many of them were affiliated with the profession of social work the phrase SOCIAL GROUP WORK, rather than simply GROUP WORK, was used to designate this activity as a social work method. In this book, we shall use the shorter expression, GROUP WORK, because it is concise and because it encompasses the full range of work with groups within the framework of social work.

Originally group workers in social work were distinguished from caseworkers in that the latter worked almost exclusively with individuals. Also, the agencies in which each worked were different in that the group workers functioned primarily in such community institutions as settlement houses while caseworkers functioned in hospitals, family agencies, children's institutions, and other welfare organizations. In the 1950's however, changes occurred in the way in which group workers and caseworkers were utilized, with group workers moving into the full range of social work institutions while many caseworkers started to work with groups. This trend is now paralleled in social work education as many schools that had formerly separated tracks for casework and group work now combine these with family work into programs such as clinical practice, direct practice, interpersonal practice, and social treatment. In light of these changes we shall use group worker to mean any social worker serving a group whether or not that person also works with individuals and families. Although we view work with individuals, families, and groups as becoming increasingly integrated, there still remain specialized aspects of the group work method. It is for this reason that we undertake the writing of this book.

Group Work, therefore, is now practiced in all types of social welfare agencies that employ social workers, including child welfare, family service, correctional, medical, mental health, and school settings as well as the more "traditional" settlement houses, community centers, and youth organizations. This book is dedicated to the idea that group services in these environments can be very effective and we shall offer evidence to support this. Thus, we should like to contribute to the ongoing effort to see that group services are distributed in appropriate ways throughout the community and that they are available to those who most need them.

This first part of the book shall elaborate on the history and scope of group work practice so that the reader may better understand the ideas that unify as well as divide practitioners of this social work method. This broad introduction shall also clarify the theoretical foundations of group work and their relationship to the approaches developed by other professions and disciplines. Specifically, in chapter 1 the author's approach to group work and how it relates to that of other writers, both within and outside the field of social work is presented.

Chapter 2 consists of a discussion of the agency settings in which group work is practiced and how the settings affect the group. We have developed a conceptual scheme for describing and analyzing the way agency functions lead to different group work approaches and this is also described in Chapter 2. Finally, that chapter also summarizes the history of group work to help the reader grasp how a practice of such scope and diversity arose.

Chapter 1

CONTEMPORARY GROUP WORK:
An Overview

GROUP WORK, as a social work method, has evolved and changed in the half-century since its origin. These changes are the result of altered social circumstances, increased knowledge, and an expansion in the number and variety of practice settings. Because of this, there is no current consensus on group work practice in social work but, rather, a number of models that compete for the allegiance of group workers.

In this chapter, we shall describe the model used in this book as well as how this approach relates to those of others. The basic principles and procedures shall be given, along with a discussion of similarities and differences among approaches. Thus this chapter should help the reader to prepare for the ideas to be presented and their relationship to those of other group writers.

THE ORGANIZATIONAL AND ENVIRONMENTAL APPROACH

Our practice model was developed from the model generated by Vinter and his colleagues at the University of Michigan.[1] This extension of the ideas of Vinter and others was originally described by Glasser and Garvin, who sought to develop principles to guide effective practice in the broad variety of social welfare agencies that now sponsor group services.[2] Their model, termed "an organizational and environmental approach," incorporates a diversity of practice procedures by declaring that the purpose or purposes for which the group is established determines the way the members will respond to their group experience and the way the worker will work with the group.

[1]Paul H. Glasser, Rosemary Sarri, and Robert Vinter, eds., *Individual Change Through Small Groups* (New York: Free Press, 1974).
[2]Paul H. Glasser and Charles D. Garvin, "An Organizational Model," in *Theories of Social Work with Groups*, eds. Robert W. Roberts and Helen Northen (New York: Columbia University Press, 1976), pp. 75–115.

Clarification of Purpose

The emphasis of the organizational and environmental approach on group purpose takes into consideration that the ultimate fulfillment of the purpose will be as a result of interactions involving the agency, the worker, the members, and even others in the environment. In certain situations, for instance, where the agency recruits members for the group, the agency's view of group purpose will precede the input of these others and thus will affect even the selection of the worker and the members.

To help the worker understand group purposes and to use this understanding in making decisions, we have developed a typology of group purposes. While this shall be discussed fully in the next chapter, we shall describe it briefly here. Our categorization takes into consideration whether the group is meant to enhance the social development of members who have joined the group voluntarily and whose development is viewed as proceeding normally *(socialization groups)* or whether the group is to remedy the social development of members whose previous socialization is viewed, in a sociological sense, as deviant and where group participation is often a consequence of some form of social pressure *(resocialization groups)*. Each of these purposes is subdivided further and this shall also be described in the following chapter.

The categorization of group purpose allows us to offer one resolution of an important concern of group work practice, as well as all of social work: to present appropriate ways of modifying both individual and environmental circumstances in order to attain individual goals. For each of the types of purposes we identify, singly or in combination, there are relevant targets of change related to the individual member, the group, and the larger social environment. Elsewhere, when we criticized the unfortunate tendency to dichotomize the choice of *either* individual or environmental targets, we made the following statements:

> The use of groups is seen either as a means to achieve social goals in a community context or as a method to encourage individual growth and change in an educational or rehabilitative context. It may be argued that this is consistant neither with modern social science theory nor with common sense. A broad view sees the social environment as a source of individual behavior patterns, as influential in maintaining such patterns, and as a useful tool in altering them. On the other hand, the individual—often together with others—can play a significant role in making more constructive use of his environment or change it in ways that will provide greater satisfaction of his or her needs.[3]

Whether the purpose of the group is to facilitate the socialization or resocialization of the member, we view all member goals as related to optimal *social functioning*. This concept refers to the way individuals seek to cope with their social situations by modifying themselves, their environment, or

[3]Paul H. Glasser and Charles D. Garvin, "Social Group Work: The Organizational and Environmental Approach," in *Encyclopedia of Social Work* (New York: National Association of Social Workers, 1977), II, 1338.

both so as to achieve the best fit among individual needs and capacities and environmental oppportunities.

We have found role concepts to be useful in an analysis of social functioning because they describe individual behaviors as responses to social circumstances. Thus the ways wives and husbands function in their marital roles, their children in their child roles, the parents in their work roles, and all family members in their roles in the community (for example, student, church member, or member of friendship groups) are examples of social functioning.

Problems in social functioning occur when a person's roles do not fit their needs and capacities, when they are not satisfied with their enactment of their roles, when the way one person performs his or her role is in conflict with the actions of others, or when others are critical of one's actions in relationship to roles. Problems can also occur when the environment fails to provide resources for role performance or hinders such performance in other ways.

Social work clients may seek to modify their role performances through acting differently, feeling differently, or thinking about their situations in new ways. They may also seek to change their environment so that it affects their role-related activities differently.

Social workers can seek to enhance social functioning on many levels. This can be done through working solely with the individual concerned or with that individual in concert with other family members. People may help each other with problems in social functioning in group situations and that is what this book is about. Individual social functioning can also be enhanced by changes brought about on a community level or by changes in national social policies. Such changes in the environment may be sought by the individual, often with the help of social workers, or may be sought by social workers on behalf of individuals, whether known to them personally or as members of such classes of people as the handicapped or of ethnic minorities.

Group workers have made contributions to alleviating many social functioning problems. For example, groups can provide people with recreational and educational resources, or group members can join with each other to obtain these. Groups can also help people who are "at risk," such as adolescents facing developmental stresses, parents who fear that their stresses may provoke them to mistreat their children, or unemployed people who seek ways to regain employment.

Focus on Goals

Another facet of our approach is its emphasis on individual goal specification and attainment—the goal being enhanced social functioning. A *goal* relates to a group member's condition, situation, or both that the member and the worker agree should be changed through group experience. A goal should be expressed in terms that are so sufficiently concrete that the member will be able to recognize when it has been reached. In order to achieve member goals, the goals regarding group and environmental conditions must also be clearly specified. Later we shall present in detail procedures and examples regarding such goal specifications.

A Mutual Aid System

Even though we see group work as facilitating individual goal attainment, we view the group as a mutual aid system. Many approaches to groups describe the worker as interacting with individuals in the context of the group. While we see this as a necessary activity of group workers from time to time, we join with other group work theorists in placing the major emphasis on how the worker facilitates the members in helping one another to achieve their individual and collective aspirations.

Evaluation of Practice

The goal attainment of the members in this approach to practice is assessed at regular intervals. This is done for several reasons: first, the effectiveness of the group process and the worker's facilitation of this process should be determined so that the individual members, the group, and the worker can, when necessary, change group conditions; second, the member, when goals have been achieved, can either leave the group or select new goals; third, the agency and the worker can gather evidence as to the effectiveness of group services as they have been offered. Throughout this book, therefore, we shall present ways of measuring changes in individual, group, and environmental conditions.

Worker Tasks

The actions the worker takes to help members achieve their goals and to create a group to accomplish this are also specified in this practice model. Since the worker is sometimes required to seek changes in the environment outside the group, this is also detailed. Although other models do not necessarily present worker behaviors in this way, our reason for doing so is that group workers should be able to generate and test propositions about the effects of different kinds of worker actions; effective ways of helping can then be identified and taught to others.

Values

There are three values basic to our practice model. First, our approach to group work shares with all others in social work a commitment to respect the worth of all people; the importance placed on self-determination is derived from this as is the importance placed on the right of individuals to obtain support from society to achieve their maximum potential. In this sense, we define our approach as humanistic while recognizing that the different group workers might define this term differently.

Self-determination requires that we uphold voluntary participation in groups and insist on a "contract" between the worker and members and the worker and the group-as-a-whole specifying goals and member and worker tasks. The worker should negotiate with members and help them to negotiate with each other whenever changes take place in these understandings. A related principle is that workers may intervene in the group in ways that do not benefit all members but must not intervene in ways that can harm any member even if others are benefited.

The second social work value inherent in group work also is the value placed on human life. This means not only the biological preservation of the individual but the nuturance of growth toward maximum utilization of capacities. Thus an alcoholic accelerates the approach of biological death and also psychological impairment, and the latter, in at least a metaphorical sense, is death. Similarly, the adolescent who embarks on a criminal careeer also has chosen a psychological death in terms of killing his or her talents even if the crimes do not lead to a threat to biological existence.

The third value issue addressed by our model arises around priorities for the development and staffing of services. Social work has always had a commitment to serve those who, as a result of being the most exploited, the most needy, or the most vulnerable, are impaired in their social functioning or are likely to become so. Group workers, throughout their history, have worked with the poor, the immigrants, and those in the cities who have grievances related to urban conditions. In a later period of group work history, workers served other oppressed groups such as mental patients, children in conflict with their schools, and prisoners.

Some writers argue that it is not the obligation or prerogative of the profession or its educational institutions to influence practitioner's choice of settings. We do not agree with this position. For example, health care institutions are often enjoined to provide medical care to people deprived of such service and lawyers are increasingly expected to advocate for persons treated unjustly by the criminal justice system. As much, if not more, than these professions, social work has a mandate to serve socially oppressed persons.

The greatest problem for the practitioner seeking to function ethically is that following some of the values mentioned can conflict with others. In later chapters we shall discuss the resolution of this issue.

DIFFERING APPROACHES TO PRACTICE

In the following discussion our model shall be related to other contemporary approaches to group work, in an effort to place it in both historical and contemporary contexts. One of the earliest comparisons of these approaches was that of William Schwartz, who identified three models.

> There was a kind of "medical" model in which "the steps of the helping process are described by assuming a sequence of movements through which the worker investigates, diagnoses, and treats the problem under consideration." There was a "scientific" model "in which the steps in the helping process resemble closely the problem solving sequence by which the scientific worker moves from the unknown to the known." And there was a "model of the organic system in which the total helping situation is viewed as a network of reciprocal activity, and in which it is impossible to describe accurately any part of the system without describing its active relationship to the other moving parts."[4]

A year later, Vinter also described three orientations to group work that he believed succeeded each other historically. The first emphasized "democratic decentralization," the second "socialization," and the third, "rehabilitation."[5]

A paper that stood as a definition of group work models for at least a decade and is still influential today was prepared by Papell and Rothman for the 1966 meeting of the Council on Social Work Education.[6] In their presentation the "social goals," "remedial," and "reciprocal" models were identified.

The social goals approach, perhaps the oldest, is clearly the outcome of the democratic decentralization orientation referred to by Vinter. This model, because of its relationship to a view of social work as a "cause" and because of its relevance to contemporary struggles for human rights, continues to influence all of social work practice as well as its group work component.

The remedial model emerged during the movement of group work into rehabilitation settings. It focused on treatment goals for individuals, with the group viewed as a means and context to attain such goals. This model is the one out of which our approach emerged.

The reciprocal model approach sought to identify and enhance the processes whereby individuals, groups, and larger social systems engaged each other to undertake activities of mutual benefit. The worker, therefore, was described as a "mediator," involved, for example, in the ways a group member seeks to use the group, the demands the group places on the members to ensure its own survival, the pressures the group places on the agency, and the agency requirements that are transmitted to the group and its members.

The assumption that group work practice included three models was influential for a number of years; the editors of two consecutive editions of the *Encyclopedia of Social Work* in 1971 and 1977 commissioned three articles to

[4]William Schwartz, "Social Group Work: The Interactionist Approach," in *Encyclopedia of Social Work*, (New York: National Association of Social Workers, 1971), II, 1255.

[5]Robert D. Vinter, "Social Group Work," in *Encyclopedia of Social Work* (New York: National Association of Social Workers, 1965), pp. 715–24.

[6]Catherine P. Papell and Beulah Rothman, "Social Group Work Models: Possession and Heritage," *Journal of Education for Social Work* 2, no. 2 (Fall 1966), 66–77.

present the state of group work theory: one by William Schwartz, the exponent of the reciprocal model, one by Garvin and Glasser, who wrote in the tradition of Vinter's remedial model, and the third, "The Developmental Approach" by Emanuel Tropp, which although not identified by its author as the "social goals" model, was described as "starting with a strong emphasis on the common group goal and the democratic process of group involvement."[7]

The most recent effort to codify models of group work was the publication of *Theories of Social Work with Groups.* This volume was planned as a companion to *Theories of Social Casework*[8] and was executed with the expectation that the explication of "single systems theoretical models" (that is, casework, group work, family treatment) "will serve as the major building blocks of multi-system integrated practice theories."[9]

It was quite clear to Roberts and Northen, who edited the group work volume, that the papers included did not represent distinct approaches to group work although some authors' values or other foundations of their theories contrasted sharply. In a final review chapter, Roberts and Northen compared the articles on such dimensions as behavioral science foundations, target populations, criteria for group member selection, and worker activity. They found that authors who had a similar position on one of these dimensions often had different postures on another. Clearly, while the authors may claim, with some justification, to have internally consistent models, all seek to achieve this by assembling a basic set of practice elements in different ways.

Therefore, we would like to encourage the reader to choose appropriate strategies for group composition or group formation from among various alternatives. It is premature to assemble all group work ideas into a master plan in which the group circumstances and the array of group work approaches can be totally accommodated, although some have tried.[10] In this book, therefore, while we do favor one model, we shall often identify alternative approaches. Whatever else may be argued, all groups have beginnings, middles, and endings, even though different ideas exist as to how to approach these events.

[7]Emanuel Tropp, "Social Group Work: The Developmental Approach," in *Encyclopedia of Social Work* (New York: National Association of Social Workers, 1977), II, 1322.

[8]Robert W. Roberts and Robert Nee, eds., *Theories of Social Casework* (New York: Columbia University Press, 1970).

[9]Robert W. Roberts and Helen Northen, eds., *Theories of Social Work with Groups* (New York: Columbia University Press, 1976), p. xi. The volume includes the work of the same authors from the *Encyclopedia of Social Work* (Tropp, Schwartz, Garvin, and Glasser) and, in addition, proponents of still other group work practice theories. Some wrote group work texts (Northern, Hartford); one is a proponent of the "functional" (Rankian) approach; several were individuals associated with casework models with group work applications (McBroom on socialization groups, Parad and colleagues on crisis intervention in groups, and Garvin, Reid, and Epstein on task-centered groups). A chapter by Gertrude Wilson on group work history and by Mary Louise Somers on approaches to problem solving in groups completed the volume.

[10]See, for example, Norma Lang, "A Broad Range Model of Practice with the Social Work Group," *Social Service Review* 46 (1972), 76–89.

INFLUENCES BEYOND SOCIAL WORK

Criteria for Use

Group activities for personal growth are proliferating and include many elements not included in the social work models we have just described. Group workers in social work, as well as their counterparts in psychiatry, psychology, nursing, and education do not live in a vacuum. Professionals read each other's works and borrow ideas across institutional boundaries. When new ideas such as gestalt therapy or transactional analysis are promoted, practitioners from all disciplines hear of them through books and workshops and seek to utilize what they have learned. Clearly, then, no set of techniques fully distinguishes any profession's work with groups, and goals and methods overlap.

The social worker with groups will, therefore, utilize techniques from many sources if they are (1) compatible with social work values; (2) helpful to those who are customarily served by social workers; (3) appropriate to the institutions that employ social workers; and (4) encompassable in the educational program prescribed for social work. Those techniques that are easily integrated into the practitioner's preferred model will be the most utilized.

Needs of Social Work Clients. Any discussion of the use of non-social work approaches must begin with a reiteration of the idea that social work focuses on individual-environmental transactions. Thus, social work approaches should be concerned with enhancing not only the behavior of individuals but enhancing the way environments meet their needs as well. In a sense this is inevitable in group work since the group has been widely viewed as a social microcosm that can reflect many of the forces the individual copes with in other situations. The group is one aspect of the member's environment. It is possible, of course, to use groups so that the social component is minimized. Group workers sometimes use the phrase "case work in the group" to describe groups that primarily focus on worker–member communications rather than communications among the members. Approaches from outside of social work that operate in a similar way are inappropriate to group work in social work because of its concern for social functioning.

Requirements of Social Work Agencies. An even more difficult issue is to determine approaches that are appropriate to the institutions that employ social workers. The following organizational variables have implications for this:

1. Social work agencies often have limited budgets. Approaches that require training that is well beyond that usually received by social workers, expensive equipment, several workers working simultaneously, or consultants who normally demand very high fees may be unfeasible.

2. Social work organizations should operate with an emphasis on voluntary participation, on personal freedom, and on noninfliction of pain. Some approaches are of limited applicability in such agencies because of their use of compulsion or of aversive measures. Even the strong confrontation style sometimes used in correctional and drug programs may be unacceptable to many social work agencies.

3. Social workers may have less power over their organizational environments than members of other professions. Approaches that require control over broad aspects of that environment may also not be feasible for group workers.

4. Some approaches require more training in order for the worker to acquire even minimally acceptable competence than can be encompassed in a social work curriculum. Some social workers, after receiving their degree, may secure such training. The purpose of this text, however, is to portray ways of working that can be taught to social workers in the normal course of a professional program. Thus, for example, the full scope of gestalt therapy, transactional analysis, or analytic group psychotherapy cannot be offered in a social work program. Nevertheless, there are techniques and concepts, drawn from these treatment systems, that can be so incorporated.

The following discussion describes some of the major approaches to work with groups developed outside of social work. In presenting each approach, we shall note those aspects that can be integrated into social work practice and taught in a social work curriculum. We shall focus on eleven approaches, grouped into four clusters, that we believe incorporate most of the major contemporary trends in work with groups for personal growth and change. Some of this material shall be elaborated on in later chapters when we discuss practice issues. We omit some ideas (for example, rational emotive therapy and reality therapy) which, while they may have group applications, are not conceived of primarily as ways of working with groups.[11]

Approaches Utilizing or Originating from Psychoanalysis

Gestalt Therapy. The framework of gestalt therapy owes its origin and much of its development to Fritz Perls.[12] Its theoretical foundation draws from gestalt psychology, particularly the idea that perception is organized around attention to some aspect of a total situation (figure) with the balance (the ground) forming a context. A particularly important concept for the gestalt therapist, then, is *awareness* inasmuch as one's needs and feelings may often be blocked and remain as *ground* and, thus, out of awareness. These

[11]For a thorough discussion of many of the approaches commented on here see, John B.P. Shaffer and David Galinsky, *Models of Group Therapy and Sensitivity Training* (Englewood Cliffs, N.J.: Prentice-Hall, Inc., 1974).

[12]Fritz Perls, R. F. Hefferline, and Paul Goodman, *Gestalt Therapy* (New York: Julian Press, 1951).

concepts are also closely related to the notion that the individual may deny aspects of his or her own desires, potentialities, or experiences that might be drawn upon to enhance one's life.

Techniques developed by Perls and his colleagues to increase awareness and subsequent integration of rejected aspects of one's self include drawing a person's attention to body positions and movements and role playing components of his or her own body, dreams, fantasies, or attitudes. The individual may then actually hold a "dialogue" among these aspects, while "occupying" what is referred to as the "hot seat." The workers in a gestalt group may also use "exercises" to help members increase self-awareness.

Perls involved group members to a very limited degree with each other as the person in the "hot seat" worked primarily with the therapist. Many contemporary gestalt therapists, however, use awareness exercises in which group members interact with each other; they may also encourage the group to discuss with the individual issues raised while in the "hot seat."

Whether or not group workers fully understand gestalt therapy, they can use gestalt exercises to promote awareness. For example, exercises can be used at the beginning and ending of the group so that feelings about these phases can be elicited. Group workers can also use these techniques to help members to "own" beliefs and feelings such as anger or rejection, which they project onto others. Ambivalence, also, is a very frequent problem that inhibits decision making, and gestalt approaches such as double chairing are useful in exploring issues around alternative choices facing members.

Group workers have studied nonverbal activities in groups. These are drawn upon to enhance relationships, encourage expressiveness, and build skills. The gestalt concepts regarding awareness may help group workers to add another dimension to their understanding and use of program experiences.

Transactional Analysis. Eric Berne, the founder of transactional analysis, like Fritz Perls, was originally trained and experienced in psychoanalytic therapy.[13] His system is based on an analysis of how transactions among people are affected by their "ego states," which are defined by Berne "as a set of coherent behavior patterns; or pragmatically, as a system of feelings which motivates a related set of behavior patterns." Most readers are probably familiar with the ego states that Berne has labeled as the *child, parent,* and *adult.* Through Berne's writings and those of many of his followers, the indicators of these ego states and many subtypes of each ego state have been identified. These concepts are used in the transactional analysis therapy situation to analyze transactions of the individual with others.

Such transactions are also found in longer interactions, and Berne

---

[13]For Berne's own explication of his system, see Eric Berne, *Transactional Analysis in Psychotherapy* (New York: Grove Press, 1961).

developed ways of conceptualizing these. One particular technique used sequences that substitute for "intimacy" called *games*. Long-lasting interactional patterns in life are labeled *scripts* and means have evolved for identifying these. The intent of this conceptual framework is to help people to examine transactions so that both immediate interactions as well as life-long patterns may be consciously modified.

In the group therapy situation, members are trained in the analysis of ego states, games, and scripts. Subsequently, with the help of the therapist and each other, they apply this analysis to behavior in the group as well as to the environment outside of the group.[14]

Within the social work group, it is often essential to examine the transactions between the worker and the members or among members. There are many approaches to this ranging from those that simply call attention to what is taking place to those that utilize a generalized set of concepts as in transactional analysis. Without any research on how effective one approach is compared to another, the worker will have to draw upon what seems most appropriate to the population represented. Therefore, some workers will use transactional analysis concepts, when appropriate.

Psychoanalytic Group Therapy. With the exception of some early experiments with tubercular patients and World War I veterans, group psychotherapy was developed within a psychoanalytic framework. The early group psychotherapists adopted many approaches to group therapy that were drawn from individual psychoanalysis, including free association and the analysis of transference. One group of writers, namely Foulkes, Ezriel, Whitaker, and Lieberman sought to understand how affects and drives were related to group forces.[15] The following are some of the propositions from these analytically oriented theories:

1. Members of groups will identify common ideational and emotional reactions among themselves and direct their discussion to these. These often relate to individual drives and psychological states.

2. Reactions to therapists include both realistic elements as well as distortions determined by members' past experiences.

3. Conflicts occur between a desire to fulfill individual needs and a fear of the consequences of striving to meet these needs, and these are often shared by members. The concensus reached as to the resolution of such conflicts may be compatible with the goals of therapy or may be a hindrance on both group and individual levels.

---

[14]*Ibid.*, pp. 165–187.

[15]H. Ezriel, "Psychoanalytic Group Therapy," in *Group Therapy*, L.R. Wolberg and E.K. Schwartz (New York: Intercontinental Medical Book Corporation, 1973); S.H. Foulkes, *Therapeutic Group Analysis* (New York: International Universities Press, 1965); and Dorothy Stocok Whitaker and Morton A. Lieberman, *Psychotherapy Through the Group Process* (New York: Lieber-Atherton, Inc., 1965).

The role of the therapist is to stimulate examination of these issues and to make the kinds of interpretations that will bring about conflict resolution through reality oriented therapist–member interactions. Common psychological themes can be dealt with and resolved in ways that can help members with their individual difficulties.

The application of these concepts is dependent on the therapist's understanding of psychoanalytic theory and how it illuminates group phenomona. Group workers have not had such training in depth but are usually taught basic information on human development, often from a psychoanalytic (usually ego psychological) perspective.

Group work clients are also not prone to the long-term verbally and psychologically oriented activities that group analytic approaches require. Nevertheless, an understanding that members may distort the reality of the worker and each other and that such distortions may hinder group and individual problem solving is important to effective work with groups. The ability of the worker to identify group themes and to analyze the meaning of these in terms of affects and drives is also useful in order to "make sense" out of the many pieces of information provided by group members. Workers should have a point of view with regard to member's personality manifestations and the meaning of their behavior, and psychoanalytic and ego psychological theory certainly provides one such system.

The Tavistock Approach. When we refer here to the *Tavistock approach,* we primarily have in mind the work of Wilfred Bion.[16] Bion was psychoanalytically trained and subsequently became impressed with group phenomona. One of Bion's major ideas was that groups often avoid "work" by operating according to "basic assumptions." A major reason for responding to a basic assumption is a reaction to the authority of the leader. Basic assumptions include dependence on the leader, fight–flight responses, and pairing among members. Typically, in a Tavistock group, the leader, who is analogous to the psychoanalyst with individuals, remains relatively inactive so that the basic assumptions, as they emerge, do so presumably out of the members' needs rather than worker reality.

This model may be useful for people seeking to understand these emotional processes in groups. The short-term, more focused nature of social work groups militates against this as a central framework. Nevertheless, in order to work toward their goals, all groups must be helped to free themselves from emotional reactions that are hindering, especially those toward leadership. The leader who has participated in a Tavistock-type experience will be particularly sensitive to this issue and will be able to impart this understanding to group members.

---

[16]W.R. Bion, *Experiences in Groups* (New York: Basic Books, 1959).

Approaches Utilizing or Originating from Social Psychological Theories

Guided Group Interactions. The guided group interaction approach has been utilized primarily with delinquent adolescents in institutional settings.[17] One of the earliest studies of the guided group interactions concept, published in 1958, reported on its use in a New Jersey insitution, Highfields.[18] There is also another related approach that has been called *positive peer culture.*[19]

Guided group interaction was designed by sociologists who believed that delinquent behavior was determined in the main by peer group rather than psychological processes. Efforts to encourage change must, therefore, be directed at these social processes. Interventions in the guided group approach require frequent, usually daily, interactions among group members who are also aware of each other's extra-group behavior, usually within an institutional program.

The group is given considerable salience for the youth in that major decisions regarding current privileges and future plans are evaluated there. These decisions are based on whether members have identified and worked on *problems.* A terminology for such problems is either developed by the group or, as in positive peer culture, taught to it. This "language" describes problems in direct, often colloquial, ways.

A major norm that is developed in the group is one of *candor* (as opposed to *conning*). Staff members motivate the group to develop such norms by creating initial ambiguity regarding the group, by confronting the group, and by fostering the dependency of members on the group. As one text on guided group interaction states, a program based on sociological theory will have to concentrate on "changing reference group and normative orientations; utilizing ambivalent feelings resulting from the conflict of conventional and delinquent standards; and providing opportunities for recognition and achievement in conventional pursuits."[20]

In some ways, these ideas can be drawn upon by group workers; in others, they are problematic. Those that are most usable relate to how the group shapes norms and how workers can mold this process, since group workers *do* work with people branded by society as deviant and placed in institutions on an involuntary basis. On the other hand, the manipulative style and the type of confrontation that is encouraged pose value dilemmas to social workers. Currently, social workers involved in using these techniques are evaluating them in an effort to resolve such issues.

---

[17]LaMar T. Empey and Maynard L. Erickson, *The Provo Experiment: Evaluating Community Control of Delinquency* (Lexington, Mass.: Heath, 1972).

[18]Lloyd W. McCorkle, Albert Elias, and F. Lovell Bixby, *The Highfields Story* (New York: Holt, Rinehart & Winston, 1958).

[19]Harry Vorrath and Larry Brendtro, *Positive Peer Culture* (Chicago: Aldine Publishing Co., 1974).

[20]Empey and Erickson, *The Provo Experiment,* p. 7.

Self-help Groups. A recent study of self-help groups estimated a membership of several million in the United States with the number of different organizations as large as 216.[21] The actual number of such groups is much larger if all the local affiliates of such organizations as Alcoholics Anonymous, Weight Watchers, and Parents Anonymous are considered. The range of concerns addressed by such groups is vast and includes addictions (Synanon, Alcoholics Anonymous), aggressive behavior (Parents Anonymous), mental illness (Recovery, Inc.), disability (Emphysema Anonymous), loss of children (Compassionate Friends), loss of spouse (Parents without Partners), gamblers (Gamblers Anonymous), weight control (Weight Watchers), and sexual orientation (Gay Liberation Front).

This type of group activity is classified as a sociological approach for several reasons. The emphasis of the groups is on interpersonal support rather than psychological uncovering; a major component of what such groups have to offer is successful role models; these groups also often have social action goals, such as securing better services or overcoming the stigma directed at group members. The use of these groups is also a social phenomenon as members are likely to have been rejected by mental health professionals and are often viewed as deviant.

Among the groups, although vast differences in programs exist, several similarities are found; these include procedures to give support to members between sessions, an opportunity to tell one's full "story" in an accepting atmosphere, an occasion to enhance one's self-esteem by helping others, and the availability of successful role models. The groups are also, with a few exceptions such as Parent's Anonymous, without professional leadership and, in fact, are often suspicious of it. While supportive, many of the groups also, at times, are quite direct and confronting in their style; it is presumed that those who take this stance have earned this right by having shared similar problems and overcome them.

The importance of the approaches to group work used in self-help groups is severalfold. These groups remind us of the great value of peer helping and this challenges professional self-importance. Even in professionally led groups, the techniques of peer support, as well as confrontation, can be cultivated to a greater degree than is usually done. There is value in non-professionally led groups, in their own right, because of the sense of competence that they nurture. The task of the group worker is to support and offer consultation to such groups without taking them over.

Psychodrama. The psychodrama approach has been associated largely with the work of one man—J.L.Moreno.[22] Many of the techniques now in use, particularly gestalt and encounter sessions, were anticipated or even

[21]Morton A. Lieberman, "Group Methods," in *Helping People Change,* eds. Frederick H. Kanfer and Arnold P. Goldstein (Elmsford, N.Y.: Pergamon Press, 1975), p. 440.
[22]J.L. Moreno, *Psychodrama* (Beacon, N.Y.: Beacon House, Inc., 1964), I.

stimulated by Moreno's work. We classify this approach as social psychological because of Moreno's stress on the "public" aspects of one's activities rather than the psychological components.

The methods of psychodrama include casting the individual into a problematic role and other individuals present into related roles and then enacting actual and potential scenes. Out of this, insights are elicited, emotional catharsis is secured, and other group members benefit through discussion as well as vicariously.

Moreno also developed another concept, sociodrama, where the focus is on social factors such as intercultural conflicts. In fact, Moreno was interested in applying his techniques to the resolution of issues raised by the civil rights movement.

Dramatic devices have always had a place in group work; nevertheless, the type of emotional expression and confrontation brought about in psychodrama is not usually elicited by social work practitioners. However, the emergence of gestalt and encounter techniques has probably made us less apprehensive about such events although lack of proof of their effectiveness may sometimes create skepticism.[23] Because of this effectiveness issue, group workers should return to the study of the carefully specified and illustrated techniques developed by Moreno and his successors.

Approaches Developed from Educational–Psychological Frameworks

Behavior Modification in Groups. One of the greatest impacts on the human service field today comes from the contemporary behaviorists. Drawing from the laboratory work of many people, particularly experimental psychologists, a vast array of behavioral procedures has emerged for treatment of the same problematic conditions at which other approaches are directed. It is not surprising, therefore, that behavioral therapists, like other practitioners, saw the potential of group contexts for behavioral treatment.

Behavioral therapy in groups shares several features with individual behavioral therapy, including a commitment to precise goal specification and initial (baseline) and subsequent measurement of the behaviors to be modified. These changes in behavior are obtained using interventions planned as applications of the principles of conditioning,[24] such as those having to do with behavior that is a result of antecedent or consequent events (operant conditioning) or as a conditioned response (respondent conditioning). The precise procedures to be used are selected after an analysis to determine the controlling conditions for the relevant behaviors.

Group settings offer a number of additional possibilities for the ap-

[23]For research on the effects of these groups, see M.A. Lieberman, I. Yalom, and M. Miles, *Encounter Groups: First Facts* (New York: Basic Books, 1973).

[24]For a discussion of such principles, see F.M. Kanfer and J.S. Phillips, *Learning Foundations of Behavior Therapy* (New York: John Wiley, 1970).

plication of the principles of behavior therapy. Members can help each other to assess behaviors and can reinforce one another for change. In addition, since many of the behaviors to be modified occur in interpersonal contexts, members can engage in assessment and change activities for behaviors occurring in the group.

The group worker can draw on many behavioral techniques in social work groups, and new behavioral approaches are being developed to facilitate this. Specific procedures, such as assertiveness training, social skill training, and communication training, draw on behavioral concepts and are frequently and appropriately utilized in a variety of social work groups.[25]

Laboratory Training (T-Groups). While behavior modification grew out of an effort to apply psychological principles to therapeutic situations that had first been studied in laboratories, laboratory training evolved serendipitously from observations of "natural" group situations. Specifically, the laboratory training approach developed out of experiences of members of the staff of the Research Center on Group Dynamics at a workshop held in 1946 to help community leaders implement the Fair Employment Practices Act. Evening sessions were held at which interactions that occurred during the day were analyzed. From the participants attending it became apparent that a powerful force for change was unleashed as members examined their behavior in the group and the reactions of others to it. Initially, the intent of the participants was to mold an effective social action device but soon the major emphasis was placed on individual learning.[26]

Laboratory training typically took place at a two-week residential experience where the individuals were isolated from their usual activities. In the beginning of the period, few instructions were given and the members struggled with this ambiguity. After such efforts, members were helped to examine the interpersonal behaviors elicited by this situation. The learning thus induced was utilized to develop applications to real-life situations outside the laboratory. Some of the key ideas of the trainers who facilitated this experience were that participants in groups can learn "how to learn" from experience; that this learning is facilitated by a "here and now focus"; and that feedback from members on their reactions to each other's behavior is an essential condition for interpersonal learning. The people associated with the National Training Laboratories have studied and researched these processes and out of this has come a better understanding of group development, composition, leadership, problem solving, and many other group phenomona.[27]

[25]For an extensive discussion of the application of behavior therapy in social work groups, see Sheldon Rose, *Group Therapy: A Behavioral Approach* (Englewood Cliffs, N.J.: Prentice-Hall, Inc., 1977), and Sheldon Rose, *Treating Children in Groups* (San Francisco: Jossey-Bass, 1972).
[26]This discussion of laboratory training draws heavily on Shaffer and Galinsky, *Models of Group Therapy,* pp. 189–210.
[27]K.W. Back, *Beyond Words: The Story of Sensitivity Training and Encounter Movement* (New York: Russell Sage, 1972).

Laboratory training typically took place at a two-week residential experience where the individuals were isolated from their usual activities. In the beginning of the period, few instructions were given and the members struggled with this ambiguity. After such efforts, members were helped to examine the interpersonal behaviors elicited by this situation. The learning thus induced was utilized to develop applications to real-life situations outside the laboratory. Some of the key ideas of the trainers who facilitated this experience were that participants in groups can learn "how to learn" from experience; that this learning is facilitated by a "here and now focus"; and that feedback from members on their reactions to each other's behavior is an essential condition for interpersonal learning. The people associated with the National Training Laboratories have studied and researched these processes and out of this has come a better understanding of group development, composition, leadership, problem solving, and many other group phenomona.[27]

The ideas generated by laboratory training, selectively employed, can enrich all work with groups. Giving and receiving feedback is an important tool when used appropriately, but it can produce a great deal of anxiety if introduced into the wrong group or at the wrong time. Members can also be seduced into avoiding the very real purposes of groups by too extensive a focus on internal processes. Nevertheless, some attention to process is valuable in all groups and essential in therapeutic groups. Group workers involved in training and program development may at times recommend an examination of their group process to staff and professional groups when problems in group functioning occur.

Approaches Developed from Social Movements

Social Change Movements. In discussing some approaches, the designation *social movement* is relevant. By this phrase, we mean an organized set of people dedicated to a social ideal that is often viewed as "radical" by status groups in the society. The term "radical" is justified by the principles embodied in the movement as well as the fact that it is usually directed against specified ills of the society and seeks a society devoid of such problems. In this respect, it is important to reflect on the fact that during the early period of its history, group work had many of the characteristics of a social movement and this was also true of the entire profession of social work.

Other movements have also developed approaches that have relevance to social group work. Black, Chicano, and similar ethnic groups have formed organizations that emphasize themes of group pride and conduct activities consistent with these themes. Social workers often work with groups composed of members of ethnic minorities and these people's problems relate strongly to lack of social support for their identities. A similar phenomenon found among women's movement groups in their approaches to consciousness raising, group support, and confrontation of sexism as ways of meeting members' needs has relevance for groups conducted by social workers. Even political groups committed to specific ideologies provide important normative climates and supports for their members that have parallels in social work situations. The programs of these groups utilize techniques similar to those employed in "grass roots" community organization and group workers should be familiar with these.

The Encounter Movement. So-called encounter groups probably form a continuum from those identified as sensitivity groups. Many encounter groups quite clearly present at least the rudiments of a social movement and have been so characterized by many writers.

The movement aspect of encounter groups, according to Shaffer and Galinsky, is "designed to put the normally alienated individual into closer contact—or encounter with himself, with others, and with the world of nature and pure sensation."[28] The socially critical stance of writers on encounter groups stems from their charge that our society and its institutions alienate individuals from themselves and their bodies. Values, such as spontaneity, honesty in interactions, and the validity of one's own feelings, are offered as a basis for the encounter experience. As with many other aspects of the "counterculture," authority is downgraded, particularly that based on the training and certification of the group leader. Instead, there is an emphasis on what can be gained from the creation of a sense of community.

Workers in encounter groups usually come from sensitivity group, psychoanalytic, and psychotherapeutic backgrounds and are often influenced by writers such as Wilhelm Reich, who stress the relationships between physiological and emotional states. They inevitably draw from individuals who hold social values different from those trained in these psychological approaches.

The techniques used in encounter groups include encouragement of direct emotional expression, physical exercises, physical interaction among participants (for example, hugging, arm wrestling, communication by touch), as well as the use of exercises drawn from approaches such as gestalt. The leader is active in introducing these procedures and is often a participant, thus lessening social distance between the leader and group members.

Some of the techniques used in encounter groups will not be accepted by social work clients who come from working class as opposed to academic and professional backgrounds and who seek help with specific circumstances and behaviors. On the other hand, the lowering of social barriers may be accepted by many clients of social work groups, particularly children and young people. Also, clients who are inhibited in emotional expression can be helped by various nonverbal exercises and clients with bodily tensions can profit from learning ways to relax these. Finally, many clients do seek ways to develop

[28]Shaffer and Galinsky, *Models of Group Therapy,* p.211.

closer ties with others by freeing themselves from various restraints and seeking new life styles.

SIMILARITIES AND DIFFERENCES AMONG APPROACHES

A number of similarities can be found among virtually all group work writers, including the following:

1. *Purposes:* All approaches to group work incorporate the professional purposes of preventing breakdown of social functioning, providing resources to meet human needs, and rehabilitating individuals whose functioning has been impaired. Some writers focus on one or another of these purposes but none deny the legitimacy of social work's responsibility for all of these purposes and the contribution that group work can make to each.

2. *Knowledge and Theory:* All approaches to group work draw from a common source of knowledge from the behavioral sciences. Some lean more heavily upon one kind of knowledge than others but all utilize small group theory as it describes group development, group leadership, group problem solving, and other group conditions. All also, utilize an understanding of individual development and ways of coping, primarily related to participation in small groups. Role concepts abound in the group work literature and are used to describe positions occupied by group members such as leader, expert, or scapegoat. Role concepts are also used to discuss the processes of socialization as affected by group participation.

Group work writers will differ, however, in the degree to which they draw on concepts from behavioral theory, systems theory, or ego psychology. In these, the differences among group workers parallel those among all human service professionals.

3. *Problem Solving:* Although differing somewhat on how the problems confronting groups and their members are to be analyzed, group workers are usually problem focused. As Somers states, "Problem solving characterized the formulations of social group work practice across the spectrum of fifty years."[29] Somers explains this focus, not only in terms of the intellectual history of group work but also because "The social and intellectual history of the United States is replete with examples of the pragmatic philosophy and experimental approach that form the matrix in which problem solving is embedded, and that provide the source of its essence and continuing energy."[30]

4. *Intervention:* Different group work writers describe many similar

---

[29]Mary Lousie Somers, "Problem Solving in Small Groups," in eds. Roberts and Northen, *Theories of Social Work with Groups,* p. 331.
[30]*Ibid.,* p. 333

worker interventions. These actions, which shall be discussed thoroughly in subsequent chapters, include enhancing program activities, eliciting the expression of affect, and supporting honest presentation of one's experiences and beliefs. Workers help members to try out roles in the group in order to rehearse for their performance outside the group and to give suggestions and feedback to one another regarding their behavior *both* within and outside of the group.

A number of ideas have been developed and used more extensively by the adherents of one approach as opposed to another. We shall now summarize some of these.

William Schwartz

William Schwartz, the initiator of what he has called the *interactionist approach,* which draws more strongly than others from systems concepts to portray members, groups, agencies, and other complex environments in interaction with each other and in a constant process of mutual adaptation. The social worker facilitates this process by functioning as a *mediator.*[31]

The interactionist model focuses on the process whereby individuals engage with others to meet mutual needs. An emphasis of this approach is on the quality of the process rather than on the long-term consequences (goals). Schwartz's analysis of process enriches all of group work practice, particularly his portrayal of phases[32] and the tasks of group workers in relationship to such phases.[33]

Robert Vinter

Robert Vinter developed some of the major aspects of what he referred to as a *social treatment* or a *problem oriented* model although others have referred to it as either the *remedial* or *preventive and rehabilitative approach.*[34] As mentioned previously, his approach was a major forerunner for this book. This work is based on the idea that the individual group member is the focus of change and the group is the means and context of such change. Vinter and his colleague's ideas contrast with those of Schwartz in that they place a strong emphasis on establishing individual goals, often long term in nature, that are precise and operational.

This model calls for an empirical base for practice: practice principles

---

[31]William Schwartz, "Between Client and System: The Mediating Function," eds. Roberts and Northen, in *Theories of Social Work with Groups,* p. 178.

[32]*Ibid.,* pp. 186–194.

[33]William Schwartz, "The Social Worker in the Group," in *New Perspectives on Service to Groups* (New York: Columbia University Press, 1961).

[34]For writing on this approach, see Glasser, Sarri, and Vinter, eds., *Individual Change Through Small Groups.*

should be scientifically tested for effectiveness and can and should be employed in the service of goal attainment. Philosophically, therefore, this framework is closer to a positivist rather than an existential stance. The writings of Vinter and related theorists have been of value in the development of group work because of their efforts to specifiy group worker activities and their effects. These have included worker acts (1) at different phases of group development,[35] (2) in relationship to different group processes,[36] (3) for various program approaches,[37] and (4) toward the social environment.[38]

Emanuel Tropp

Emanuel Tropp considers his approach as in the "mainstream" of the development of group work in social work; he regards many other group work writers as "special offshoots."[39] Tropp sees the mainstream as stressing the principle that "group self-direction toward a common goal is the most effective group vehicle for the social growth of its members";[40] the individual is helped to achieve growth through participation in establishing and accomplishing the group's goal or purpose. Because Tropp sees the group as the vehicle of such growth, he describes the worker (or "leader") as helping to establish group goals and to attain them.

In sharp contrast to Vinter's conceptualization, Tropp does not seek to articulate his model with social science and other research findings. He believes that these endeavors have not created and are not likely to create a basis for social work practice. Rather, he finds the empirical evidence for group work in the experiences of its practitioners.

Finally, Tropp does not describe group work as "treatment" and its beneficiaries as "abnormal or pathological." As he states, "All are seen as people who face stressful developmental stages, life situations, challenges, and crises with which they must cope in some way."[41] Thus, Tropp has made major contributions to an understanding of how workers function when their intent is to provide the group context for individual growth experiences.

[35]Rosemary C. Sarri and Maeda Galinsky, "A Conceptual Framework for Group Development," in *Individual Change Through Small Groups,* eds. Glasser, Sarri, and Vinter, pp. 126–48.

[36]Charles D. Garvin, "Group Process: Usage and Uses in Social Work Practice," in *Individual Change Through Small Groups,* Glasser, Sarri, and Vinter, eds. pp. 209–32.

[37]Robert D. Vinter, "Program Activities: An Analysis of their Effects on Participant Behavior," in *Individual Change Through Small Groups,* Glasser, Sarri, and Vinter, eds. pp. 233–43.

[38]Paul Glasser and others, "Group Work Intervention in the Social Environment," in *Individual Change Through Small Groups",* Glasser, Sarri, and Vinter, eds. pp. 292–306.

[39]Emanuel Tropp, "Developmental Theory," in *Theories of Social Work with Groups,* Roberts and Northen, eds. pp.198–99.

[40]Ibid.

[41]Ibid., p. 213.

Alan Klein

Alan Klein, an author whose books on group work span almost three decades (the most recent published in 1972),[42] like Tropp, emphasizes the potential of group experience to help individuals acquire interpersonal skills. Klein, however, refers to his model as a "matching" one in which individual needs are related to environmental opportunities. Klein, as well as Tropp, places strong emphasis on the role of the group in nurturing and encouraging the freedom and autonomy of the group member. In this respect, Klein and Tropp draw on the extensive heritage in group work of analyses of the democractic process in society.

Margaret Hartford

Margaret Hartford has developed concepts that place group work in the context of generic practice,[43] in that the worker "uses the methodological approaches most appropriate for the given situation." She sees common as well as unique elements to all social work with groups and for this reason has developed a typology of the full range of such services. Her classifications include, for example, work focused on individual participants, problem solving or task achievement, the group context, the institution outside the group or the wider society.[44] In this respect, Hartford differs from other writers who might see either only one function for workers wherever they are located (for example, as mediators) or who limit their model to selected functions (for example, prevention and rehabilitation). Hartford describes "stances" for group workers depending on the type of group and the specific circumstances of the group (for example, stage of development). These stances include directing, facilitating, permissive, and flexible postures.

Boston University School of Social Work

The work of Saul Bernstein and other persons associated with the Boston University School of Social Work has also been very influential for current practice.[45] Their impact is due to their identification of key practice issues. Their approaches and solutions are drawn from their extensive experience as well as from theory. Examples of this are their discussions of

---

[42]Alan F. Klein, *Effective Group Work* (New York: Association Press, 1972).

[43]Margaret Hartford, "Group Methods and Generic Practice," in *Theories of Social Work with Groups,* eds. Roberts and Northen, pp. 45–74. Also see her effort to portray knowledge about groups for all social workers, in *Groups in Social Work* (New York: Columbia University Press, 1972).

[44]Margaret Hartford, "Group Methods and Generic Practice," pp. 54–55.

[45]Saul Bernstein, ed., *Explorations in Group Work* (Boston: Boston University School of Social Work, 1965).

worker activities in different stages of group development, in group conflict situations, and in decisions on group purpose.

Helen Northen

Helen Northen has incorporated systems theory into group work in order to provide a theoretical foundation for a *psychosocial* model.[46] She employs concepts regarding individual assessment and goal setting that are also used in the preventive and rehabilitative model. Her model also emphasizes the concept of group development and the ways worker tasks vary in relationship to the group's developmental stages. She presents a comprehensive review of the way changes in group conditions and member behaviors relate to the processes of goal setting, interpersonal relationship development, confrontation, and feedback.

Behavioral Group Work

Roberts and Northen in explaining how they chose the models they included in their book on contemporary group work theory justify excluding behavior modification as a model.[47] It is seen, rather, as a set of procedures initially developed by psychologists and incorporated into many models. This is true; yet the reader's attention should be drawn to the writings of Sheldon Rose and Martin Sundel, and Harry Lawrence,[48] all social workers who have identified themselves with group work as well as with behavior modification. The behavior modification approach, like the preventive and rehabilitative model, focuses on individual behavior change to achieve mutually agreed on goals. Procedures for achieving such changes are usually introduced by the worker and are derived theoretically from conditioning concepts. (These were discussed earlier in this chapter where the influences of behavior therapy were summarized.) Change is carefully monitored and data is used as feedback for modifying the procedures. Rose's work differs from that of many behaviorists, however, in that it incorporates small group theory and describes how group conditions (for example, cohesiveness, leadership, deviance) may be modified so as to enhance individual goal attainment. These writers, as well as many others who use behavior modification in social work with groups, had been closely associated at one time or another in their careers with Vinter, Glasser, and Garvin at the University of Michigan.

[46]A recent statement of her model is Helen Northen, "Psychosocial Practice in Small Groups," in *Theories of Social Work with Groups,* eds. Roberts and Northen, pp. 116–52. An earlier and more extensive presentation of her ideas is found in Helen Northen, *Social Work with Groups* (New York: Columbia University Press, 1969).

[47]Roberts and Northen, eds., *Theories of Social Work with Groups,* p. 373.

[48]See Sheldon Rose, *Group Therapy*; and Harry Lawrence and Martin Sundel, "Behavior Modification in Adult Groups," *Social Work* 17 (1972), 34–43.

SUMMARY

We began this chapter with a presentation of the model of group work utilized in this text. This presentation included an explanation of how this model seeks to be relevant to the many settings in which group work is practiced through the use of a typology of group purposes. Each of these purposes requires adaptations of the model including variations in procedures directed at individual members, the group, and the extra-group environment. Other features of the model that were discussed include the view of the group as a mutual aid system and the requirement that goals and means of achieving them be specified behaviorally and that outcomes be evaluated. The professional values embedded in the model were enumerated.

Subsequent sections of the chapter described other group work models, approaches to group facilitation by non-social workers, and the similarities and differences among group work approaches. In these latter discussions, the criteria for the usefulness of an approach in social work settings were enumerated.

Chapter 2

GROUP WORK ACTIVITIES AND SETTINGS

THE SIGNIFICANCE OF THE AGENCY

MOST GROUP WORK, as well as social work, is practiced under the auspices of a social agency. These agencies have been established either by government or private citizens to meet a variety of social needs such as those related to physical and mental health, to specified populations (children, the aged), to resource deficits (financial assistance), or to the enhancement of the quality of life (education and the use of leisure time).

Some social workers, including group workers, engage in private practice in which the worker directly recruits clients who then pay a fee. Private practice, therefore, tends to serve the more affluent. Because of the emphasis of our model on service to the oppressed, we do not discuss private practice—although many group work principles do apply to it.

The agencies that offer group services include those in the public sector, such as departments of welfare or community mental health, state institutions for the mentally ill, and schools, and those maintained by private boards (often with government assistance), such as many family agencies, child guidance clinics, and community centers. These agencies do not merely promote a group in a neutral way and then disengage from it; they influence the group at all stages of its development from conception to termination. A worker cannot effectively work with a group, therefore, without understanding, utilizing, and sometimes seeking to change agency conditions. Major issues related to this are how to involve the group and how to cope with the fact that the worker is an employee of the agency as well as a professional.

As a consequence, in this book we identify with what Hasenfeld calls "an organization practice model" and not a "clinical practice model."[1] The latter "focuses primarily (and often exclusively) on client-change agent relations and the purposeful use of these relations for change, with minimal at-

---

[1] Yeheskel Hasenfeld, "Organizational Factors in Service to Groups," in *Individual Change Through Small Groups,* eds. Paul H. Glasser, Rosemary Sarri, and Robert Vinter (New York: Free Press, 1974), p. 307

tention given to the organization within which such relations exist or to the impact the organization has on the entire change process."[2] This chapter shall be devoted to helping the reader to understand organizational effects on group work: Chapter 7 shall present change strategies.

The current range of group work activities and their relationship to the sponsoring agencies will be more meaningful if the history of the group work is understood. This history is an exciting one in which group workers struggled to develop their ideas and to overcome opposition to them. An understanding of the history involved should also help the reader to see why the models described in the previous chapter were created as well as the controversies surrounding them.

GROUP WORK HISTORY

In discussing the history of group work, we must describe events that occurred before the phrase *group work* was even used. This is because important developments took place that would later be labeled "group work" and the individuals involved in these would later come to call themselves "group workers." This history, then, can be divided into four periods: the emergence of group work (1861 to 1927); the method (1928 to 1946); the growth (1947 to 1963); and the generic (1964 and after).

The Emergence of Group Work: 1861 to 1927

Developments in American society during this period that gave the greatest impetus to group services were the emergence of the United States and other countries as industrial societies, the shift of large populations from rural to urban living to support such industrialization, and the immigrations from Europe, Mexico, and Asia. This led to the entrapment of people in communities that were overcrowded, unhealthy, and deteriorating. Many of the residents of these communities were also handicapped in improving their occupations and they experienced themselves as powerless to change these conditions. These factors stimulated the creation of organizations to ameliorate these circumstances through progressive social reform activities.

One of the first agencies to respond to these problems through group services was the Young Men's Christian Association, organized in the United States in 1851 "to improve the spiritual condition of young men in the drapery and trades"; this developed into the broader objective of improving the "mental, social and physical condition of all young men of good moral character."[3]

The Young Women's Christian Association was founded in the United States 15 years later. In the years after that, many additional organizations

---

[2]Ibid.

[3]Gertrude Wilson, "From Practice to Theory: A Personalized History," in *Theories of Social Work With Groups,* eds. Roberts, Robert and Helen Northen (New York: Columbia University Press, 1976), p. 6.

with similar orientations emerged such as the Girl's Friendly Society of the United States (1877) and the Boy's Clubs of America (1906). According to one writer, these organizations "looked to the face-to-face group to restore opportunities for the good life taken from people by the speed and ruthlessness of post-Civil War industrialization."[4]

A more vigorous reform thrust, however, was provided by the introduction of the settlement house into the United States, inspired by similar institutions developed in England. Stanton Coit, after a visit to Toynbee Hall in London, established the Neighborhood Guild on the lower east side of New York in 1886. The settlement idea spread rapidly and in 1891 there were six settlements in the United States; by 1900 the number was more than 400.

The idea behind the settlements was that the problems of the poor could be understood better by participating in their community life. Settlement sought to create a variety of programs to ameliorate the specific problems of their communities. Thus settlements sponsored such diverse activities as kindergartens and preschool sessions, adult education, leisure time and cultural arts groups, social action committees, and neighborhood councils—all group-oriented activities. Settlements, in contrast to many other social services that emphasized adjustment to the social order, had a social focus. Their workers sought changes in social conditions as a way of attaining their objectives.

Closely related to the development of the Ys and the settlements was the emergence of the Jewish community centers, and Young Men's and Women's Hebrew Associations. These organizations had philosophies that were similar to those of the Ys. A difference, however, was that they were often sponsored by the more affluent western European Jews who, having come to this country before the Jews from Eastern Europe, used these associations as a means to "Americanize" the latter group.[5]

During this period, there was a lack of professional identification among workers in these various agencies; they were known by their setting such as Y or Scout leaders or settlement workers. While people from a number of professions, such as education, psychology, sociology, and social work, discussed with each other how to utilize groups, there was no agreement among them regarding a professional auspice.

Within social work itself, beyond those people who worked with groups, there was little appreciation of the value of group experience. However, Mary Richmond, one of the pioneers in the development of casework practice, began, in her later works, to emphasize a broad conception of social work practice and in 1920 wrote of the importance of "small group psychology"[6]

[4]William Schwartz, "Social Group Work: The Interactionist Approach," in *Encyclopedia of Social Work* (New York: National Association of Social Workers. 1971), II, 1253.

[5]For a discussion of this, see Irving Howe, *World of Our Fathers* (New York: Simon & Schuster, 1976), p. 230.

[6]Mary Richmond, "Some Next Steps in Social Treatment," *Proceedings of the National Conference of Social Work* (Chicago: University of Chicago Press, 1920), p. 256.

One writer who influenced these early workers was Mary P. Follett, a political scientist. In her book, *The New State*, Follett stated that she thought solutions to social problems would emerge from the creation of groups in neighborhoods and around social interests.[7] Another thinker who was important to these workers was John Dewey, who developed the idea of progressive education. According to one view of the period, the social group work method "was an application of the principles of progressive education to small informal groups in leisure time settings."[8]

Group work, at first, was closely associated with community development concepts, and, in fact, the origins of community organization method and its citizens participation focus cannot be distinguished from the beginnings of group work. Another writer who influenced these developments was Eduard C. Lindeman, who was interested in the fostering of community groups, also, and their role in a functioning democracy.[9]

Although these ideas and programs were developed in an atmosphere of excitement among reformers, educators, and social workers involved in them, it was not until the end of this period that a course in group work was introduced into a school of social work. The first course was taught by Mildred Chadsey at Western Reserve University in 1923. This began a long and productive period of that school's commitment to the development of group work. Virtually all of the pioneers among group-oriented social workers either taught at Western Reserve or were closely associated with its faculty.

The year 1927 was chosen to mark the end of this period of group work history as in that year, Western Reserve University enlarged its group service curriculum. By then the large number of agencies offering group services and the use of these experiences by social workers like Kaiser, Newstetter, and Williamson to conceptualize a theory of practice made this step possible.

The Emergence of Group Work as a Method: 1928 to 1946

The further development of group work from 1928 until the end of World War II was affected by two major cataclysms that occurred at the beginning and ending of this period: the depression and the war. The depression posed a challenge to social reformers who believed that their efforts had contributed to progress toward a humanitarian society. Social workers now were forced to question the validity of adjusting people to the existing social order. This gave impetus to many group workers who saw groups as a vehicle for promoting social change. It is not surprising, therefore, that these years were productive ones for group work.

---

[7]Mary Parker Follett, *The New State* (New York: Longman, 1926).

[8]John Dewey, *How We Think* (Lexington, Mass.: Heath, 1933).

[9]Harry Lawrence, "The Origins of Social Group Work" (unpublished manuscript, p.13), quoted in Scott Briar, "Social Casework and Social Group Work: Historical Foundations," *Encyclopedia of Social Work*, p. 1241.

First, this increased awareness of the importance of group services was associated with an enhanced professional identity. Gertrude Wilson relates an interesting anecdote associated with this process. In 1927 Wilbur Newstetter of Western Reserve University and Walter Pettit of the New York School for Social Work (now Columbia University School of Social Work) were traveling together on a long train ride to the National Conference of Social Work. Newstetter could only describe the group work project at Western Reserve that had just begun as he did not know what to call it. "Pettit said that it sounded to him as if the project would demonstrate the delivery of social services through groups and that at his school they call the delivery of social services to individuals *casework*; why not call this Western Reserve project *group work*."[10] Wilson explains that the phrase "group work" had been used before this time, in a programmatic sense, in religious education, and adult education contexts. Newstetter was innovative in using "group work" to designate a social work method.

During the 1930s and 1940s the bulk of group work continued to be found in the settings in which it had arisen: the Ys, settlements, Jewish centers, and scouts. The main controversies were not among personnel employed in these agencies but rather among the range of professionals and educators whose concern was building a practice theory and a professional identity for group workers.

Even with a label, the emergence of a social work identity for group workers was difficult. People interested in group work, such as Coyle, Kaiser, Wilson, and Newstetter, were closely related to social work; but it took several years for their efforts to take organizational form. The years 1935 and 1936 were important ones in this respect. In 1935, the National Conference of Social Work agreed to institute a section on group work and a number of important papers were delivered at the 1935 meeting.[11] Group workers were also active on another organizational front. The National Association for the Study of Group Work was formed in 1936, beginning a period in which group workers possessed an organizational form for furthering their practice interests.

As group work pioneers advanced their ideas through social work channels, major conflicts did appear. One speaker at the 1935 National Conference saw group work as a "social mechanism perfectly competent people utilize to achieve their own ends."[12] He saw social workers' use of groups as

[10]Wilson, "From Practice to Theory," p. 18.

[11]These include Coyle's classic presentation of a philosophy for group work entitled "Group Work and Social Change," Grace L. Coyle, *Group Experience and Democratic Values,* (New York: Women's Press, 1947); and Newstetter's clarification of semantic and conceptual issues: W.I. Newstetter, "What is Social Group Work?" in *Proceedings of the National Conference of Social Work* (Chicago: University of Chicago Press, 1935), pp. 291–99. Coyle in her presentation stressed the dual function of group work to transmit cultural values to individuals while at the same time helping people to transform these values through democratic processes. Newstetter identified group work as a "field," a "process," and a "set of techniques."

[12]Schwartz, *Encyclopedia of Social Work,* p. 1254.

an adaptation of something broader and more basic than simply a social work method. At the same time, caseworkers took issue, not with group work philosophy, but with the seriousness of group work as an enterprise. Wilson describes the stereotyped way group workers were viewed as people who "play with children" or "run dances."[13]

Nevertheless, by 1937, ten schools of social work offered courses in group work. Even then, others rejected this type of education because of its ties to recreation, within the next two years the number of schools offering group work education grew to seventeen. Six more schools taught about group work but did not provide a field experience in it.[14]

Coincident with these organizational activities was the development of group work practice theory. An audience was recruited when the National Association for the Study of Group Work established a publication—*The Group—in Education, Recreation, Social Work,* in 1939. A number of texts were also written in the 1930s that continue to have their influence felt to the present day.[15]

We consider this period to have ended in 1946 when group workers consolidated their emergence as practitioners of an established method: by forming the American Association of Group Workers, by producing a consensus document on professional standards, and by expanding their activities into new settings. This latter development was an important hallmark of the next period.

A Period of Growth: 1947 to 1963

As a result of the depression and the war, the idea of large-scale government involvement in programs and services led to the expansion of social work practice. On the other hand, the state of foreign affairs, particularly the cold war with the Soviet Union, was associated with fears of an "internal communist menace," the accusation that reformers were "subversive," and the hindrance to the social reform spirit of the previous period. Since many group workers were associated with this spirit, this period had an effect on their endeavors.

These decades of the forties and fifties, while not ones in which group workers sought to attain social change, were ones in which they sought to clarify and expand group work practice theory and the movement of that practice into new settings. The connection of group work with social action was muted. An example is provided by the comparison of two discussions of

---

[13]Wilson, "From Practice to Theory," p. 25.

[14]Ibid., p. 18.

[15]For example, Grace Coyle, *Studies in Group Behavior* (New York: Harper & Row, Pub., 1937); Clara A Kaiser, *The Group Records of Four Clubs* (Cleveland: Western Reserve University, 1930); S.R. Slavson, *Creative Group Education* (New York: Association Press, 1937); and Margaretta Williamson, *The Social Worker in Group Work* (New York: Harper & Row, Pub., 1929).

social action printed during this era. The first, written by Grace Coyle in 1948, describes a situation in which a group of young people planned a lobbying strategy for Fair Employment Practice legislation.[16] Five years later, Alan Klein, in his discussion of social action, gave the example of a member of a group who was expelled by the police from a park. Through subsequent visits to the police station, the group was helped to develop a closer relationship with the police.[17] This latter type of accommodation to society was typical of the fifties in contrast to the practice illustrated by Coyle.

At the beginning of this period, ambiguity existed as to whether group work was a social work or an educational specialization. A crucial decision was reached at the meeting of the National Conference on Social Work in 1946 in support of Grace Coyle's conclusion that "group work as a method falls within the larger scope of social work *as a method.*[18] Coyle came to this conclusion through her analysis of the common concerns of caseworkers, group workers, and community organizers. The decision was to form the American Association of Group Workers (AAGW) as a professional membership organization, with membership based on the possession of professional training.

In this organizational environment theoretical developments received great encouragement; many influential books were published and *The Group,* now under AAGW sponsorship, continued to play an important role.[19] With this type of conceptual progress, it was inevitable that group workers would bring their skills to the performance of new tasks in new settings.

While the predominant employment of group workers continued to be in settlements, Ys, and youth organizations, demonstrations of the group technique were conducted in psychiatric services, hospitals, family agencies, correctional institutions, and schools. This was enhanced by the use of groups with reported beneficial effects for the treatment of World War II veterans with psychiatric problems.[20] Support for many of these experiments with group work was provided by government funds as well as by the National Association of Social Workers.[21]

The entry of group workers into rehabilitation settings, nevertheless,

---

[16]Grace Coyle, *Group Work with American Youth* (New York: Harper & Row, Pub., 1948).

[17]Alan Klein, *Society, Democracy and the Group* (New York: Morrow, 1953).

[18]Harleigh B. Trecker, ed., *Group Work: Foundations and Frontiers* (New York: Whiteside, Inc., 1955), p. 340.

[19]For example, Gertrude Wilson and Gladys Ryland, *Social Group Work Practice* (Boston: Houghton-Mifflin, 1949); Harleigh B. Trecker, *Social Group Work* (New York: Women's Press, 1948); Grace Coyle, *Group Experience and Democratic Values;* Gisela Konopka, *Therapeutic Group Work with Children* (Minneapolis: University of Minnesota Press, 1949); and a few years later Helen Phillips, *Essentials of Social Group Work Skill* (New York: Association Press, 1957).

[20]Wilson, "From Practice to Theory," pp. 32-33.

[21]*Use of Groups in the Psychiatric Setting* (New York: National Association of Social Workers, 1960).

led to considerable debate during the 1950s. Writers such as Robert Vinter aruged that the preponderance of group workers in community agencies was a "retreat from the profession's historic mission of service to those most in need."[22] On the other hand, some group workers saw this shift as withdrawal from social action responsibilities.[23] Some also feared that the preventive function of group work would be lost.

A factor that created other dilemmas for group workers was the idea that the social work method could be viewed in a generic sense. The "generic" idea was paralleled and enhanced by the 1962 decision of the National Association of Social Workers to eliminate "sections" devoted to separate methods such as group work. The next phase of group work history, which brings us to contemporary times, is one in which there is a rich and diverse body of theory for work with groups existing alongside efforts to conceptualize social work as a single method.

Group Work and the Generic Method: 1964 and After

The events in the society that affected the development of group work in the sixties and seventies were the War on Poverty and the Civil Rights Movement. Both of these led to pressures on social workers to see problems from new, often more sociological, perspectives and to seek ways to solve such problems that were not restricted by the traditional dogmas.

Thus the government was committed to supplying money to be used for experiments with new solutions to delinquency, poverty, and mental illness. In conceiving of such experiments, professionals were influenced to consider comprehensive interventions by the Civil Rights struggles. In addition, data from the evaluation of previously utilized interventions led to serious concern about their effectiveness. This concern covered the utilization of *all* social work approaches. Thus one idea that emerged was that a combination of these methods would be more effective than the utilization of only one.

Developments in group work practice theory during the 1947 to 1963 period facilitated the development of a generic approach. Because group work was increasingly practiced in psychiatric, medical, child welfare, correctional, and other "special" settings, group members were now similar to casework clients. Approaches evolved to group work practice that utilized concepts familiar to caseworkers. For example, Robert Vinter, in his writings in the 1950s, described treatment goals for individuals served in groups and related these to individual diagnoses. He saw the group as a means for achieving such treatment goals rather than as an end in itself. Writers such as Fritz Redl and Gisela Konopka also wrote about group work utilizing the same psychoanalytic concepts employed by caseworkers.[24]

These trends in group work practice led also to the recognition that

<hr />

[22]Robert D. Vinter, "Group Work: Perspectives and Prospects," in *Social Work with Groups* (New York: National Association of Social Workers, 1959), pp. 128–49.

[23]Wilson, "From Practice to Theory," p. 33.

[24]Konopka, *Therapeutic Group Work;* Fritz Redl, "The Therapeutic Ingredients in the

there were now "schools" of group work practice, namely the ones described in the preceding chapter. Some of these schools were compatible with the generic practice idea, but writers associated with other schools feared that the essence of group work would be lost in a generic approach.

The current controversies that surround group work stem from the historical events just described. Those who maintain that the group as an entity has a vital role in a democracy and, as such, should be nurtured by social workers are the heirs of the tradition of Follet and Lindeman, who wrote at a time when democracy was seen as threatened by rapid industrialization, war, and economic depression. Others who are more likely to emphasize the group as a means to individual change are in the tradition of Redl and Slavson, who were allied with psychology and psychiatry. The development of group work as therapy began during the individually oriented years of the 1920s[25] and continued in the 1950s when an ideology of individual rather than social responsibility for one's problems was strong.

In conclusion, when the social climate is one in which the concern in the society is for its democratic functioning, the role of the worker as facilitator of group process is favored, such as in the thirties when Grace Coyle's work was influential and in the sixties when Schwartz's ideas influenced group workers profoundly. In contrast, in the more conservative atmosphere of the fifties, group work was defined by one writer as "the systematic ways in which the worker affects social and group process to achieve specified objectives," and group process in social work groups was defined as "group process when consciously affected by the worker toward specified ends."[26]

In the later 1970s, when movements for social change were in abeyance, behavior modification approaches were of considerable interest and a leading theorist on social work with groups wrote that "treatment planning involves choosing from a number of highly specific procedures that have been demonstrated to be related to achieving behavioral change goals."[27] The intent here is not to express criticism of these sets of ideas but rather to place them in the social and historical contexts that were conducive to their development.

The expert versus facilitator dichotomy is also affected by the state of social science knowledge regarding human behavior and its control. As London points out so well: "...means are being found, in all the crafts and sciences of man, society, and life, that will soon make possible precise control over much of people's individual actions, thoughts, emotions, moods and wills."[28] Both practitioners and philosophers have speculated on the possibil-

Group Work Program in a Residential Treatment Center for Children," in *Group Work in the Psychiatric Setting*, ed. Harleigh Trecker (N.Y.: Whiteside, Inc., and Morrow, 1956), pp. 43–46.

[25]See, for example, T. Burrow, "The Basis of Group Analysis," *British Journal of Medical Psychology* 8, Pt. 3 (November 1928), 198–206.

[26]Marjorie Murphy, *The Social Group Work Method in Social Work Education* (New York: Council on Social Work Education, 1959), p. 312.

[27]Sheldon Rose, *Group Therapy: A Behavioral Approach* (Englewood Cliffs, N.J.: Prentice-Hall, Inc., 1977), p. 9

[28]Perry London, *Behavior Control* (New York: Harper & Row, Pub., 1971), p. 4.

ity that such a development can be halted because of the threat posed to liberty. London, however, is pessimistic in his statement: "It is plain to anyone who troubles to look that once the potential for a particular technological development is clear, the actual technology follows, sometimes sooner, sometimes later, but without fail."[29] London's inevitable conclusion is: "The future, already upon us, must be controlled."[30]

As far as group work is concerned, group workers considered themselves as facilitators of group process before the emergence of technologies of behavior control. Some workers, now, with the creation of behavioral techniques seek to implement group work procedures that have immediate and potent effects.[31] In this respect, group workers join the ranks of teachers, psychologists, and the creators of the mass media who can be divided into those who maintain a facilitative and educational stance as opposed to those who seek to attain predetermined goals by the most expeditious means possible.

Now that we have examined the evolution of group work theories and practice settings, we shall analyze in detail the way such settings currently affect practice. This discussion, as we stated earlier, should help the practitioner to see ways of using agency conditions as well as, on occasion, seeking to change them.

AGENCY CONDITIONS THAT AFFECT GROUP WORK

Why Agencies Establish Groups

In order to supply a foundation for the worker's evaluation of agency conditions that affect group services, we will first list and discuss such conditions. We will then describe the current range of group work activities in terms of a classification of types of agency purposes.

Example: The X Family Agency decided to offer a "drop-in group" to help mothers with young children discuss concerns around child rearing. Baby sitting services were also provided to them while they attended the group.

Example: The Planned Parenthood Clinic offered "rap sessions" for teens concerned about sexuality and sexual behaviors.

Agencies always have a reason for allocating staff time to group work services as the above examples imply. Sometimes these reasons are explicit and embodied in formal proposals or descriptions of services. Thus an agency may state that it supports groups to enhance the classroom behavior of school children or to assist previously hospitalized psychotic patients to cope with a return to the community. At other times, there is no specific statement

---

[29]Ibid., p. 7.
[30]Ibid., p. 21.

about the group work program and one must refer to the overall program descriptions of the agency to infer agency purposes for groups. There also can be "hidden" purposes, such as the transfer of clients from individual treatment caseloads because their workers no longer wish to work with them. Purposes may also be stated in very general terms, such as "helping children adjust better to institutional conditions" or they may be very specific, such as "helping unwed mothers decide whether or not to place their children for adoption after delivery."

The agency purposes for the group will have a strong influence on group processes throughout the life of the group. They will influence who is referred to the group, how the member is prepared (or not prepared) for the group, what kinds of group activities are reinforced, and how the agency is likely to respond to requests from the group and its worker.

An example of the way purpose is influential is that of a group of ten- and eleven-year-olds meeting in a community center. The agency composed the group from children who were referred from the local public school because of complaints about their classroom behavior. The agency had contacted the youths and their families, explained the *purposes* of the group, and inquired as to the youths' interest in participation.

When the youngsters got together, they asked if they could take trips. They were informed that this was not the *purpose* of the group, as the worker had explained prior to the group's first meeting. A trip might be taken, however, to reward the group for working out the details of how the group's meetings will be used to accomplish its *purposes*. The agency had equipped a room with some school supplies so that the youngsters might, at some point, simulate their school room. The worker had asked for this resource because of the *purpose* of the group.

Group workers have the responsibility, before the beginning of a group, to help the agency to consider purposes that can be accomplished through groups. Some purposes should not be implemented such as attempting to cause members to accept agency injustices, other purposes may be unethical, such as manipulating members to accept goals that they might otherwise reject. The worker should also help the agency to evaluate how its purposes are being achieved through groups so that unfeasible ones might be modified. Workers should be clear to members about the purposes and should help members to negotiate with the agency regarding these purposes either through the worker or directly.[31]

How Members Are Referred to or Recruited for the Groups

Example: In a psychiatric clinic, a worker asked other workers to refer socially isolated young adults to him as he planned to start a group to help such persons make friends.

---

[31]For example, see Rose, *Group Therapy.*

Example: In a child and family service agency, a policy was announced that all unmarried, pregnant women asking for help with decisions about placement will be offered membership in a group established for that purpose. Those who expressed concern about group participation or who had other reasons for not being included in a group will be offered individual service.

Example: In a residential treatment center, a group worker offered to hold weekly meetings with the youths living in Cottage D.

These examples illustrate several of the ways people may be secured for group work services. The agency usually establishes recruitment procedures that have substantial influence on the future of the group, including agency intake itself, and when this process eliminates clients of specified ages, ethnic groups, social statuses, or with certain problems, the range of group services is predetermined. Subsequent to agency intake, the way clients are recruited for groups varies; for example, people may be offered individual services first and then may be referred to groups by "caseworkers." This may be before or after individual services have begun. Alternatively, group work may be presented as an option when individuals enter the agency.

When the agency stresses individual services, Hasenfeld hypothesizes that group work services will be considered marginal and group work practice "...confronts the problem of formulating a common basis for clients to interact as a group."[32] Thus the worker and clients will spend a substantial amount of energy identifying and maintaining the rationale for the group's existence.

In some cases, the agency interacts primarily with all its clients on a group basis as, for example, in residential institutions, where the group worker will often be in competition with other people who also transact with groups, such as teachers, nurses, and custodial personnel. This can blur the particular functions that are to be served by the group work experience.

When enrollment for groups is decided at the point of agency intake, who decides and how this is decided are important. One of the major influences a worker has on group events is through the composition of the group (see page 68) and this depends on a sufficiently diverse pool of potential members. The composition procedures the worker utilizes can be implemented better when they are part of decision making for services rather than when they are "political" and must depend on the beliefs of staff to whom the clients have been assigned and who must relinquish them.

Another major dimension of the intake process of concern to group workers is whether agency services as well as group work services are voluntary or compulsory. Again, according to Hasenfeld, in the latter case "the

---

[32]Hasenfeld, *Individual Change Through Small Groups,* eds. Glasser, Sarri, and Vinter, p. 309.

group is likely to develop apathy, self-aggression, frustration, and inability to adapt to free situations, which could undermine any treatment objective."[33]

For example, group services are offered frequently in prisons and psychiatric treatment facilities where group members are pressured to attend. Much time is then spent by the worker discussing member reactions to determine if a basis for working together can be developed. (This process of identifying such a basis—the development of a contract—is discussed in Chapter 4; a more extensive discussion of issues in working with involuntary clients is presented in Chapter 12.)

The way each member experiences entering the agency and then the group is important. As Yalom demonstrates, members will be more committed to the group and will interact more with each other if prepared individually for the group.[34] This procedure, however, takes time prior to the first meeting of the group, and the agency must facilitate this.

The ability of the worker to have an effect on these intake events is a function of his or her status in the agency, an issue which we turn to now.

What Are the Status and Role of the Group Worker in the Agency

Example: John's job assignment included work with individuals, families, and groups. He was seen as a professional equal by the other social workers in the Community Mental Health Center.

Example: Bill was one of a staff of workers in a large settlement house. When the caseworkers in the agency saw her, they always jokingly asked her where her whistle was to call the children to activities.

Example:Bill was one of a staff of workers in a large settlement house. All of the workers spent most of their time either working with groups or supervising people who did.

The way the agency defines the job of the group worker and the location of this person in the agency hierarchy will have impact on the group. If the major technology in the agency is one-to-one treatment, a separate cadre of workers usually offer group services and initial assignments of cases are made to caseworkers; the activities of the group worker is then likely to be seen as relatively unimportant. Members of groups often perceive the low status of their worker and react accordingly, even to the extent of rejecting group services.

The status of group workers can vary beyond the division of labor between work with individuals and work with groups. People with expertise and interest in work with groups may or may not be represented in the administra-

---

[33]Ibid.

[34]Irvin D. Yalom, *The Theory and Practice of Group Psychotherapy,* 2nd ed. (New York: Basic Books, 1975), p. 294.

tion of the agency. On the other hand, group workers might be either supervised by people defined as caseworkers or else segregated into a separate unit. Even though this pattern may become less dominant as social work practice becomes generic, it will be found in a number of agencies. The impact of such arrangements is less power for the worker to secure resources for the group, influence the pattern of referrals to the group, and have his or her ideas taken into consideration in agency determination of group purposes.

The resolution of this issue is affected by whether group workers define their "method" as a unique one amidst the "methods" of casework and community organization or whether work with groups is seen as a skill developed by all workers. In the former case, it is important that group workers have as much power as other practitioners to influence policy, particularly policy on how services are offered. In the latter case, people who work with groups will, by definition, have as much power as any other worker. As indicated earlier, we prefer to conceive of group work as part of a generic range of skills to be developed by most workers.

Which Resources Do Agencies Allocate to the Group

Example: The Child Guidance Clinic rented the gymnasium of a nearby YMCA for the use of an adolescent group.

Example: The family agency furnished one of its rooms with comfortable sofas and arm chairs for use as a group therapy room.

Example: The probation service established a small budget for refreshments at group meetings.

Group activities are enchanced if the worker has available space, equipment, consultation, and other resources. With the possible exception of play therapy and other treatment modalities for use with children, there is more of a tradition regarding the use of material objects and space in group work than in other social work approaches. This is because of the use group workers have made of a variety of program media to provide new experiences for members. Group workers have often required suitable space to engage, for example, in games with children or to help adults feel that this is a different experience than a class or committee meeting. Group members in residential situations may want to visit places outside of the institution as part of their learning experiences and this leads to such costs as transportation and worker time beyond the "therapeutic hour." All of these contingencies require agencies to consider the costs involved in group sessions. Group workers, in helping agencies establish such services should be forthright in making this known to agency administration.

How Targets for Change Are Selected by Agencies

Example: A school system defined the targets of its school social work program as those classroom behaviors that were immediately associated with learning. Family and peer relationship problems were not to be dealt with. Workers were expected to refer such situations to other agencies.

Example: The Child Guidance Clinic, because of the psychiatric orientation of its administrator, the focus of its consulting psychiatrist, and the material asked for on agency recording forms oriented its efforts to parent-child, parent-peer, and child-authority transactions. Little attention was paid to job, housing, or community resource issues also of concern to clients.

As illustrated by these examples, agency conditions may predispose a worker to select some aspects of client–agency–environment transactions rather than others as targets for change. This is related to our proposition that social work problems are created by the interactions of people in situations. This is similar to the contention of many family therapists that "problems" in families are defined by the family in ways that are based on the family's systemic requirements.[35]

The workers have a number of options as to how to approach this issue of the agency's preferred targets. One way is to describe agency definitions of problems to clients, who may then chose to seek services elsewhere. On the other hand, some clients may wish, often with the help of the worker, to seek to change the agency's orientation so that support is given to the client's targets. When the agency's and client's preferred targets coincide, either fortuitously or as a result of negotiation, it is more likely that necessary resources for the group and the worker will be forthcoming. The worker, then, will not be caught in a conflict between member and agency desires that can be immobilizing for all concerned.

What Effect Agencies Have on Groups' Social and Physical Environment

Example: In the Child Guidance Clinic, the agency assigned the social relations group, a group formed to help socially isolated teenagers, to one of the agency's club rooms. The group was given a set of drawers in the room in which to keep records of how members were performing "social tasks" chosen by members. They were also given a bulletin board to pin up clippings and quotations selected by members.

[35]James Framo, "Symptoms from a Family Transactional Viewpoint," in *Progress in Group and Family Therapy*, eds. Clifford Sager and Helen Kaplan (New York: Brunner/Mazel, 1972), pp. 271–308.

Example: A community center assigned several workers to "reach out" to teenage gangs in the area. When one of these groups decided to come to the agency for meetings and activities, the agency assigned one hour a week in the gym for the group's exclusive use.

Again, according to Hasenfeld, "the capacity of the group to develop well-defined boundaries and identity is partly determined by its ability to establish and shape its own 'territory' according to its needs."[36] The same writer also states that "development of the group requires a space that provides some insulation from the environment and protection from excessive external disturbances."[37] As we shall see in Chapter 4, a sine qua non for the effectiveness of the group to help its members is the attraction it holds for them, that is, its cohesiveness. An often neglected factor in enhancing this is the environment the agency offers the group. This includes the physical setting for the group meeting as well as the following:

1. The ways that other people in the agency, in addition to the group worker, interact with group members. These people include other clients, receptionists, other professional staff, secretaries, and maintenance workers.

2. The decor of the agency. Whether the agency looks orderly and maintained is often interpreted by members as showing the esteem with which clients are held; also relevant is the meaning to the members of visible objects in terms of their culture. For example, one agency placed pictures of its benefactors in its rooms and these were mostly caucasians. The largely black clientele did not feel the agency valued them until important people in black history were also honored by having their pictures prominently displayed.

3. The "social" aspects of the agency. Workers should attempt to "see" the agency through the eyes of the group members who will usually be willing to share their perceptions when asked. The "social" environment of the agency includes the degree to which the staff members function as a team, understand and support one another, and have high morale. The workers cannot ignore these variables any more than they can ignore internal actions in the group.

How Agencies Interact with Groups' Indigenous Leaders

Example: In Agency A, the director sent a letter to the group asking it to nominate people for an advisory committee on group services from among its members.

Example: In Agency B, the worker notified the group that the type of services received by the group were to be discontinued by the agency. Several group members sought out the agency director to discuss this decision but

[36]Hasenfeld, *Individual Change Through Small Groups,* eds. Glasser, Sarri, and Vinter, p. 318.
[37]Ibid.

were told by her receptionist that she would not be available for an appointment for several weeks.

People tend to emerge in groups who have greater influence over group processes than others, who function as spokespersons for the group, or who are authorized by other group members to represent the group in external affairs. Agency definitions of clients' status will affect these individuals. In some group work situations, however, members conceive of themselves as recipients of a service and do not expect to be involved in any processes with the agency after they have joined the group. This is most often true of those voluntarily seeking help with personal problems in psychiatric outpatient facilities.

In other cases, group members conceive of themselves as constituents rather than clients, in the traditional sense of the word, and *do* expect to be consulted by the agency and involved in its affairs. This is usually true in community centers. In yet another type of agency, clients may feel alienated and powerless in relationship to social institutions (for example, welfare agencies or prisons). The noninvolvement of these persons in the agencies offering them group experiences is more evidence of their powerlessness. In these cases, such involvement may be therapeutic in itself.

An asset of the group experience is the group members' awareness that they may share similar concerns. Out of this springs the possibility of joint action and this creates even more power for members. Some agencies may seek to reinforce this possibility while others may fear the consequences of group pressures and may act to inhibit them.

This issue of involvement of group members in extra-group processes is related, also, to how much control the agency has over clients. The agencies that have the most control are those in which the client is institutionalized, such as mental hospitals, residential treatment centers, and prisons. Substantial control is also exercised by agencies given legal legitimation for control, such as probation and psychiatric aftercare programs. The least control is, of course, exercised by agencies in which the client is there voluntarily (a community center) or where the client may be performing a service for the agency (adoptive parents of hard-to-place children).

Group members are often least involved in those agencies with the greatest degree of control over them. The control issue will have effects on the way members exercise options related to group program, create indigenous leadership, respond to worker decisions, and participate in selecting group goals and targets.

What Are Agencies' Attitudes to Service Ideologies and Technologies

Example: An institution for adolescents was committed to the use of positive peer culture. Staff received training in this approach and referral agencies were informed of this emphasis. As soon as youths were admitted, other group members explained the way the PPC group was conducted.

Example: The Child Guidance Clinic was directed by a psychoanalytically oriented psychiatrist. Workers were hired based on their knowledge of this theory. At case conferences, clients were assessed in terms of ego functioning. Group experiences were recommended when these were seen as enhancing such functioning.

Most agencies have preferences for particular theories, ideologies, and techniques. These are manifested in the way services are defined, people are interviewed for staff positions, assumptions are made about intake, consultants are recruited, and agency record forms are conceived. Such preferences govern the way workers are expected to act in groups.

Agency clarity regarding preferred treatment approaches can be supportive of workers and group members as the workers will know what is expected of them and will receive rewards for meeting these expectations. Clients will know what the available service is. In some instances, clients may even be informed of the effects and effectiveness of the approach through research evidence or case example.

Problems can arise when approaches to group work are utilized that are either ineffective, inappropriate, or not desired by workers, clients, or both. Under these mandatory circumstances, short of leaving the agency, workers can do the following: they can seek to hire staff trained in appropriate technologies; they can secure additional training for themselves; or, together with group members, they can creatively develop new group procedures.

The involvement of group members in the decision of service technologies presupposes that they have some knowledge of such matters. We believe that this information ought to be made routinely available and that, in addition, workers should find ways of explaining to group members the nature of the services offered.

How Intraorganizational Relationships Affect Groups

Example: The worker for a young boys' treatment group in the Community Mental Health Program was told by his supervisor that the group had been too noisy and rambunctious in recent meetings. The supervisor thought that the worker should exercise firmer controls. The worker, in turn, lectured the boys at the next meeting about their behavior.

Example: The morale of the staff in the school was low because a recent millage election had failed and many services were to be cut. The worker, in the next few meetings of the group, was lethargic, did not pursue new topics of importance to the members, and was not very empathic with the members.

Hasenfeld raises an important, yet subtle, issue when he states that "a process of 'isomorphism' occurs in which worker-group relations come to reflect the same structural properties of worker relations with staff members in the agency".[38] This phenomenon occurs because other agency personnel, particularly those in authority, provide models for the worker. Agency conditions affect the worker's emotional state, also, and set norms for what is and is not rewarded. Workers have several options in regard to this issue:

1. When problems arise in the group, the worker should analyze whether they parallel agencywide situations.

2. The worker can then consider whether action should be initiated at an agency or group level or both.

3. The worker, as agency concerns are discussed at a staff level, can consider their effect at a group level.

4. At times the worker can "buffer" the group from agency conditions by acting in ways that are at variance with these conditions. For example, workers should consult with group members on decisions even if they are not, themselves, consulted by administrators.

5. At times it becomes necessary to inform members about agency conditions that lead to undesirable consequences for the group; the members may then seek to initiate changes in such conditions, sometimes in concert with the group worker; they may try to isolate themselves from the effects of the conditions; or they may decide that the conditions are really not a problem for them or may even be constructive.

Thus far in this chapter we have outlined selected agency conditions that may have an effect on group work practice. We believe that all of these are relevant to group work in any agency but also that agencies with certain types of functions are likely to approach these variables in ways that differ from agencies with other functions. Some of these ways enhance group services; others hinder them. We shall now turn to an analysis of agency "types."

A TYPOLOGY OF AGENCY PURPOSES

In order to facilitate this analysis, as well as to illustrate the possible range of group work activities, we have developed a classification of agency purposes. To us, the phrase "agency purpose" means either the purpose the agency fulfills for the society, for the clientele, or both. Sometimes the agency purposes are directed toward societal objectives that are not, at least initially, sought by clients (for example, prisons). At other times, the purposes are mutual (a job training agency established to reduce unemployment for clients who wish jobs). In presenting this classification, we also draw on the following considerations:

---

[38]Hasenfeld, *Individual Change Through Small Groups*, eds. Glasser, Sarri, and Vinter, p. 316.

1. It is rare, if not impossible, to find an agency whose services represent only one purpose. Thus all agencies have several purposes, but many are likely to emphasize some more than others.

2. An issue for any agency is the extent to which it has clarified for itself, if not for its clientele or the general public, what its purposes are.

3. When an agency seeks to fulfill a purpose, some of its activities may conflict with other activities because the agency has conflicting purposes. An example of this is a school program. Schools are both society's way of socializing youngsters into roles through imparting skills as well as society's way of ensuring that behavior follows societal norms. Sometimes these two functions conflict, as when a youngster seeks a future role (for example, social radical) that some teachers believe is inconsistent with their value of maintaining the system.

Vinter[39] and Hasenfeld[40] describe the two major purposes of agencies as socialization and resocialization of the client. The former category involves the purpose of helping persons viewed as "normal" and who are progressing from one status to another. Examples of this are assisting adolescents to assume adult responsibilities, middle-aged persons to plan for retirement, and school children to make better use of their learning environment. The latter category, resocialization, refers to the purpose of helping people who are not viewed as experiencing "normal" phases of development or role transitions, who are often labeled "deviant," and who, by virtue of this position, experience conflict with others. Examples are working with inmates of prisons and mental hospitals and some clients of mental health programs.

Subpurposes

Upon further consideration of these two categories, socialization and resocialization, we concluded that each category should be further subdivided. Under the heading of "socialization," one subpurpose should be to help individuals who are having difficulty deciding on socialization goals. Because this is frequently, as Hartman states, due to *anomie,* which is "a state of societal demoralization—of normlessness—created by the disjunction of goals and norms for reaching these goals" we have termed this subpurpose *anomie reduction.*[41] One example of a client who required this type of service was a woman trying to raise her level of consciousness of emerging and changing women's roles so she could pursue them in a personally more satisfying way; another was a gay person who also sought to identify and follow newly emerging norms; and another adolescent confronted with the chang-

---

[39]Robert D. Vinter, "Analysis of Treatment Organizations," *Social Work* 8 (1963), 3–15.
[40]Hasenfeld, *Individual Change Through Small Groups,* eds. Glasser, Sarri, and Vinter, p. 308.
[40]Ann Hartman, "Anomie and Social Casework," *Social Casework* 50 (1969), 132.

ing and conflicting patterns for youth. It is interesting that in our discussion with practitioners of this categorization, they noted that almost all agencies to a degree have to deal with the problem of anomie; that is, clients frequently seeking to understand and relate themselves to changing and conflicting norms. This may, therefore, be a highly significant phenomenon in our culture that always affects agency services.

Once people have decided on socialization goals and values, the next logical step is to achieve their goals. We have termed this subpurpose *role attainment*. This type of helping is in recognition of the fact that many people need help in meeting role requirements in positions such as citizens, employees, students, parents, and adults.

In considering the category of resocialization, we also recognized two subpurposes. The first refers to people who have not yet determined that they wish to fulfill a nondeviant, socially acceptable role. Because society established institutions such as courts to work to bring about resocialization, we have termed this subpurpose *social control*. We do not include in this book any discussion as to whether or not or to what degree social work as a profession is an instrument of social control. It is evident, however, that social workers frequently are employed in agencies with social control functions parenthood clinics, women, and minority groups, consciousness raising organizations, and many counseling programs associated with universities. In addition, a number of private organizations and institutes (some for profit) have formed to make this type of service available to the large number of people who desire it. Such clients, are generally self-referred and highly motivated to participate, although they may not always be clear about the group experience they seek.

In a process similar to "socialization," some clients who become group members do accept or come to accept resocialization goals. The purpose of helping such people we call *alternative role attainment*; the types of people helped in this manner include many clients of outpatient psychiatric facilities, aftercare programs, and treatment-oriented correctional programs.

In the remainder of this chapter, we shall describe the kinds of agencies and groups that seek to fulfill each of these subpurposes. Again, the reader is reminded that there is no assumption that agencies fall into only one category. At any given moment, however, a worker should be able to identify which purpose an agency, a program, a group, or a group session is fulfilling. This framework, then, is a means to describe the range of group work activities so that later we can describe the different ways workers should act in relationship to the purposes appropriate to the situation.

Anomie Reduction

Example: A group of nine women in their twenties met together in a "Young Mothers' Club" in a community center. They had all been recently married and had either a young child or were pregnant. All had worked to supplement their family's income, most at occupations such as secretary, sales person, or waitress. They came together, originally, as a social club because several had gone to school or worked together. In the process of informal discussions, they discovered that they were all experiencing similar problems. These included the kinds of expectations their husbands held of them that denied them the equality they expected in their marriages. On the other hand, many did believe that mothers had more responsibilities than fathers for child rearing and they were uncertain how this related to the issue of equality. They asked each other for help in resolving some of these concerns and, when the Community Center was told of this, it offered them the services of a group worker.

In the first few meetings, the worker helped these young women to describe to each other how these issues were manifested in their own families. At times, they were embarrassed to describe some of their experiences, but the worker helped them through discussing norms of confidentiality and through sharing some details of her own life. The worker also used value clarification exercises to help the members to decide what each believed most about her rights in her marriage. When it became apparent that most of the members had trouble explaining their beliefs to their husbands, the worker introduced some role plays to help them to practice a greater degree of assertiveness. The worker also assisted them in planning a joint meeting with their husbands to discuss the roles of each partner in a marriage.

Similar types of experiences to help members identify conflicting norms to which they are exposed are now offered in a number of agencies. Examples of organizations that have arisen to respond to these needs include teen "rap centers" associated with community mental health agencies and planned parenthood clinics, women's and minority groups' consciousness raising organizations, and many counseling programs associated with universities. In addition, a number of private organizations and institutes (some for profit) have formed to make this type of service available to the large number of people who desire it. Such clients are generally self-referred and highly motivated to participate, although they may not always be clear about the group experience they seek.

Several aspects of group work service focused on anomic situations are illustrated by the example of the "Young Mothers' Group." The group was formed around people who experienced similar normative problems. Because they quickly recognized that they were dealing with parallel issues, they were able to be supportive to and yet could also confront one another. They had somewhat different ideas about the resolution of value conflicts affecting young women today and, therefore, could help each other to examine alternative solutions. These characteristics made a group rather than an individual counseling experience a particularly valid one.

Role Attainment

Example: A high school was aware that a number of students were motivated to complete their high school program but had various handicaps: (1) poor preparation, as they had been educated in less adequate grammar schools than other students; (2) insufficient support from families, as most had only one parent; and (3) hostility from school personnel who labeled them unmotivated and incompetent and failed to give them the help they needed.

One of several programs the school used to reverse this cycle of failure was group work on a voluntary basis; such individuals were invited to join a group conducted by a social worker that met on a weekly basis. In the first meetings, the students helped each other to chose short-term goals for themselves. These included regular completion of homework assignments, better quality of work as attested to by higher grades, and decisions regarding future employment and education. The members then each decided on "tasks" to help them reach their goals. Each member's goals were discussed by the entire group and suggestions were made as to appropriate tasks. For example, a young woman whose goal was better grades on tests chose as her tasks to study two hours a day after school and to complete two homework assignments during this period.

Members used their discussions at meetings to help each other accomplish their tasks. The student who wanted to improve grades spoke about interruptions from her family and friends while she was studying. The group members gave her suggestions as to how she could respond to these interruptions and she practiced their ideas during group meetings in role plays.

Organizations that emphasize role attainment include schools, settlement houses, family life and sex education agencies, nursery and preschool programs for children, and senior-citizens centers. The emphasis in this type of helping is not on giving up old attitudes, values, and behavior but on anticipatory socialization and building on already present knowledge and skills.

Adult clients who make use of these agencies tend to come voluntarily. Although children are required to participate in some programs, there is an overall assumption that client motivation is high and resistance to learning low. The focus of service is on career development providing as many opportunities for learning as possible. Ideally, agency rules are open and flexible, and there is opportunity for democratic decision making.

The preceding example of a role attainment group is illustrative of the fact that such groups usually consist of members who seek similar socialization goals and are striving to overcome similar barriers to such achievement. Members will, therefore, be prone to identify strongly with and give support to each other. The approach used in the example of picking "tasks" is only one of several that may be used. Such procedures, however, tend to focus on specific goals and means to attain them.

It is also common, in socialization-oriented groups, to discover barriers in the environment to such socialization (in this case, the attitudes of teachers). As we shall see later, there is a tendency for workers to focus on member behaviors rather than environmental conditions, thus leading members into activities in which their desires will be frustrated. Socialization-oriented groups should draw on the long tradition in community center and settlement house work with such groups that have strong social action components.

Social Control

Example: Group meetings were required of adolescent boys who were committed to the Training School. One such group consisted of ten boys between the ages of fifteen and seventeen. They had been sent to the institution for such offenses as repeated theft and destruction of property. In the second meeting of the group, the members sat in postures that showed their boredom and resentment. A few boys looked fearful. As the worker waited until all boys had arrived to begin the meeting, those present complained about the institution and about being required to attend the group. The worker began the discussion by empathizing with the boys' feelings. After a short period, however, he confronted the members with the statement that their complaints were "going nowhere" and that, perhaps, they could figure out something they could do to help themselves. In the discussion, he also commented that their difficulty in knowing what to do in tough situations may have landed them in the Training School. Many of the boys ridiculed this idea and said it was another example of the kind of preaching they always heard. One boy, however, did not join in this discussion and yet the worker knew that he was respected by the others. The worker sought to draw him out by commenting that maybe he saw things a little differently.

The social control purpose illustrated here is employed in an organization because society, usually through legislative and judicial processes, has sanctioned the agency to limit deviant behavior. Organizations that emphasize social control purposes include mental hospitals, residential treatment institutions, training schools for the delinquent and the retarded, drug centers, child guidance clinics, and community mental health facilities.

Central to social control goals for clients is behavioral change, that is, the diminution or elimination of behavior for which the client was in trouble with society. Service to clients is often involuntary, as the agency's control over its clientele is relatively high. The development of new and more functional modes of performance to replace the dysfunctional behavior should be, but is not always, a focus of the agency's program. The rules of these organizations tend to be authoritarian and coercive, especially in closed settings, and clients are allowed relatively little option on a number of issues.

Clients recruited to social control organizations are often resistive to change and rebellious to the agency itself. This is sometimes fostered by the rigidity of agency rules and sanctions as well as by peer group pressure to engage in aggressive behavior. Thus the initial motivation for change among such clients may be low or even nonexistent. Further, it is usually necessary to deal with peer group resistance to change by seeking to change the norms and values of the group.

A major issue for the professional is the potential conflict betwen the social control purpose of the agency and the professional commitment to self-determination of clients. However the worker resolves the issue, it must be with honesty so that members know the limits of their situation as well as the worker's personal stands. Members must receive recognition for their desire to confront agency policies together with support to do this in a constructive manner; moreover, the agency must be helped to respond with understanding and flexibility.

Group treatment in these settings can be very effective because previous group forces often have molded the individual's norms, values, and behaviors. The opportunity afforded to individuals to change their behavior with the support of a benign group situation is invaluable.

The illustration beginning this section shows many of these issues; for example, the understandable resistance of the group members to the compulsory features of the situation. The worker empathizes with their feelings about this and yet does not deny the agency's power and its use to attain agency objectives. The worker uses confrontation more often than in other settings to point out the member's behavior and its possible effects. In this way the worker presents, none the less, the concept that the members have choices to make. Even though the worker may favor some choices as opposed to others, he employs the value of self-determination so that the members ultimately are responsible for their own decisions.

Alternative Role Attainment

Example: A psychiatric outpatient clinic has established a group composed of seven men and women who voluntarily came to the clinic. One was a man who had had a succession of relationships with women in which the woman had broken off with him for reasons he did not understand; another was a man who expressed a great deal of anxiety about starting relationships with either men or women; a third was a woman who was fired from a number of jobs with the charge she did not get along with co-workers; and others were a woman and man who were in the process of divorce from their respective spouses and expressed strong feelings of loss and sadness around this. All of these people had an interest in being members of a group conducted by a social worker on the staff; as part of the intake process into the group, the worker had explained to them that their problems appeared to be related to how they interacted with others and that in a group they could learn about, get feedback on, and modify such transactions.

At early meetings of the group, the members elaborated on the problems just described. In the way they presented their problems, some of the reasons for their difficulties can be seen. The man, for instance, with the succession of lovers backed off from discussions in the group as soon as another member expressed too much "caring." The woman who had been fired from her job asked very intimate questions of other group members and tended to ridicule their answers. Gradually, with the help of the worker, the members began to point out these kinds of patterns to each other. Some, then began to try out other ways of responding in the group.

When alternative role attainment is the primary purpose, the focus in the group is on the development of new values, knowledge, and skills to replace outdated or dysfunctional ones. While the client is, or is likely to be, in trouble in his or her environnment, there has usually not been a major violation of social norms with subsequent legal sanctions. While there may be considerable environmental pressure on clients to do something about their situation, they usually seek help voluntarily because of personal discomfort. Organizations serving these populations generally allow clients many more opportunities for choice than when social control functions are being exercised. An exception to this analysis is when inmates of correctional programs move voluntarily toward seeking rehabilitation. Under these circumstances, clients are rarely resistive to change, and their motivation to learn alternative roles is often high. However, they may find change difficult because of previous, even lifelong, patterns. The worker's efforts are directed at building on the motivation already present and increasing the clients' comfort with this process. The peer group is used to increase client motivation by reinforcing individual change efforts. The peer group is also useful because clients' resocialization problems are intimately connected with their relationship patterns that are enacted in group situations which simulate life outside the group.

Groups that function as instruments of social control often proceed to become alternative role attainment groups. This occurs when group members identify a common ground between their needs and interests and those of the agency. Such a transition demands, however, that the agency be benign, have a therapeutic orientation, and be prepared to negotiate a common ground with groups and group members.

Other organizations that emphasize alternative role attainment purposes as part of resocialization include sheltered workshops and similar skill-development programs for the physically handicapped and the retarded, retraining programs for the unemployed, family service agencies, psychiatric clinics, medical social work departments, and family life education programs.

The preceding example illustrates how members in groups not only talk about their relationships but actually enact these behaviors because the group *is* a social situation and members find that people in the group remind them of people outside. Members can also stereotype each other and hinder change as well as enhance it and this poses a problem to the group and the worker. Thus a wide range of learning possibilities occur in an alternative role attainment group as members understand not only how to experiment with change but how to respond to people who seek to hinder it. This is especially true in resocialization as opposed to socialization experiences, as new behaviors must replace old ones.

Because the group is, as stated, a social situation, members will also behave in socially conventional ways: they will resist commenting on each other's behaviors or revealing their own thoughts and feelings. As the previous example indicates, it takes a considerable amount of worker skill to help the members of such groups make good use of the group for change even when motivation is present; this is because the possibility is ever present that members will reinforce existing behaviors rather than new ones.

SUMMARY

This chapter began with a discussion of the importance of agency conditions in relation to group work practice. These conditions have evolved over more than half a century and an understanding of this provides many insights into the current group work situation; therefore, an extensive presentation of group work history was offered.

Following the section on group work history, the specific organizational conditions that can either enhance or hinder the group work experience were described. These conditions include purposes assigned to the group, the selection of members, the status of the group worker, and the agency allocation of resources to the group. A number of additional organizational conditions were also described.

The final section of the chapter included a full discussion of the range of group services based on a typology of such purposes. This typology subdivides purposes into socialization (further split into anomie reduction and role attainment) and resocialization (further split into social control and alternative role attainment). Throughout this book, we shall use this set of categories to clarify the variations in group work practice that exist. A major emphasis shall be placed on this scheme in the third part of the book.

Exercise: ASSESSING AN AGENCY'S EFFECT ON GROUP WORK

The following questionnaire can be employed to help the reader assess the impact of agency conditions on group work services:

PURPOSES:

1. What do agency documents state the purposes of the agency are?

2. What group purposes are compatible with agency purposes?

3. What types of clients are likely to come to the agency in view of its purposes? How will this affect group composition?

4 What will members perceive is expected of them in the light of agency purposes?

5. How will agency purposes affect the activitiers of the group and the content of group deliberations?

AGENCY REFERRAL PROCEDURES

1. Are members recruited for or referred to groups before, during, or after agency intake?

2. Which agency staff are responsible for referral? How are people who work with groups in the agency involved in this process?

3. Is some service of the agency (for example, one-to-one casework) actually the preferred or predominant one?

4. Does the agency interact with its clients predominantly on a group, one-to-one, or family basis?

5. Is members' attendance at group meetings voluntary or compulsory?

6. How are potential members approached and prepared for the group?

7. What are the effects of this approach and preparation on (a) members' perceptions of the group, (b) members' attitudes toward the group, (c) the kinds of people likely to be referred to the group?

STATUS OF THE GROUP WORKER

1. Does the group worker only work with groups? If not, what are his or her other tasks?

2. Are social workers who work with groups or who are highly

knowledgeable about group work represented in supervisory and administrative positions to the same degree as social workers who are not?

3. What is the effect of the group worker's status on recruitment of group members, power to make decisions on ways of serving the group, and ability to secure resources for the group?

RESOURCES ALLOCATED BY THE AGENCY TO THE GROUP

1. What kind of room (that is, location, size, equipment) has the agency assigned to the group? To what other uses is it put? Is it regularly assigned? Are the group members allowed to alter the room in any way (for example, by putting up posters, shifting equipment)?

2. What kind of equipment is the group likely to require? Will it be readily available?

3. Will the group be likely to require other material resources (for example, transportation) and will the agency provide these?

4. Will the group require other human resources (for example, consultation) and will the agency provide this?

5. What are the effects of points 1–4 on group activities, morale, and climate?

TARGETS FOR CHANGE SELECTED BY THE AGENCY

1. Does the agency perceive its groups as primarily directed at changing the members? If so, is this conceived of as changes in self-understanding, attitudes, knowledge, and/or behavior?

2. Does the agency perceive its groups as seeking changes in the agency itself and/or in the environment outside of the agency?

3. What are the effects of points 1 and 2 on the activities of the group and on the attitudes of the members to the group?

INTERACTION OF THE GROUP
WITH THE AGENCY AND STAFF

1. With which staff members, in relation to the group worker, are members of the group likely to interact? What will be the nature and effect of this interaction on the member and on the group?

2. How is the agency decorated and how well is it maintained? What will be the effect of this on the group?

INTERACTION OF THE AGENCY
WITH THE GROUP'S INDIGENOUS LEADERS

1. Are group members involved in any way in agency decision making?

2. What are the effects of this involvement or lack of involvement on the group?

AGENCY'S PREFERRED SERVICE TECHNOLOGY

1. Does the agency have a preference regarding a theory or an approach to work with groups and/or individuals? What is it? How is it explained to members? What is the effect on the members?

2. How do the agency and the worker interact around preferred approaches (for example, consultation, training)?

3. Is the preferred approach consistent with approaches used in other services (for example, one-to-one, family, childcare, custodial)? What is the effect on the group of this consistency or inconsistency?

INTERORGANIZATIONAL RELATIONSHIPS

1. How does the group worker interact with staff peers and administrators? How does this affect him/or her? How does this ultimately affect the group?

2. What is the morale of the staff? How does this affect the group?

PART TWO

The Phases of Work

INTRODUCTION

IN THE FIRST PART of this book, we provided the reader with information on what group work is, how approaches to it vary, and how these approaches emerged historically. We also described the nature and effect of agency settings. As the next step, this second part shall contain a detailed presentation of the principles and procedures that guide practice with groups. The background provided earlier should help the reader to see how these practice specifications are drawn from our practice model and how they relate to agency conditions affecting practice.

Our discussion of group work shall be a sequential one based on two kinds of sequences found in group work practice. The first is the phases of group development; in the relevant chapters we shall summarize the conditions that usually emerge at different phases in the life of the group. The second is the movement from identifying the goals of the group work experience to planning, executing, and evaluating the means employed to achieve these goals. Consequently, each chapter in this part shall integrate aspects of group development and goal attainment in a time progression.

Accordingly, Chapter 3 shall describe the activities in which the worker is engaged, some with prospective members, prior to the first meeting of the group. A few approaches to group work practice do not emphasize preplanning as much as we do because of their assumption that facing the unplanned events in the group parallels the way one copes with the uncertainties of life. We believe that this idea may be valid at times, such as in the training of group facilitators, but is not appropriate for helping many applicants for group work services who usually have limited time, resources, and motivation. Therefore, we shall discuss a number of worker actions that enhance the ease with which members begin to define their goals and ways of achieving them.

In Chapter 4 we shall present the role of the worker during the first phase of group development: group formation. This phase must be well understood as what happens during it is vital to the success of the group. This is the period when the correspondence between member goals and group goals is developed and the members try, in the process, to form the kinds of relationships among themselves and with the worker that will sustain the group. When these and related issues are not satisfactorily resolved, the group either falls apart or remains frustrated in its efforts to meet the needs of its members.

Chapters 5 through 7 shall be developed as a series devoted to describing how the worker helps the members attain their goals. In part, the worker accomplishes this, by seeking changes in group conditions; the ways workers do this shall be described in Chapter 5. Another aspect of the worker's role is to promote changes in individual members and this shall be dealt with in Chapter 6. Finally, changes must often be sought in the environment outside the group and this is the topic of Chapter 7. This latter content has often been neglected in group work literature and we hope to offset this by the attention we give to environmental change procedures through group work.

A theme that pervades the entire book is that effective service is closely related to measurement of the effects of worker and member actions. Each chapter is meant to contribute in some way to this idea. Thus in Chapter 8, we shall present how changes in individual members, the group, and the external environment can and should be assessed.

In Chapter 9 this part of the book shall conclude with a discussion of group endings. The content of this chapter is based on the premise that careful attention to the tasks of termination will lead to more lasting and more beneficial results of the group experience.

Chapter 3

THE PREGROUP PHASE

AS STATED in the introduction to this part, we believe there are a number of tasks the worker can perform before the first group meeting that will make group experience more likely to be successful. In addition, there is research to show that the way these activities are performed will affect how rapidly and effectively the group moves forward to accomplish its goals. The reader should remember, however, that unpredicted events can always occur, as many group workers' diaries will attest. Sometimes even the most carefully laid plans must be cast aside. The intent of preplanning is not to eliminate uncertainty about group events but to reduce it.

One of the first tasks of the worker is to conceptualize the purpose of the group, at least in a general sense. As we stated in Chapter 2, agencies often have purposes for sponsoring particular groups and the worker must take these into consideration or risk losing agency support. As we shall describe, however, sometimes agencies wish to relate their purposes to a needs assessment of clients, and we shall suggest means for accomplishing this. The reason for conceptualizing purpose before attempting other pregroup tasks is the relationship of purpose to such other decisions as those on composition and group size.

Because purpose is so closely allied to composition, we shall treat this topic next and shall discuss how to compose a group so that the selection of members will support the purposes for which the group was established. A topic that shall also be considered in relationship to composition is whether a group experience is even the appropriate one for the individual concerned.

The major topic that we shall extensively discuss is how to prepare members for the group. This is often done in one or more sessions before the group begins when the worker also seeks to better understand the problems or concerns that brought the individuals to enter the agency and subsequently to contemplate a group experience. We shall describe ways in which the worker prepares other staff members to welcome the group as well as how the worker establishes physical conditions conducive to the group's beginning.

GROUP PURPOSES

By *group purposes,* we mean the specific reasons for which the group was established, usually expressed as the type of goals that the group will try to help its members attain. Group purposes may be conceived in different ways by the worker and the members; even each member may have a different perception of the purposes of the group. Purposes for the group may also be stated in terms of long-range plans or for a shorter span of time, even a given meeting.

These distinctions are important ones. Each of these aspects of purpose will have strong impact on group events. Thus group purposes affect and are affected by decisions on group composition, group program, worker interventions, number of meetings planned, and even choice of a worker for the group. An example should help to clarify these propositions about group purposes.

Example: A welfare department formed a group composed of parents of high school students. The agency's reason (*agency purpose*) for establishing the group was to help to provide support to their children to remain in school. In order to compose a group for this purpose, the agency asked workers to refer parents to the group worker who had expressed concern about this issue (*composition related to purpose*). Agency purpose thus became worker's purpose. The agency wanted the members to have the opportunity to describe their situations in detail and a small group—about five members—was decided on (*size related to purpose*). The worker believed that parents gathering for this purpose would want to focus on the issue quickly and learn how to deal with it and, thus, eight group meetings should be sufficient (*number of meetings related to purpose*).

When the group members were told about the group, several were of the opinion, privately, that the agency's "real" purpose was to check on how they were spending their welfare grant (*member's perception of purpose*). The worker anticipated that this might be what they thought and planned to discuss group purpose thoroughly at the first meeting to allay perceptions of purpose that would hinder the group's achievements.

At the first meeting, one member indicated a desire to be a member of a group that would help in making friends; the worker responded that, perhaps, another group could be formed for this purpose (*member's purpose*). The members, by the end of the first meeting, agreed that they had problems with keeping their youngsters in school and they wanted to be in a group established for this reason (*members' consensus on long-term purpose*). In planning for the second meeting, they also decided that the purpose of that meeting would be to report on the difficulties their children had told them they were experiencing in school (*short-term purpose*).

The reason for distinguishing among worker purpose, member purpose, consensus among members on purpose, and short-term and long-term purposes, is that a logical relationship must exist in order for the group to progress smoothly toward its goals. Thus if members and workers have different conceptions of group purpose, they are unlikely to find it very easy to work cooperatively together; similarly, if members do not agree on purpose, they are also unlikely to reach agreement on group goals or activities; if short-term purposes do not relate to the longer-term ones, the group will not be able to build on its experiences to create significant accomplishments.

As reasons for discrepancies among purposes are discovered, these may suggest that purposes that were originally decided for the group should be changed. This is more valid than the idea that the members should forgo ideas they have about the group's purpose. While modifications in group purposes can and do occur, the process is time consuming and the potential for severe conflict is present. Much of this can be obviated by careful planning about group purposes prior to first meetings and it is to this that we shall now address ourselves.

Needs Assessment

One way of establishing purposes that will lead to viable groups is through assessing the needs of people who are or might be served by the agency. The following is a sample of a series of items developed for a family agency. Such questions can be raised in an interview, a questionnaire, or by other professionals who refer people to groups.

Group Needs Assessment Questionnaire: We plan to start a group to help people with a variety of concerns they may have, such as relationships with family and friends, job situations, and so forth. It will help us to set up groups that will be of interest if you will answer the following questions. If you wish to be notified about a group of interest to you, a place is provided for you to sign your name.

1. Please indicate your interest in being in a group:

    _____ very interested

    _____ somewhat interested

    _____ not interested at all

2. Please check any areas you might like to discuss in a group:

    _____ relationship to husband/wife

    _____ relationship to person with whom you live
    (specify relationship) _____

    _____ relationship to friends

_____ job concerns

_____ feelings of discomfort (sadness, fears, worrying)

_____ concerns about your future (job, schooling)

_____ concerns about making an important decision (where you will live; go to school; leave school or home)

3. Have you been in a group before to discuss personal concerns?

_____ yes   _____ no

4. If yes to question 3, what did you think of the experience?

5. Which of the following describes what you are like in groups? Check as many as apply.

_____ I talk a lot.

_____ I seldom say anything.

_____ I make acquaintances easily.

_____ It takes me a long time to get to know others.

_____ My feelings get hurt easily.

_____ I easily tell personal things about myself.

_____ It is very hard for me to tell personal things about myself.

_____ I think I have a good idea of what others think of me.

_____ I like to stay on the subject.

_____ I have little influence on others.

_____ I can influence others a great deal.

At times, workers have little influence over the composition of the group and this makes it difficult or impossible prior to the first meetings to determine the purpose of the group. This is true when there are very few referrals to the group, when the group is already established (youth gangs), or when the group has been created for other purposes (cottage groups in a residential treatment center). In these cases, the question is reversed: Instead of "given a purpose, how shall the group be composed?", the worker asks "given group composition, what purposes can be achieved?" However, the worker can still use items such as those in the needs assessment instrument to help the group determine a purpose consistent with the purposes of the agency.

Organizational Functions and Group Purpose

To help the reader to understand the range of purposes, we present some examples in relationship to each of the types of organizational functions we described in the preceding chapter. In examining this list, it should be remembered that groups may also be composed of members with different needs; thus a group, on occasion, may serve several purposes.

Anomie Reduction Purposes

1. To decide what type of sexual life style is consistent with each member's current identity as well as future aspirations.
2. To select the kinds of roles in marriage that conform to each member's values and desires regarding marriage.
3. To clarify the meaning of masculinity (femininity) and what this implies for each member's behavior, life style, and crucial decisions, such as marriage, child rearing, and occupation.

Role Attainment Purposes

1. To learn how to fulfill the role of a parent.
2. To learn how to succeed in school, both through changing personal behavior as well as school policies when the latter impede personal progress.
3. To learn the social skills necessary to function in adolescent (young adult, adult) situations.
4. For foster parents to become better substitute parents.

Social Control Purposes

1. For individuals who are on parole, to make choices regarding legitimate occupational careers.
2. For a student in primary school grades to learn cooperative rather than disruptive classroom behaviors.
3. For a patient in a mental hospital to cease behaviors that are disruptive of hospital routines and/or aversive to other patients.

Alternative Role Attainment Purposes

1. For mental patients who have been socially isolated by virtue of unacceptable or bizarre behavior to learn behaviors appropriate to the social roles they desire.
2. For child-abusing parents to learn to discipline their children in nonabusive ways.
3. For obese persons to learn eating habits that will lead to lower food intake and weight loss.

GROUP COMPOSITION

In situations where the purpose of the group is determined before it is created, the next step is to select the members. Some workers will have a large pool of people from whom to chose and will be able to consider many factors in this choice; in other situations, few prospective members are available and the worker may even conclude that a selection from this limited set of people cannot possibly lead to a viable group.

The worker, in considering group composition principles, must be aware that there are many unknowns regarding the combination of member characteristics that will produce optimal groups. Also, there are many forces that affect group outcomes (for example, techniques employed by the worker, available resources in the agency) so that attention should be paid to composition, but the worker should not become obsessed by compositional decisions. As Yalom states "Time and energy spent on delicately casting and balancing a group is not justified given our current state of knowledge; the therapist does better to invest that time and energy in careful selection of patients for group therapy and in their pre-therapy preparation."[1] Nevertheless, we do not advocate inattention to group composition and we shall now discuss some major considerations for accomplishing this task. We also include an exercise at the end of this chapter to demonstrate the principles of composition.

Purpose and Group Composition

The central issue that workers should consider in composition is the purpose of the group. Some purposes cannot be addressed in groups composed in certain ways while for other purposes, composition may be less crucial. Some examples of compositional issues related to the major categories of group purposes are now given.

Anomie Reduction. A group in which members seek to determine or change their values should have members whose values are different enough to provide a range of ideas for each member to consider. One group for women seeking to clarify their female roles provided many models for the members because it included women who were career oriented, home oriented, as well as those who sought to combine both. The group also included women who were militant in their pursuit of their objectives as well as women who were not.

Role Attainment. In situations where groups are used to help members learn the necessary knowledge and skills to attain some role, it is best for

---

[1] Irvin D. Yalom, *The Theory and Practice of Group Psychotherapy* (New York: Basic Books, 1975), p. 272.

members to have similar aspirations. Thus a group of adolescents, seeking to attain school success, provided a good deal of reinforcement to each other. Role attainment groups are also facilitated if, in addition to commonality of objectives, different knowledge and skills related to these objectives are possessed by each member. Members can thus help one another overcome personal as well as social obstacles to fulfill their roles.

Social Control. A group whose members hold similar values in regard to an antisocial behavior can provide reinforcement to maintain that behavior. Dissimilarity in this regard is often sought. An important principle can be demonstrated here; namely, that when composition cannot be varied (as is often true in institutions serving offenders) new approaches to intervention must be developed. Thus in fairly homogeneous social-control-oriented groups, workers use confrontive approaches and encourage members to confront each other regarding their attitudes and behaviors. A compositional "technique" to secure some heterogeneity in these groups is to "seed" them with people who have been members of other groups and have already begun the process of normative change.

Alternative Role Attainment. As in role attainment groups, similarity of resocialization objectives is sought so that members can help one another in that process. An example is that of a group of clients in a half-way house who had been previously diagnosed as schizophrenic and were now in the process of job training.

Group Cohesiveness and Composition

In order for a group, certainly a voluntary one, to remain in existence, the members have to be motivated to attend, participate, and complete tasks. The concept that encompasses these variables is *cohesiveness*, usually defined as "the resultant of all the forces acting on all the members to remain in the group."[2]

Members can have many reasons to remain in a group, including attraction to other members, the worker, the goal, the activity, or the status asssociated with membership. Thibaut and Kelley have identified yet another variable, "the comparison level for alternatives," which is defined as "the standard that an individual uses to decide whether to remain in or to leave an interpersonal relationship."[3] This variable causes us to recognize that individuals not only choose to remain in groups because of what the group has to offer but also because of how these offerings compare with other opportunities.

[2]L. Festinger, "Informal Social Communication," *Psychological Review* LVII (1950), 274.

[3]J.W. Thibaut and H.H. Kelley, *The Social Psychology of Groups* (New York: John Wiley, 1959), p. 15.

The cohesiveness of a group is analogous to the concept of *relationship* in one-to-one interactions. According to research findings, it is one of the most important forces accounting for the effectiveness of a group.[4] In reference to this, Yalom states, "If an individual experienced little sense of belongingness or attraction to the group, even when measured early in the course of the sessions, there was little hope that he would benefit from the group and, in fact, a high likelihood that he would have a negative outcome."[5]

Although there are many bases of cohesiveness, the one that is most often studied, as well as sought after, is the attraction of members for each other. One way this attraction is enhanced is when members perceive each other as being similar to themselves. The worker can maximize cohesiveness, therefore, by composing groups of persons who are as similar as possible both on attributes (age, sex, race, socioeconomic status) as well as behaviors (types of problems, skills in problem solving, interests in the same activities).

An issue that has troubled group workers is whether people will be reinforced for their dysfunctional ways of solving their problems if they are too similar in their behaviors. Thus many workers have argued that members should differ in their ways of coping. This will lead, presumably, to the kinds of constructive disagreements and tensions among members that will maintain interest in the group and stimulate members to consider new ideas and behaviors. Yalom has labeled this compositional model the "dissonance" one.[6]

Yalom concludes, based on his examination of both research and clinical experience, that "there is no evidence that deliberately heterogeneously composed groups facilitate therapy,"[7] and this has also been our experience. We, therefore, agree with Yalom's proposal that"...cohesiveness be our primary guideline in the composition of therapy groups."[8] This conclusion has been reached with the awareness that people differ considerably from one another and even the greatest efforts at matching will still produce an array of individuals with different experiences, ideas, and ways of responding to their environments.

Yalom asserts that cohesiveness should be emphasized in *therapy* groups. Thus he has a specific practice model in mind—one in which members are encouraged to remain in the group for a long period of time and treatment is accomplished through members' intensive examination of interpersonal processes in the group. Social workers often work with other kinds of groups. In these cases such an emphasis on homogeneity leading to cohesiveness may not be as necessary. Examples are:

1. groups formed for a specific short-term purpose, such as preparation for discharge or orientation,

[4]Yalom, *Group Psychotherapy,* pp. 49–52.
[5]Ibid., p. 52.
[6]Ibid., p. 270.
[7]Ibid.
[8]Ibid., p. 271.

2. groups employing a structured format, such as those for assertiveness training, and

3. groups with a strong educational component, such as parent
training.

Deviance and Group Composition

Although we have stated that the worker should strive to select
members who are similar when a cohesive group is sought, this is often not
possible. The question then arises as to how dissimilar a member can be from
others. The danger is that a member who is very different from others will be
perceived as undesirable or, in sociological terms, deviant by the other
members. When the difference is based on some attribute such as age or race,
the members may avoid communicating with this person, thus creating a
group isolate. When the difference is based on a behavior such as topics
discussed, personal disclosure, or social skills, the members may become
critical of the individual and then scapegoat the person, who will then develop
negative feelings toward the group, avoid its influences, and eventually drop
out. In some cases, the member will try instead to modify his or her behavior
so as to become more acceptable to others in the group but the risk still remains that such a person will become alienated from the group.

When the group is quite heterogeneous, the worker must avoid introducing someone who differs substantially from the other members in a
way that group members consider salient to their interests. What constitutes
such a salience must often be anticipated by the group worker based on experience with the population in question. For example, athletic skill may be
an important consideration in an adolescent but not in an adult group;
religious attitudes in a group to discuss child rearing but not in one to discuss
employment; and types of sexual experience in a marital counseling group
but not a preparation for retirement one.

There are several things the worker can do when there is a likelihood
that group composition will lead to creating a deviant member. One is to seek
to enroll another member who is either similar to the person in question or
who is somewhere in the "middle," thus creating a continuum of member
characteristics. This continuum then avoids the image and experience of a
group that has extreme differences in attributes or behaviors between one
person and the rest.

There are some situations where the worker may wish to use constructively the way a member differs substantially from others. One example was
that of a "friendship" group of adolescent boys in a community center. The
worker asked them to accept as a group member a boy with cerebral palsy.
After much discussion, this was accomplished. Some months later, when this
boy had become well integrated into the group, another member mentioned
that the boys will never again use the word "spastic" as a way of ridiculing
someone.

One device used to compose groups to avoid creating a group isolate or deviant is to rate each member on a series of scales. Each scale represents an attribute or behavior deemed significant by the worker.[9] This graphic device, as illustrated in Figure I, has the property of making it easy to identify this type of undesirable situation. The way that we have used such data is to examine each attribute or behavior to identify individuals who are "extreme" on that variable. Other variables are then examined to see if that person is also extreme with regard to these. If not, we assume that these other conditions will provide the bases for the commonality necessary for interpersonal attraction and group cohesiveness. When an individual is placed at an extreme on several "scales" in relationship to other group members, it is best to introduce others who are similar in some ways or to seek another group for him or her.

Name	Age	Race	Degree of Verbal Aggressiveness	Presenting Problem	Interest In Group
Sam	14	Black	Low	Severe conflict with teachers	Moderate
Bill	15	Black	Moderate	Theft from school	Moderate
Frank	15	White	Moderate	Runaway from family	Low
Carl	13	White	Moderate	Poor peer relations	High
Dick	17	Black	High	Frequent physical fights	Low

Figure 1 *Composition of an Adolescent Boys' Group*

In our illustration (Figure I), Dick is older than the other boys; he is also verbally aggressive, engages in frequent physical fights, and is less interested in the group. His main area of identification is likely to be his race. On the other hand, he might serve as a model for the younger, particularly black members, in ways that are problematic. In this example, the worker introduced two additional members to the group: another black 17-year-old who had been a runaway from his family and a 14-year-old white youth who had been involved in thefts—this latter member was not very aggressive, verbally or physically. The modified group composition, therefore, avoids the likely creation of an antisocial leader (Dick). It also avoids the equally likely creation of an isolate (Carl).

[9]For more details on this procedure, see Harvey J. Bertcher and Frank Maple, "Elements and Issues in Group Composition," in *Individual Change Through Small Groups,* eds. Paul Glasser, Rosemary Sarri, and Robert Vinter (New York: Free Press, 1974), pp. 194–95.

Program Activity and Group Composition

In most group situations, the major activity is group discussion, and verbal and cognitive approaches to treatment predominate. In group work, even before the advent of encounter and other groups that use nonverbal exercises, a variety of activities was used to achieve group purposes, including games, crafts, music, dance, and so forth. While many of these "programs" are chosen by groups after the group has been formed, the likelihood of their selection can often be predicted.

When the type of media that are likely to be used is anticipated, this influences group composition. If discussion is to be employed, verbal skills must be assessed. Similarly, if the members are likely to communicate through drama, art, or athletics, the interest and level of skill in these must be rated.

Assessing Members in Relationship to Group Composition

The preceding discussion of factors to consider in composing groups is based on the idea that aspects of a person's behavior can be predicted. This is a difficult task because a person's behavior is determined both by personal characteristics and by the forces present in a situation.[10] For this reason, the best indicator of a person's behavior in a group is his or her actions in a similar group situation.[11] Some group serving agencies, to secure this kind of information, have set up "waiting list" groups[12] or diagnostic groups.

Another possibility, suggested by Yalom, is an interpersonally oriented initial interview.[13] In this procedure, the worker assesses to what degree the clients can comment on the interpersonal process going on between them and the worker and how they assess and respond to the therapist's views of them. Also examined in such an interview is information about the clients' relationships with peers as well as the kinds of roles they have assumed in groups.

Various psychological instruments have been used to select members for groups but probably the best-known one is Schutz's FIRO-B (Fundamental Interpersonal Relations Orientation) scales.[14] Schutz based his instrument on the proposition that everyone seeks to relate to others so as to satisfy three needs: *affection, control, and inclusion. Affection* pertains to close personal relationships, *control* to power over others, and *inclusion* to being with others. Everyone, according to Schutz, can be described as to the degree with which each of these is expressed and whether it is manifested toward others as well as expected from them.

[10]For a discussion of the point, see Marvin E. Shaw, *Group Dynamics: The Psychology of Small Group Behavior* (New York: McGraw-Hill, 1976), pp. 175–86.

[11]A. Goldstein, K. Heller, and L. Sechrest, *Psychotherapy and the Psychology of Behavior Change* (New York: John Wiley, 1966), p. 329.

[12]Yalom, *Group Psychotherapy*, p. 255.

[13]Ibid., pp. 257–58.

[14]William C. Schutz, *Firo: A Three Dimensional Theory of Interpersonal Orientations* (New York: Holt, Rinehart & Winston, 1958).

One social work writer, William Shalinsky, utilized Schutz's scales to study the effects of different kinds of composition in children's groups. Shalinsky created some groups that were compatible and some that were not. Compatibility was defined as groupings consisting of people who were "similar to others in [their] total amount of expressed and wanted behavior in the need area of affection."[15] This researcher found that members of compatible groups liked each other more, found their group more attractive, and were even more cooperative. Also, compatible groups in competitive tasks won significantly more often than incompatible ones.

The implication of Shalinsky's findings are that these interpersonal traits should be considered in composing groups and that homogeneity should be sought in this regard. This is also consistent with Yalom's emphasis on seeking cohesiveness in therapy groups and basing this on such measures as those devised by Shalinsky.

Selection of Candidates for Groups

The process of composing groups consists of two stages: the first is to ascertain whether a group experience, at all, is an appropriate one; the second is to compose groups of people who are both appropriate referrals to *any* group as well as to the one planned. In this respect we assume that both group and one-to-one helping are equally valid for a large proportion of people served by social work agencies.

Family Treatment. Probably the most important decisional issue, then, is whether family treatment or other family involvement is required. Only after family approaches are rejected, should a worker consider whether casework or group work should be employed. It is, of course, possible to have a group composed of several families.[16] The decision to involve the family should be based on the following assessment:

1. Is the problem maintained by processes operating in the family as a system?
2. How will the family respond to changes the individual may chose to make and will these responses support or retard such changes?
3. Does the individual wish to involve the family and is the family amenable to such involvement?

If the family interaction maintains the problem or if the family opposes changes that the individual choses to make, effective helping requires the worker to seek to involve other family members. Individual and group ap-

[15]William I. Shalinsky, "The Effects of Group Composition on Aspects of Group Functioning" (unpublished doctoral dissertation, Western Reserve University, 1967).

[16]H. Laqueur, H. Laburt, and G. Morong, "Multiple Family Therapy: Further Developments," *International Journal of Social Psychiatry* (1964) Congress Issue, 70-80.

proaches should only be the worker's choice when these family considerations are lacking or minimal or when the client has rejected family involvement.

Client Preference. The next consideration is whether the potential group member wishes to be in a group. Clients usually come to agencies with expectations regarding the kinds of services they will receive and, often, this is for one-to-one help. The client's choice of individual, group, or family services should be an informed one based on information regarding different forms of interpersonal helping and what they are like. For such knowledge of group work, agencies have presented films, tapes, or even "comic books" that portray what happens in the agency's groups.

For some clients, a group experience may be desirable but is rejected by the client because of some aspect of their situation. One example of this is a concern regarding confidentiality. In some cases, this problem is very "real" in that some information regarding clients might be harmful to them if publicized. On the other hand, all groups develop norms regarding confidentiality and breaches of this are almost nonexistent. Most clients who have such concerns are reassured by discussion of this issue prior to the group and during the first meetings.

The Work of Yalom. Although workers should consider family issues, client attitudes, and confidentiality, they cannot draw from comprehensive research findings to determine the efficacy of group as opposed to individual modalities of service. Yalom, however, presents an excellent discussion of therapy group member selection that does draw on research findings.[17] The problem of generalizing from his discussion is that it is based almost entirely on research and experience from either adult therapy groups or encounter groups. Group workers often work with children's, short term, and nonverbal activity groups, to name a few, where Yalom's conclusions may not hold.

For example, Yalom cites the "clinical concensus" that the following people are poor candidates for outpatient intensive group therapy: (1) brain damaged, (2) paranoid, (3) extremely narcissistic, (4) hypochondriacal, (5) suicidal, (6) addicted to drugs or alcohol, (7) acutely psychotic, or (8) sociopathic.[18] Group workers have worked with brain-damaged people; crisis groups have included suicidal people; groups patterned after Alcoholics Anonymous have been used with alcoholics; and confrontive group technologies such as Synanon games and guided group interaction have been used with people labeled sociopathic. At least anecdotal reports suggest some success with these populations through group methods other than traditional psychotherapy.

Yalom, while referring to groups that do not represent the full range of

[17]Yalom, *Group Psychotherapy,* pp. 221–43.
[18]Ibid., p. 221.

group work activities, took an imaginative approach to the issue of selecting appropriate members for groups. Since it is difficult to determine for whom groups are best suited, he examined, instead, the kinds of people who dropped out of therapy groups after twelve or fewer meetings.[19] Obviously, if a person terminates early from a group, they are unlikely to have benefited from it. In the absence, therefore, of a replication of this study with social work groups, Yalom's findings should be considered in selecting members for such groups. The reasons, according to Yalom, for such premature termination were:

1. external factors

These included reasons such as conflict between meeting attendance and other events. Yalom implies the conflict may be a rationalization based on resistance to the group. Also, some people who present this kind of resistance to group attendance may be experiencing a crisis and wish to secure help on an immediate one-to-one basis.

2. group deviancy

As group deviancy was discussed early in this section, people who are viewed by themselves and others in the group as different in attributes relevant to the group are likely to be harmed rather than helped through the group process. As Yalom states, "There is experimental evidence, then, that the group deviant derives less satisfaction from the group, experiences anxiety, is less valued by the group, is less prone to be influenced or benefited by the group, is more likely to be harmed by the group, and is far more prone than nondeviants to terminate membership."[20] Here Yalom is describing people who are deviant in therapy groups because of their attitudes and behaviors, namely their strong use of denial and projection, their lack of interest in the intrapsychic, and their tendency to blame physical and health factors for their difficulties. From our group work experience, we conclude, also, that the worker's inability to find a group for a person in which other members have some similar attributes militates against offering group service to that person.

3. problems of intimacy

The people who Yalom included in this category included those who manifested schizoid withdrawal, too rapid and intense self-disclosure, great fear of self-disclosure, and "unrealistic demands for instant intimacy."[21] Yalom recognizes that there is a paradox in the concept of problems with intimacy as these are the reasons people are often referred to groups. The implication here, perhaps, is that some people are capable of working on these in

---

[19]Yalom, *Group Psychotherapy*, pp. 224–35.
[20]Ibid., p. 229.
[21]Ibid., p. 232.

group situations while others are overwhelmed in one way or another by the stimuli experienced in groups.

We remind the reader that Yalom is describing member problems with intimacy evoked in groups whose major focus is on the examination of relationship patterns. People with some severe intimacy problems have been helped with relationship issues in social work groups such as those where the programmatic emphasis is on activities with less verbal exchange and fewer demands for disclosure. Groups in mental health settings have utilized art, dramatics, and even games, and these have helped to shape social interaction behaviors and to desensitize people whose fears led to inappropriate behaviors regarding disclosure and intimacy. A subsequent experience may then appropriately be in a verbally oriented therapy group.

4. fear of emotional contagion

This category of group dropouts includes people who "reported that they had been extremely adversely affected by hearing the problems of the other group members."[22] Yalom believes that such people may also gradually be desensitized to this. In many group work groups in which the process is structured, such individuals may have less cause for anxiety as to how they will be affected by the behaviors and problems of others.

When Yalom's list of categories of people who drop out of groups is reviewed, the variable that seems the most pervasive for referral to any group is the likelihood that the person will find others to whom he or she can relate and who will reciprocate. In addition, expressions of difficulty in attending meetings, if not resolved, often indicate strong resistance to the group and militate against such a referral.

Yalom discusses "inclusion criteria," as those characteristics that most point to group therapy. He concludes that any person not excluded for such reasons as just listed can profit from group therapy. In one study, he found that those people who profitted the most were those who were most attracted to the group and introspective.[23] In another study specifically devoted to outcomes of encounter groups, the set of predictors of good outcomes included being valued by other members, being desirous of personal change, viewing oneself as deficient in understanding one's feelings, and having high expectations of the group.[24]

One problem with these studies is that they do not distinguish between those who benefited from group therapy and those who benefited from other group approaches. Another problem is that the findings may be confounded by therapist expectations that motivated, verbal, socially assertive persons will succeed in therapy. This also points to the strong need for research regar-

[22]Ibid., p. 234.
[23]Ibid., p. 236-37.
[24]Morton A. Lieberman, Irvin Yalom, and M. Miles, *Encounter Groups: First Facts* (New York: Basic Books, 1973), pp. 315-55.

ding the ways the many different types of groups conducted by social group workers are likely to affect their members.

PREPARING FOR THE GROUPS

Once candidates for the group have been selected, the worker will accomplish a series of tasks prior to the first group meeting. These tasks include preparing the individuals for the group, determining the optimum size of the group, and arranging the physical setting. Other people in the agency must also be prepared for the group so that they can support the arrangements that have been made. Careful attention to these details will do much to ensure the success of the group.

Preparing Members for the Group

The idea that members who are prepared for the group experience are more likely to benefit from it is receiving increased support. This had led to efforts to specify such systems of preparation sufficiently so that they can be tested. Northen, for example, recommends that the worker help the potential group member explore reactions to group placement and at the same time become acquainted with the worker. This, she asserts, will lead to a reduction in pregroup anxiety and confusion.[25]

Goldstein, Heller, and Sechrest also argue for the following hypothesis: "Giving patients prior information about the nature of psychotherapy, the theories underlying it, and the techniques to be used will facilitate progress in psychotherapy."[26] Based on this type of prediction, a number of investigations have been conducted as to the effects of explanations given to clients in a "role induction" interview. In one study conducted as early as 1964, patients who were told how to behave in therapy rated higher on attendance, relationships, and other therapy-related behaviors, as well as outcome measures, than those not receiving such instruction.[27] Based on this finding, Goldstein and co-workers suggest that any such preparation present a theory relevant to the disorder, a rationale for the treatment, and a description of the treatment to follow.[28]

Yalom developed and tested a procedure for preparation of clients for groups that conforms to the preceding criteria.[29] In his approach, he includes

---

[25]Helen Northen, *Social Work with Groups* (New York: Columbia University Press, 1969), p. 108.

[26]Goldstein, Heller, and Sechrest, *Psychotherapy*, p. 245.

[27]R. Hoehn-Saric and others, "Systematic Preparation of Patients for Psychotherapy: Effects on Therapy Behavior and Outcome," *Journal of Psychiatry Research*, II (1964), 267–81.

[28]Goldstein, Heller, and Sechrest, *Psychotherapy*, p. 250.

[29]Yalom, *Group Psychotherapy*, pp. 290–98.

the following information and questions which he tailors further to the individual being interviewed:

1. All who enter psychotherapy have problems in relationships with others.
2. The therapy group is a place for "honest interpersonal exploration" but this will not be easy.
3. There will be a "carryover" from the working out of relationships in the group to relationships outside the group.
4. To accomplish this carryover, members must be honest and direct in the group at the moment with their feelings.
5. "Stumbling blocks," such as feeling discouraged in early meetings, will occur and members should not follow an inclination to leave during this period.
6. Treatment is gradual and long.

In addition, Yalom tells patients about the history of group therapy, as well as the results of current outcome studies. They are also alerted to the issue of confidentiality. Finally, if patients form relationships with other members outside the group, they should discuss this with the group.

In a test of this procedure with sixty people waiting for group psychotherapy, members of "prepared" groups had more faith in therapy and engaged in more group interaction. This piece of research presents strong evidence for such preparation. The task now is to develop analogous systems of preparation for the different types of groups served by group workers.

Group Size

The size of the group should also be determined in relationship to group purpose. The worker should also understand the kinds of processes that occur in groups of varying sizes so that this can be accomplished. Small groups, such as those of about four to eight members, demand and produce more intimacy than larger groups. Such small groups are likely to bring pressure on members to participate. Larger groups, on the other hand, allow members to withdraw from active participation. The tendency in such groups is for a polarization to occur with some members talking a great deal while others seldom speak.

Writers on verbally oriented group psychotherapy have recommended that such groups have about seven members. This allows for a sufficient number to carry on the group when inevitable absences occur. Members have sufficient time for each to focus on his or her own issues and withdrawal from participation and intermember hostility are quickly noted and discussed.

Usually children's groups should be of a smaller size. In general, children are unlikely to postpone attention to their concerns for any length of time. In addition, if there is any likelihood of destructive or aggressive behavior, the group will be small enough for the worker to respond to this while at the same time remaining in control of the overall group situation. The same may be true of adolescent groups. On the other hand, at times, adolescents want the comfort of withdrawing from a demand for participation and this can be accomplished in larger groups.

It is possible in large groups to employ some devices to produce greater intimacy. These include extending the length of meetings so that more members have time to receive group attention and dividing the group into subgroups, or even pairs, for discussion of issues, receipt of feedback, and reinforcement.

The following are some examples of ways of relating group size to group purpose. Groups devoted to helping members clarify their values can be large if similar sets of values are examined, otherwise such groups should be small. Role attainment groups where members face similar barriers to achieving socialization goals may be large, otherwise small. Social control groups, if large, may allow members to avoid confrontation which is usually employed in such groups. On the other hand, some individuals may be "turned off" by too early confrontation and also may profit from observing other people who are able to deal constructively with such confrontation in a large group. Alternative role attainment often requires attention to the conflicts each member experiences and should be small. However, people who are fearful of disclosure might initially benefit from a large group in which models for such behavior are available.

Preparing the Physical and Social Setting

Often neglected but important details in group beginnings are the selection of the group's meeting place and the preparation of other staff for the impact of the group. If at all possible, the group should have a permanent room. This facilitates the group member's sense of group identity and permanence. The room should have pictures or other symbols that indicate the agency's receptivity to the group. These might include pictures of scenes pleasurable to the members or of people with whom members might identify. Occasionally, abstract art is used as a way of eliciting members' projections.

Bruno Bettelheim, for example, has presented the epitome of thoughtfulness regarding a rationale for the selection of decoration and objects in a therapeutic setting.[30] He discusses in great detail the objects in his agency's (a residential treatment center for children) reception room—the "living room." These include an antique crib which communicates the belief that an infant's early experiences are important, a wall hanging showing a fairy tale, some furnishings suitable for adults and some for children, and an

[30]Bruno Bettelheim, *A Home for the Heart* (New York: Knopf, 1974), pp. 104–58.

elaborately carved "throne," which skillfully supports either reality images or fantasy ones.

The size of the room should also be planned with reference to the purposes of the group and its anticipated activities. Too large a space can give members the illusion that the group has no boundaries and yet one worker "made do" in such a situation by structuring a fence of chairs across the width of a large room. This helped to set some limits for a large group of hyperactive children, otherwise likely to fan out beyond the worker's control. Too small a space, on the other hand, can cause anxiety in a group whose members are fearful of being forced into intimacy prematurely.

It has become a stereotype that a group worker arranges chairs into a circle at all meetings. Yet this face-to-face contact promotes more interaction than other arrangements. The distance between chairs can also be varied, although members will usually move chairs into positions in which they are comfortable and this will help the worker to assess the structure of interpersonal relationships. Groups with problems with interpersonal contact can, however, sit around a table as a sort of barrier.

The material objects in the room will also suggest activities to the members (for example, chalk and blackboards, games, sports equipment). For group therapy situations, either comfortable chairs or large cushions on a carpeted floor serve to communicate the idea that informal interaction is anticipated.

Other staff members should be aware of the beginning of the group. The receptionist should appear knowledgeable; attending a first meeting is anxiety-provoking enough without confusion beginning literally at the door of the agency. Members should be shown to the meeting room on arrival. The worker should be present early as the way members arrive and the timing will also disclose much about their attitudes to the group.

When other staff direct members to the room, their knowing about the group further communicates the agency's receptivity to the service. Staff, particularly those who have made referrals, will be asked questions by prospective members and, therefore, should be given information about the purpose of the group, frequency of meetings and their timing, as well as their location.

Part of the preparation for the first group meeting is the preparation of the worker, himself or herself. We all experience feelings and thoughts about beginnings—whether the experience will be what we anticipate, whether we will be able to cope with events, whether we will be liked by others, whether we will like them whether the group will be a success. Some workers handle these concerns by overstructuring first meetings; others deny these feelings and present a facade to members; still others openly admit to members that they, like the members, have concerns about the beginning of the group but that together they can work to share and resolve these. Whatever the preferred style of beginning, the worker should be aware of what his or her style is, what it is a response to, and how it affects the members as they cope with the beginning of a new experience.

SUMMARY

In this chapter, we have presented a rationale for preparing the group and have discussed various aspects of this. Preplanning includes a determination of group purpose, a decision as to which persons can be helped in a group, a determination of the size and composition of the group, and selection and preparation of the physical setting.

GROUP COMPOSITION EXERCISE

Goals

1. To learn to apply the principles of group composition.

2. To identify the steps involved in a group composition procedure.

3. To learn how to evaluate the adequacy of one's group composition procedure by assessing whether initial group processes are the ones intended by the way the group was composed.

Procedure

1. Prior to the exercise, trainees read about and discuss the principles of group composition described in this chapter.

2. Trainees (preferably about twenty but the exercise can be done with sixteen) fill out the accompanying Assessment Form. This simulates a needs assessment and group referral process.

3. The instructor divides the group in half, and the halves exchange Assessment Forms. The two halves created in this way are instructed to compose a group consisting of about five persons from the other half. (If the halves are too small, they can supplement each other to form the group.) This task is to be completed by utilizing the principles of group composition that the trainees have discussed. The group may secure additional information to accomplish this task through delegating someone to go to the other half to arrange for a private "interview" with one or another prospective member.

There are two alternatives for the next step in the exercise:

a. Each half reports on the group it has composed and the rationale for believing this is a viable one. The entire class discusses the issues this raises.

b. After composing a group, the trainees predict how the group is likely to begin (that is, topics likely to be discussed, initial exploration of commonalities, purposes which emerge, subgroupings). One or two members volunteer to be group workers and actually conduct a minisession (about twenty minutes) of the group. The trainees then present their rationale for composing the group, their predictions, and the initial group outcomes. The entire class discusses the issues posed by this.

Questions for Discussion

1. How was the initial purpose for the group determined?

2. How were individual reasons for wishing to be in a group related to group purpose?

3. What types of attributes were considered and why were they considered?

4. What types of member behaviors were considered and why were they considered?

5. How was motivation to be in a group considered?

6. How did the "workers" plan to begin the group in the light of the way it was composed? Did this plan involve some mechanism for dealing with some deficits in the composition (too great heterogeneity; insufficient basis for interpersonal attraction)?

ASSESSMENT FORM

Group Composition

Name _____

Sex _____   Age Group _____ 20–25 _____ 26–30 _____ over 30

Briefly describe a question, concern, or issue you would like to discuss in a group.

If none, write NONE.

How active are you in groups?

_____ talk a great deal   _____ talk little

_____ talk somewhat   _____ say nothing or almost nothing

What are some of your hobbies or interests?

How do you feel about being in a group composed as part of this class?

_____ very interested   _____ somewhat opposed

_____ somewhat interested   _____ very opposed

_____ neutral

Notes for Group Composition Rater

Chapter 4

BEGINNING A GROUP

IN THIS CHAPTER we shall describe the kinds of processes that occur in groups during their beginning phases and the activities of group workers to facilitate these processes. Group workers seek to understand the processes of group beginnings for several reasons.

1. All groups go through formation phases and the workers who understand these will not be overly concerned by inevitable events in the group. Rather, they will understand these as efforts of group members to cope with determining group purposes, selecting activities to achieve these purposes, and learning to trust and cooperate with each other.[1]

2. The worker can learn to differentiate between fairly typical patterns and those that require the worker and members to take special measures to save the group from inertia or destruction.

As we indicated in the Introduction to this part, the worker must learn to integrate both knowledge of phases of group development and stages of the group work process from its beginnings to its endings. This chapter, therefore, seeks to enhance this integration with reference to group beginnings.

The first section of the chapter, therefore, presents the process of group formation as it may occur in any group. Following this general discussion of group formation, we present the tasks the worker must undertake and help

---

[1] Our discussion of group formation draws on such portrayals of group development as Rosemary C. Sarri and Maeda Galinsky, "A Conceptual Framework for Group Development," in *Individual Change Through Small Groups*, eds. Paul Glasser, Rosemary Sarri, and Robert Vinter (New York: Free Press, 1974), pp. 71–88; James A. Garland, Hubert E. Jones, and Ralph Kolodny, "A Model for Stages of Development in Social Work Groups," in *Explorations in Group Work*, ed. Saul Bernstein (Boston: Boston University School of Social Work, 1965), pp. 12–13; and Irvin D. Yalom, *The Theory and Practice of Group Psychotherapy* (New York: Basic Books, 1975), pp. 301–75.

the members to undertake to accomplish the social work purposes of the group. These tasks include helping the members to decide on group purposes that will help them to achieve their goals as well as group rules that will govern behavior. Both the members and the worker will also have to gather information in order to choose effective ways of accomplishing the group's goals. Usually when the group is thought of as "treatment," this information gathering is conceived of as an *assessment*.

A number of issues regarding member emotions in beginning phases must also be understood. These emotions are often ambivalent because members are attracted to the group while experiencing some anxiety about investing in it. The members will also have feelings about the worker with which they must learn to cope, and these matters shall be discussed here.

Some practical ideas presented in this chapter for helping the group through the beginning are in the sections on group structure and on the contract. We then conclude the chapter with a discussion of how to resolve atypical formation difficulties. A group exercise based on enhancing one's understanding of group formation concludes the chapter.

PROCESS OF GROUP FORMATION

In the first meetings of groups, particularly those in which members have not known each other beforehand, there is little sharing of personal, more intimate reactions and experiences. Rather, members will interact with one another in ways based on fairly superficial attributes or experiences. For example, members will comment on the similarities and differences of places they have lived, they will talk primarily with people who are similar in obvious ways such as age, race, and sex. Members may also seek out others in the group based on common interests in sports, politics, religion, or leisure time activities.

In his discussion of group beginnings, Yalom notes that in groups defined as offering therapy, "symptom description is a favorite early issue, along with previous therapy experiences, medications, and the like."[2] He sees this "stereotyped" activity as one way of coping with the anxiety posed by beginnings.

DECISIONS ON GROUP PURPOSE

In the process of becoming acquainted, members must determine group purpose(s). This may be simple, as when a group has been formed around some highly specific issue such as enhancing assertiveness or parenting. Members in these circumstances have joined the group to learn specific social skills or

---

[2]Yalom, *Group Psychotherapy*, p. 305.

discipline techniques. The determination of group purpose may, however, be a more complex one when members have additional, alternative, or even covert reasons for joining the group.

An example of a covert reason for joining a group that affected the process of determining group purpose was a member of an assertiveness group who hoped to make friends in the group; another example was a woman in a parent education group who sought encouragement to seek employment outside her home. Another person joined a job placement group in order to recruit people for a social action project to promote a public service career program.

A thorough discussion of purposes in a group's formation period leads, in most circumstances, to the group purpose that has the strongest commitment of all members. In some instances, however, individual issues that will broaden or change group purposes do not surface until the group begins to move to the subsequent phase when activities to accomplish group purposes are determined. Problems that arise in making decisions on activities are often a result of lack of commitment of some or all members to the group purpose.

In some groups, the initial statement of purpose is vague. This is true of statements such as "enhancing interpersonal relationships." The group members in such groups must enter into further discussions of purpose in order to have the group purpose clear enough to serve as a basis for decisions regarding group activities.

ASSESSMENT IN GROUPS

Usually, in concert with determining purposes, members will find it necessary to gather various kinds of information. This activity can help members to specify group purposes in detail as they list problems that concern them individually or as a group. Such information gathering will also include securing details about individual or group problems. In groups devoted to achieving specific individual treatment goals members will obtain data related to the causes of and solutions to individual problems, thus forming as assessment of the member's individual behavior problems. In addition to or instead of a member-oriented assessment, the process of data gathering may focus on analyzing other systems, such as members' families' schools, communities, or places of employment.

There are a number of useful guidelines for the assessment of individuals, groups, and larger systems, such as those provided by Sporin, Compton and Galaway, and Rose.[3] These frameworks can be used in in-

[3]Max Sporin, *Introduction to Social Work Practice* (New York: Macmillan, 1975), pp. 219–50; Beulah Compton and Burt Galaway, *Social Work Processes* (Homewood, Ill.: Dorsey Press, 1979), pp. 232–56; and Sheldon D. Rose, *Group Therapy: A Behavioral Approach* (Englewood Cliffs, N.J.: Prentice-Hall, Inc., 1977), pp. 25–40.

dividual, family, or group work, as in all these contexts workers and clients should base their actions on an analysis of the systems that are relevant to the problem at hand.

Assessments of the problems of group members will employ the same concepts and theories as those used when working with people individually. There is no consensus, however, in social work regarding a theoretical framework for assessment, and group workers will use behavioral, ego psychological, role, or other theoretical systems in the same manner as other social workers. Group workers can draw upon the group, however, in the assessment process as follows: first, members can be trained to participate in assessments of each other; second, behavior in the group provides direct evidence regarding the member's interpersonal behavior that is not available through individual ways of helping.

Members, with or without a common conceptual framework, are likely to ask each other questions and to contribute information about their problems. Because of similarities in problems, cultures, and life experiences, members may offer more insight into each other's difficulties than the worker does and this is a major advantage of the group context. In addition, members can be taught to utilize established frameworks for assessment.

Two examples of frameworks taught successfully to members of treatment groups are behavioral assessment and transactional analysis.[4] One applicable form of behavioral assessment involves explaining to members that behavior is *caused* by its antecedents and consequences. A study of *antecedents* includes an examination of the place where the behavior occurred, when it occurred, who was present at the time, and what these people were doing. *Consequences* is a less technical expression than *reinforcement* and *punishment* but refers to both terms as well as to the likelihood that specified behaviors will be met with pleasurable or aversive responses from the environment, or none at all.

Members have been taught to recognize antecedents and consequences through explanation of these terms followed by examples and role plays which are analyzed in this manner. Because of the member's familiarity with each other's circumstances, the group is an effective place to perform a behavioral assessment.

In a similar manner, members can be taught to use the principles of transactional analysis to help each other understand the sources of their difficulties. In this type of analysis, group members learn to recognize actions that stem from parent, adult, and child ego states. An ego state as defined by Berne is "a system of feelings which motivates a related set of behavior patterns."[5] The parent ego state derives from the individual's earlier experiences with parent figures and usually involves value positions and judgemental

[4]For examples of the ways these are taught in groups, see Rose, *Group Therapy*, pp. 95–102.

[5]Eric Berne, *Transactional Analysis in Psychotherapy* (New York: Grove Press, 1961), p. 17.

responses. The child ego state reflects one's childhood experiences and is reflected in responses to authority, playfulness, creativity, and dependence. The adult ego state represents rational, information processing approaches to situations and problems.

In utilizing a transactional approach, members identify how their behaviors relate to ego states and how their ego states are responded to by others—both in the group as well as outside of it. Members can seek to change their responses to others in ways that are related to their goals and to help others do the same. They can be trained to do this with similar procedures to those used in behavioral approaches, namely, discussion, role play, and analysis of actual life circumstances.

The group, because it represents a small society in its own right, also provides direct information about the causes of member behaviors. The workers and members observe each other reacting to stress, nurturance, ambiguity, and other interpersonal circumstances. This use of the group for assessment purposes can be enhanced in several ways.

One method is role playing. Members can set up simulations of environmental situations or can replay intra-group ones. The members comment on these events, utilizing the variety of data provided. A member can even observe while another member plays his or her role and thus gain objectivity regarding the circumstances.

A second assessment device is provided by the use of activity programs. The worker can introduce crafts, dramatics, and games, to name a few, that enable members to express their concerns through these media and that display member responses to a variety of situations.[6]

A third device, usually referred to as the "fishbowl," requires part of the group to observe and give feedback to another part of the group. This procedure provides excellent training for members in the understanding of behavior. The observing subgroup or even single members who are asked to "observe" the group can be supplied with simple questionnaires or rating instruments to support this activity.

DETERMINATION OF NORMS

In the beginning phase of the group, members also make decisions regarding group norms, that is, expectations members place on each other as to proper behavior. Sometimes these normative decisions are explicit, as when a worker or member initiates a consideration of the issue of confidentiality; other times, the normative decisions are implicit, as when members and workers begin to call each other by first names without any formal decision.

A norm that workers seek to develop in groups is that all members have responsibility for the group. This includes full participation of every member

[6]Sallie R. Churchill, "Social Group Work: A Diagnostic Tool in Child Guidance," *American Journal of Orthopsychiatry* 35 (April, 1965), 581-88.

in group deliberations or tasks. A related issue is the norm that members have responsibility to be open and honest with each other. For psychotherapy groups, Yalom states also that norms regarding "nonjudgmental acceptance of others, high levels of self disclosure, a desire for self understanding, dissatisfaction with present modes of behavior, and an eagerness to change" should be instilled.[7]

The worker helps bring appropriate norms into existence through modeling. He or she, therefore, should inform members regarding communications about the group to outsiders. The worker presents himself or herself also a someone who is in the process of growth as a person as well as a professional.

Discussions about norms are introduced early and throughout the life of the group. One of the most potent aspects of group activity is the pressure exerted for conformity to norms in cohesive groups. When these are therapeutic, this is a valuable phenomona. Otherwise, the group can be a destructive experience and the worker should make this known to the group.

At times, the worker will also introduce outside reference groups in an effort to mold group norms. An example of this was discussions of sportsmanship in an adolescent group that included ancedotes about respected athletes. The group worker also established a buddy system for this purpose with members of the prominent football team of a nearby university.

EMOTIONAL REACTIONS TO GROUP FORMATION

An emotional issue present in group beginnings is the conflict between being attracted to the group and simultaneously experiencing anxiety about the group.[8] This constitutes a form of approach–avoidance conflict for the members. The attraction to the group is attested to at least in volunatry groups by the members' presence. Members come because they hope that the group will help them attain their objectives. They may also look forward to the gratification of interacting with other members and/or with the worker. On the other hand, members often have apprehensions about the group. Will it help them to achieve their purposes or will it hold them from the direction they wish to go? Will other members be hostile, unaccepting, or unlikable? Will the costs of achieving goals be too great to pay? Will the member find some position in the group that will be familiar and comfortable?

If the group, in its first meetings, appears more on the positive side compared to other ways members might satisfy their wants, the members will remain and invest themselves in it. If the group, in the same period, is seen negatively, several members will discontinue, and this may be enought to destroy the group.

The worker should comment on these ambivalent feelings which may help sustain the members through difficulties that are usually present in

[7]Yalom, *Group Psychotherapy,* p. 108.
[8]Garland, Jones, and Kolodny, in *Explorations in Group Work,* p. 21.

group beginnings. This action should have an empathic quality and this can also enhance member–worker relationships. In addition, an empathic response invites the members to work on their feelings about group beginning and to cope with fears about the group. This type of discussion may also help members to approach formation issues in a more relaxed manner.

In the beginning of groups as well as at other crucial times in their existence, members sometimes develop a tradition of a "round." This involves members, in turn, sharing their feelings at that moment. Since shared feelings often relate to common group themes, this procedure helps prepare the way for discussion of these.

RELATIONSHIP OF GROUP WORKER TO MEMBERS

Members, in an emotional sense, place the workers in a central position because of their presumed expertise and responsibility for the group. The members address a large proportion of their communications to the worker and may appear dependent on that person for solutions to individual and group problems. According to at least one writer, this early dependence on the group worker is the need for an omnipotent, omniscient omnicaring parent.[9]

Too much dependence can be confronted at an appropriate stage in the development of the group; in the beginning, however, even though the worker risks dependence, he or she should nurture a relationship with each member. At the most elementary level, this includes addressing each member by name. To accentuate this expression of interest, the worker should seek occasions to single out each member for a comment, question, or encouraging remark. The worker also takes responsibility for opening the group meeting. This shows a readiness to take a share of responsibility for the group, even when the worker's plan and philosophy calls for the group's eventual assumption of responsibility for itself.

A large literature has demonstrated that the outcome of helping processes are strongly related to the degree to which the worker demonstrates three types of behaviors—empathy, genuineness, and warmth.[10] While much of the research on these variables has been done in the one-to-one counseling situation, some substantiation of their potency in group situations is available.[11]

[9]See Yalom, *Group Psychotherapy,* Chapter 6.

[10]Morris B. Parloff, Irene Elkin Waskow, and Barry E. Wolfe, "Research on Therapist Variables in Relationship to Process and Outcome," in *Handbook of Psychotherapy and Behavior Change: An Empirical Analysis,* 2nd ed., eds. Sol L. Garfield and Allen E. Bergin (New York: John Wiley, 1978), pp. 242–52.

[11]C. B. Truax, R. R. Carkhuff, and I. Rodman, Jr., "Relationships Between Therapist Offered Conditions and Patient Change in Group Psychotherapy," *Journal of Clinical Psychology* XXI (1965), 327–29; C. B. Truax, J. Wittmer, and D. G. Wargo, "Effects of the Therapeutic Conditions of Accurate Empathy, Non-possessive Warmth, and Genuineness on Hospitalized Mental Patients During Group Therapy," *Journal of Clinical Psychology* XXVII (1971), 137–42.

Empathy

Empathy refers to the accuracy of the worker's feedback regarding the feelings the member experiences. Accuracy includes not only the feeling but the context in which the feeling was aroused. Some techniques, such as the exact repetition of members' statements, are often aversive to many people who view this as a mocking quality. The worker must, therefore, choose a sincere and natural way of paraphrasing member feelings. An example of an empathic response of a worker to a member's statement that "I was frightened when I went home and found my wife had gone out," was "It was a scary feeling for you when you got back from work and found your wife wasn't home." The member then continued by saying "That's right and I didn't know what to do."

An important experience in a group is for members to offer and receive empathic responses from each other. This also increases the cohesiveness of the group. The worker increases the likelihood that members will be empathic with each other by the model he or she presents. In addition, the worker explains the value of empathy and trains members to make empathic responses to each other. This training can be done through calling attention to his or her own responses, role playing empathy, or giving feedback to members when they naturally interact in this way.

The frequency of the total number of empathic responses in a group can be increased. This is accomplished by having a member or observer count the number of empathic acts. If the group believes this too low, an increase can become a group goal and the group can reward itself for achieving it. This type of self-monitoring is usually done in early stages of groups or when members are concerned about the group atmosphere.

Genuineness

Genuineness consists of the honesty and openness of the worker with the members. To be genuine the worker must have a substantial amount of self-awareness, otherwise he or she may unknowingly behave in inconsistent or covert ways. Genuine behavior will be devoid of contradictions among various aspects of the worker's behavior. The worker who is genuine, for example, will not deny being angry with members when this emotion is present. Similarly, when the worker feels warmly towards members, he or she will be free to say so. The worker will also engage in appropriate self-disclosure. While evidence exists of the value of the worker revealing aspects of his or her own experiences in order to model openness for members and provide useful data, a great deal of judgment must be exercised regarding when and how much disclosure should take place.[12]

Another aspect of genuineness is the willingness of the worker to provide feedback to members regarding perceptions of *their* behavior. The

[12]See Parloff, Waskow, and Wolfe, in *Handbook of Psychotherapy*, pp. 242–52.

worker who withholds personal reactions to individuals in the group as well as to the group itself will not be evaluated by the members as having been honest with them. The worker must use judgment as to the way such reactions are shared and whether they are reflective of his or her biases in ways that are destructive to the members. Some examples of workers' reactions are given to illustrate this point.

Example: A worker told a group of young adults with socialization problems that they were wasting *their* time when they avoided discussions of their relationships to each other.

Example: A worker for a group of parents who sought better ways of raising their children pointed out to them the amount of time they spent complaining about their children rather then seeking better ways of responding in difficult encounters with them. The worker said they were doing some of the kinds of things they complained about their children doing.

At the same time the worker must help the members to behave more genuinely to each other. The following is an example of this.

Example: When Robert turned his back on Sam as the members were discussing Sam's problem, the worker pointed this out to him (helping Robert to be aware of the contradictory messages he presents to Sam). The worker then encouraged Robert to discuss what about Sam was upsetting him (helping Robert to engage in appropriate self-disclosure). In this discussion, the worker also supported Robert in telling Sam that whenever he (Robert) tried to help Sam, he (Sam) also turned away (helping Robert present his perceptions of Sam honestly to Sam).

Warmth

Warmth, usually referred to as non-possessive warmth, is somewhat harder to operationalize than empathy and genuineness because much of its expression is in the form of feelings. As Schulman points out also, "several characteristics are included in the concept of warmth—equal worth, absence of blame, nondefensiveness, and closeness."[13] A rating scale Schulman uses divides warmth, for this reason, into two dimensions: positive regard and respect.[14]

Positive regard is the degree to which the worker shows interest in the group member and concern for his or her welfare. It also includes the acceptance, by the worker, of the members' freedom to be themselves. This does not preclude the worker's expectation that the members will seek to realize their fullest capacities.

[13]Eveline D. Schulman, *Intervention in Human Services*, 2nd ed. (St. Louis, Mo.: C. V. Mosby, 1978), p. 225.
[14]Ibid, p. 231.

Respect, on the other hand, is reflected in the way the worker appreciates the members' efforts. Even when they fail at these efforts or behave in some fashion that is unpleasant to others, the worker recognizes the fact that the members are trying to cope with difficult situations.

Example: When Mary reported to the group that she failed her examination, she was in tears as the worker placed her arm on Mary's shoulder. At this, Mary, even while crying, angrily attacked her teacher as a "mean old bitch." The worker, while her arm was still around Mary, said she could see why Mary felt this way. The worker also asked Mary how the group could help her. Mary said she knew that Sue had had a "run in" with the same teacher and she asked Sue how she had handled it. The worker, in this way, facilitated Mary's securing expressions of warmth from other group members.

RELATIONSHIPS AMONG MEMBERS

The feelings members have toward one another, if primarily positive, will be the major reason they return to the group. The trust they develop in one another will also be the major determinant of their ability to help one another with personal difficulties or with tasks.

Seeking Similarities

The worker seeks to develop relationships among the members by helping them to discover similarities in their life experiences, their difficulties, and their ways of responding to situations. This is initiated by encouraging the members to tell about themselves, while observing that a few members do not monopolize the first sessions, thus causing other members to lose interest in the group. One relevant question could be how they came to join the group. In a child guidance clinic, children in a group used small dolls to describe their family composition; in a group of handicapped people undergoing physical and occupational rehabilitation, members described the kinds of rehabilitation programs in which they had participated.

In some groups where the intent is for the group to continue for a long period and complex interactional patterns are likely to be discussed, the worker may draw attention to more subtle similarities. In a group of people served by an out-patient psychiatric clinic, one member spoke of his difficulties in setting out for the group meeting that evening; another spoke of problems in starting school; and a third talked of how difficult it had been in the beginning of her marriage. The worker perceived the common theme of feelings about difficult beginnings and stated this.

Talking to Each Other

One of the major issues in first meetings is the tendency for members to talk to the worker rather than each other. This may be inevitable when the worker offers information to orient members. On the other hand, members must be encouraged to talk to each other and in the group's beginning this should be raised as an issue. The worker can draw attention to this in several ways: first, by redirecting questions placed to him or her back to group members; second, by directly pointing out the value of members helping each other; third, by identifying commonalities among the members. The worker may also choose to raise the issue of overdependency on the worker for discussion.

Reducing Distortions

Members should be helped to separate distorted perceptions of each other from realities. While this process continues over the life of the group, it is important to begin it early. Some workers accelerate this by asking members to select a member who reminds them of someone. Members then discuss this either in pairs or with the whole group. A less direct form of this exercise is to ask members in rotation to focus on one member at a time and associate colors, animals, and so forth, with that member. This experience is then discussed and can lead to an awareness of the kinds of emotions and meanings members project onto each other.

During these kinds of early processes, the worker should be aware that closeness among members, or for that matter among any human beings, is not easy to attain and may be particularly difficult for the types of people served by social workers. The worker should acknowledge this in as empathic a manner as possible. One of the ways to facilitate closeness is to enhance the way members listen to each other.

Careful Listening

Some of the approaches mentioned in this chapter are likely to encourage such careful listening. Thus identifying one's fantasies about other members helps in being more attentive to the actual rather than imagined statements of the other people. Being sensitive to common concerns also has this effect. In addition, however, some techniques directly relate to the listening issue. One is to help members to be aware of times when they are not listening and out of this awareness to commit themselves to practice listening.

For training in listening, some workers use the exercise of asking members, for a limited period, to repeat the previous comment before continuing on with their own. Another is for members to rotate the role of "summarizer." The group will then be asked to turn to the "summarizer" whenever it wishes to examine its recent process.

When the worker confronts members who have failed to listen, they can be asked to talk about feelings they had at such times. Members, particularly children who are being taught group discussion skills, can be rewarded with tokens by other members of the group when such other members feel understood.

GROUP STRUCTURE DURING FORMATION

Another task of the worker in the beginning of a group is to enable the group to have the kinds of structures conducive to further group development. Group structures consist of the patterns of relationships among members. We shall deal here with group structure issues relevant to group beginnings; in the next chapter, we shall elaborate on structural issues occurring in groups at later stages.

Types of Structures

Some of the major group structures are the following:

1. communications structure: who speaks to whom about what and under what circumstances;[15]
2. sociometric structure: who likes or dislikes whom in the group (These emotional patterns contribute to the creation of subgroups. Groups are often subdivided into cliques of members who interact with each other more frequently than they do with others outside of the subgroup.);[16]
3. power structure: who influences whom in the group and in what manner.[17]
4. leadership structure: who contributes most to the determination and accomplishment of groups tasks as well as who contributes most to reducing tensions, enhancing group cohesiveness, and securing compliance with formal and informal rules;[18]
5. role structure: who occupies formally recognized positions, such as chairpersons, secretaries, and so forth, who fills positions created by group activities (for example, pitcher, expert in sewing), and who fulfills categories growing out of even more informal group interactions (for example, mediator, clown, rebel).[19]

---

[15]Margaret E. Hartford, *Groups in Social Work: Applications of Small Group Theory and Research to Social Work Practice* (New York: Columbia University Press, 1972), pp. 218–27.

[16]Ibid., p. 196.

[17]Ibid., pp. 261–69.

[18]Ibid., pp. 264–67.

[19]Ibid., pp. 216–18.

Structural Changes

The worker should examine each of the types of structure just listed in terms of their effects on group beginnings. The communications structure should become one in which the maximum number of members participate and in which members respond to each other. Rose, for example, suggests a number of devices to measure communication patterns,[20] including simple tallies of the number of times each member talks. We have also used a form of recording (see Table 4-1) that captures who is spoken to as well as the people speaking. Rose also uses behavioral approaches to change these patterns such as the person on the speaker's right reinforcing low-frequency speakers with tokens and restraining high-frequency speakers with a hand on their shoulder.

Sociometric structures in groups in which members are new to each other are not likely to be defined rigidly early in the group's life. The exception may be when members have some definite cleavages among them determined by an attribute such as race, age, or sex. The worker's task is to avoid creating such cleavages by devices such as assigning group task or encouraging participation so that members have as much contact as possible with members who differ from themselves.

Table No. 4-1
COMMUNICATION STRUCTURE RATING FORM

Person Speaking	Person Spoken To						
	John	Bill	Sam	Frank	Several	All	O
John		|||					
Bill	||||						
Sam									
Frank						||	||

Similarly, some members may appear to have more power than other members by virtue of their expertise, control over resources (for example, a car, sports equipment), ability to punish (for example, use of sarcasm), or ability to inflict even physical harm. The worker strives to help members to use power in ways that help them attain their treatment goals without interfering with other members' attainment of theirs.

Some individuals who experience themselves as relatively powerless should be helped to gain a share of influence in the group. This can be done through helping such members assume useful roles in the group, coaching members on ways of being more assertive in the group, and also giving sup-

[20]Rose, *Group Therapy*, pp. 133–40.

port to these members' contributions during group meetings—thus adding the worker's "power" to the members'.

In reference to leadership structure, Sarri and Galinsky have pointed out that the beginning phase is characterized by "leadership roles played by the more assertive and aggressive individuals."[21] This may be functional at the early stage in group development but the group must have the flexibility, as purposes and tasks are clarified, to allow inputs from other people. The worker, consequently, should try to keep the leadership structure fluid by emphasizing temporary assignments to tasks and rotation of any influential positions in the group.

Finally, in regard to role structure, the worker must examine how all of the types of roles just described are performed. In the situation where members have joined the group to solve problems through discussion, the group is unlikely to chose "officers" in any formal sense. On the other hand, in anomie reduction and role attainment group situations, the members' assumption of group leadership positions may be an important type of experience. In groups with formal leadership roles, the worker in the group formation stage helps the members to determine the nature of such positions, the ways in which members will be chosen to fill them, and the attributes that members should possess in order to be chosen for positions.

A broader issue, in terms of role structure, is how to fill positions created by group activities. For example, when the group utilizes role play, members should be selected for the roles consistent with their goals. Similarly, in a game, members may have different tasks and the worker should try to match people to positions in constructive ways.

During the process of group formation, the worker will utilize the role structure of the group to help members become committed to the group and deal with ambivalence about the group. The worker can also use role assignments to obtain information about the problems of members. The following are a few examples of this use of role structure.

Example. In the second meeting of a parents' group, the worker suggested that the members take turns summarizing the discussion taking place. The worker did this because she thought it would help members to think about and take more responsibility for the problem-solving activity of the group.

Example. In the third meeting of a group of ten-year-old boys who had problems in following school rules, the worker introduced a game in which the group was divided into two teams. He asked a boy who had been rebellious against rules to be the scorekeeper. The worker was interested in seeing how this boy handled rules when he had some responsibility for their execution.

---

[21]Sarri and Galinsky, in *Individual Change,* p. 75.

The worker watches to see what kinds of informal positions members enter into through various transactions among themselves. Some of these will be conducive to the further development of the group while some will not. Some members will function as tension relievers through humor (group "clowns"), through compromise (group "diplomats"), or through promoting social activities ("social directors"). The group will turn to these individuals when such needs arise and the ability of some members to function in this way is beneficial to the group and should be supported by the worker.

On the other hand, some members are placed in positions that are likely to be harmful to themselves or the group. This includes scapegoats and *overactive deviants*—a term used by Bales to describe people who are verbally very active yet do not contribute positively to resolving task or social-emotional issues.[22] The worker should quickly identify the emergence of these phenomona so that their causes can be assessed and coped with.

In regard to scapegoating and deviance, the worker should try to prevent some members from becoming locked into such roles in early meetings as it is difficult to remove a deviant label once it has been affixed. It is even possible that such members will either be pushed out of the group or leave voluntarily. These issues are complex and often difficult to manage. We shall, therefore, discuss management of deviance in group situations in more detail in later chapters devoted to middle phases of the group's evolution.

In early stages, one activity of the worker with regard to such issues as scapegoating is to promote the group norm that members should take responsibility for their actions toward each other and they should seek to help one another. This does not mean that members should not be confronted with the consequences of their behavior.

The worker should also initiate a group norm that the group will *examine* how it responds to deviant members. Each member should, in this way, take responsibility for his or her role in this process.

INDIVIDUAL AND GROUP GOALS

Research evidence is strong that clarity of goals elicits actions to achieve these goals and clarity regarding such intended actions helps to secure their enactment.[23] While this principle is sound, there are many ways that workers and members can select goals and means to achieve them.

Frequently members in early meetings are not ready to select and agree on goals stated in specific terms. In these cases, the worker should attempt to

[22]Robert F. Bales, "Task Roles and Social Roles in Problem Solving Groups," in *Readings in Social Psychology,* 3rd ed., eds. Eleanor E. Maccoby, Theodore M. Newcomb, and Eugene L.Hartley (New York: Holt, Rinehart & Winston, 1958), pp. 427–46.

[23]Janice H. Schopler and Maeda Galinsky, "Goals in Social Group Work Practice: Formulation, Implementation, and Evaluation," in *Individual Change Through Small Groups,* eds. Glasser, Sarri, and Vinter (New York: Free Press, 1974), pp. 126-48.

secure agreement that one of the "goals" of early interactions is to identify and agree on individual and group goals. According to Croxton, this is often "no more than agreement to try out the process."[24] This can include an agreement to attend a few meetings, explore whether goals that can be met through the group experience exist, and sample the types of activities and interactions that will occur in the group.

The group worker considers several orders of goals. This is a complex matter because both goals for individuals and goals for the group exist and must be related to each other. Individual goals are the changes that the members would like to achieve in themselves, their situations, or both as a result of participation in the group; group goals are the changes that the group agrees to seek to achieve in its members, itself, or its environment as a result of the group activity. An example of an individual goal is a desire of a group member to act more assertively with fellow students. The same group chose the group goal that all of the members should act more assertively in their social situations. This was a group of high school students and they chose another group goal: to change school conditions that punished assertive behavior.

Our approach to group work[25] is oriented toward describing goals as specifically and as early as possible. We characterize a well-formulated goal statement as including a specific description of the behavior desired in oneself or others, the conditions under which the behavior will occur, and the criterion of successful performance. Rose gives an example of such a goal statement: "By the end of treatment, George will carry on conversation with his friends while maintaining eye contact with them at least 50 percent of the time."[26] This statement meets the requirements of a goal statement as it specifies the behavior (carrying on a conversation while maintaining eye contact), the circumstances (with friends), and the criterion of successful performance (50 percent of the time).

Other group work approaches place less emphasis on specific individual goals as an outcome of the group work experience. These tend to see this goal-oriented approach as false to their view of reality that individuals continuously modify their aspirations on the basis of current experience. Adherents of that view argue that too much of a future orientation prevents the fullest and finest involvement in and acquisition of benefits from contemporary ("here-and-now") events. Schwartz, for example, speaks of "valued outcomes" during different phases of the group's work.[27]

[24]Tom A. Croxton, "The Therapeutic Contract in Social Treatment," in *Individual Change Through Small Groups,* eds. Glasser, Sarri, and Vinter (New York: Free Press, 1974), p. 180.
[25]Robert D. Vinter, "The Essential Components of Social Group Work Practice," in *Individual Change Through Small Groups,* eds. Glasser, Sarri, and Vinter (New York: Free Press, 1974), pp. 13-15.
[26]Rose, *Group Therapy,* p. 76.
[27]William Schwartz, "Social Group Work: The Interactionist Approach," in *Encyclopedia of Social Work* II (New York: National Association of Social Workers, 1971), 1260.

Our view incorporates both positions and conforms to our perception of how people cope effectively with their situations. People often seek to fulfill their wants through a choice of future goals that have been selected through thoughtful appraisal of personal and social realities. In pursuing such goals, however, a great deal may be learned about those realities and as a result of this goals may need to be altered. The group work process, therefore, can operate both with a goal orientation and a withdrawal of commitment to such goals when they are determined to be inappropriate, unattainable, or no longer relevant because of the changing nature of the situation.

THE GROUP WORK CONTRACT

The idea of a group work contract draws on ethical as well as research considerations. The ethical issue is that the dimensions of the group work experience are agreed to and not imposed on group members by the worker. These include goals, means of achieving goals, and actions to maintain the group such as helping other members, attending meetings, and paying fees. The research considerations relate to the finding, noted in the discussion of goals, that clarity of goals, as well as means of attaining them, enhances the effectiveness of the group experience.

Increasingly, workers with individuals, families, and groups utilize the concept of contract. Contracts in group work are of five types:

1. between the group-as-a-whole and the agency;
2. between the group and the worker;
3. between a group member and the worker;
4. between one member and another;
5. between a member and the group.

The term *contract* has been used to describe an actual written document signed by the separate parties; it has also been used to describe verbal agreements that are specific as to the terms; finally it has been used to describe agreements that are not as formalized as the former types but are or can be acknowledged as operative by the group members and the worker.

We believe all of these formats to be valid under different circumstances. Schwartz, for example, refers to a contract between the group-as-a-whole and the agency when he states that the worker asks both to "reach some consensus about the members' needs and the agency's stake in offering the service." He seems, however, to be addressing the group-worker contract when he writes of a "contracting phase" in which a concensus is sought on "purposes, roles, and procedures." Finally, Schwartz sees the worker monitoring the terms of the contract and asking the group and agency to "renegotiate" when this becomes necessary.[28]

[28]Ibid.

Garvin and Glasser in their discussion of contract refer to an agreement between the members and the worker regarding the problems to be dealt with by each individual and the means that will be employed to attain these ends.[29] Neither Garvin and Glasser's nor Schwartz's conceptions refer to written documents and, in fact, Garvin and Glasser specifically write that "the group work contract, in contrast to the legal contract, is not a fixed document; rather it is a process with many subtle components." Modifications, therefore, can occur from session to session or "even during a given interaction."[30]

Sheldon Rose, in contrast, favors a written instrument. An example he presents includes commitments of the member regarding fees, attendance, punctuality, completion of homework assignments, attention during meetings, and participation in research. The workers commit themselves to the time of meetings, the clarification of member problems, the facilitation of members' use of resources, the provision of effective procedures, respect for confidentiality, and the refund of fees under specified circumstances.[31]

At times workers will become even more specific about aspects of the contract. This includes goal statements, procedures to be used, reasons for believing in the procedures' effectiveness (for example, research studies), and potential "side effects" (possible negative effects of participation in the group).

Member-to-member contracts are often used in phases of the group that occur after formation when members attempt to attain individual goals. These contracts are commitments of members to reward other members for an activity or the completion of a task. One such procedure, for example, is for two nonverbal members to agree to reward each other with money they have put into a common pool if a specified increase in group participation takes place. This type of reinforcement can also take place with the group-as-a-whole giving a reward for the accomplishments of members.

PROBLEMS IN BEGINNING GROUPS

The preceding material may appear to suggest that beginnings of groups are easy. Actually, beginnings are always somewhat difficult because of the risks people feel they are taking in entering any new enterprise. For some people, however, their mistrust of others and their fears of the unknown are so great that the worker must put forth great efforts to accomplish the tasks associated with formation.

One such situation occurs when the members are highly resistant in the

---

[29]Charles D. Garvin and Paul H. Glasser, "Social Group Work: The Preventive and Rehabilitative Approach," *Individual Change Through Small Groups,* eds. Glasser, Sarri, and Vinter (New York: Free Press, 1974), p. 37.

[30]Ibid.

[31]Rose, *Group Therapy,* p. 23.

beginning. This resistance can be manifested in refusal to participate verbally, in direct expressions of hostility, or in indirect expressions such as disagreeing with the purposes of the group in ways that do not appear sincere. The worker, in these circumstances, does not deny the reality of what is happening; rather the worker poses it as a problem for solution.

Above all, however, the worker does not make the mistake of thinking the group can move ahead before these kinds of resistance are diminished. Workers must not convey, on the other hand, that they are paralyzed by expressions of resistance as this can communicate that "something dreadful" exists that justifies all the self-protection the members can muster.

At times, the worker can diminish initial resistance by reducing members' anxiety. Ways of doing this include relaxation training[32] as well as introducing activities that are fun. Direct discussions of feelings can also be promoted. Finally, the relaxing way the worker handles the stresses of beginning the group is also important.

Another problem that can confront the group worker is the group that seems to remain too long in its formation phase. Such a group will continue to argue about, question, or frequently shift its goals; the same members do not attend consecutive meetings and group cohesiveness remains low. This state may be a result of agency conditions, such as those prevailing in some residential settings where persons do not remain very long. It may also be a result of group composition factors, incorrectly chosen group purposes, a truncated process of negotiating group goals, or a group norm of resistance to the agency or worker. When formation is prolonged, all of these as well as other possible contributing factors should be examined so that barriers to the further development of the group may be removed.

It is possible, also, that a group that never goes beyond formation can also be intentionally established. Some groups formed to provide a moderate amount of support to people leaving a program fall into this category. Some very short-term groups (five sessions or less) may move quickly beyond formation if they are carefully composed and have clear yet modest objectives.

SUMMARY

In this chapter we reviewed the events that occur in a group during its formation phase. This includes deciding on group purposes, formulating individual and group goals, gathering information that will be necessary to achieve these purposes and goals, and determining norms. During this phase, the worker helps the members with emotional reactions to beginnings as well as with relationships among themselves and with the worker. The latter relationship is enhanced by the worker's empathy, genuineness, and nonpossessive warmth.

[32]Douglas A. Bernstein and Thomas D. Borkovec, *Progressive Relaxation Training: A Manual for the Helping Professions* (Champaign, Illinois: Research Press, 1973).

The worker is aided in facilitating the group's development by an understanding of structures and processes as they occur when the group is forming. A contract is often developed between the worker and group as well as among the members as to expectations of each other. Problems can occur in formation that will prevent further group development and these were also discussed.

GROUP FORMATION EXERCISE

Goals

1. To understand group tasks during the group formation stage.
2. To identify ways of helping a group accomplish formation tasks.
3. To learn to assess the degree to which the group has accomplished group formation.

Procedure

1. Prior to the exercise, trainees read about and discuss the principles of group formation described in this chapter.

2. Five trainees are asked to volunteer to form a group which will hold a short meeting in the center of the class. An interest in a common topic is desirable (for example, how group members will apply this course to their work; finding better housing; dealing with "burn out").

3. Members of the group are centered in the front of the class and instructed to act as if they are having a first meeting of a group related to the issue selected in step 2. No group worker is present.

4. After about 10 to 15 minutes, the group discussion is suspended. The accompanying Group Formation Assessment Form is utilized to discuss how well the group is handling the tasks of formation. Ways of helping the group with formation tasks are also discussed. (Depending on time, the trainer may choose to emphasize some but not all items on the form.)

5. Another member of the class (or two members if co-workers are desired) volunteers to be a group worker to help the group in the ways suggested in step 4.

6. After about 10 to 15 minutes of the group meeting with a group worker, the group stops and the class, utilizing the Group Formation Assessment Form, discusses further progress in group formation and the role of the worker in this.

GROUP FORMATION ASSESSMENT FORM

Group Purposes

1. For each member, indicate the purpose the number expresses for being in the group and the degree of relationship to the stated purpose of the group, utilizing the following table.

Member's Name	Member's Purpose	Relationship to stated purpose[a]

[a]Code: A for highly related; B for moderated related; C for slightly related or not related at all.

2. Which of the following should a worker do in the light of 1?

_____ Because purposes are clear and a consensus exists, move to plan activities related to purpose.

_____ Because there is a discensus on purpose, renegotiate either purpose or composition.

_____ Purpose of members in relationships to group purposes are not yet clear; continue discussing purpose.

_____ Other (specify) _____

_____

Gathering Relevant Information

3. Has the group decided on the type of information it needs to plan activities to accomplish purpose?

_____ yes   _____ no

Specify the type of information to be sought.

4. Has the group decided how it will secure this information?

   Specify how the group will secure this information.

5. What should a worker do to initiate or enhance the collection of information? (More than one of these activities can be listed.)

   _____ Suggest the type and source of information.

   _____ Instruct the group about an individual assessment procedure [behavioral analysis; transactional analysis; kinds of motivation, capacity, opportunity, and so on].

   _____ Instruct the group about an environmental assessment procedure.

   _____ Other (specify) _____

_____

Determination of Norms

6. Check which norms are relevant and rate the degree of agreement.

	Relevant		Agreement[a]
	Yes	No	
Confidentiality			
Attendance			
Honesty with each other			
Help each other			
Other (specify)			

[a]Code: A for all or most; B for some; C for few or none.

7. What should the worker do in light of step 6?

   _____ Ask for discussion of norm.

   _____ State his or her position on norm.

   _____ Other (specify) _____

_____

Emotional Reactions to Group Formation

8. Rate the percentage of members who are experiencing the emotion at a high level of intensity and indicate how the worker might respond to this.

Emotion	Percentage Strongly Experiencing	Suggested Worker Response[a]
Attraction to group		
Fear		
Anger		
Mixed attraction to & rejection of group		
Other (specify)		

[a]Code: A for discussion of emotion; B for utilization of relaxation procedure; C for offering of self or others as models; D for other (specify).

Relationship to Group Worker

9. Which of the following characterizes the reaction of some members to the worker? Indicate how the worker should respond to this.

Reaction of Some Member to Worker	Suggestions for Worker Response
Dependency	
Anger	
Liking	
Fear	
Rejection	
No visible reaction	

Relationship Among Members

10. Have members sought for and formed similarities among one another?

11. For a 5-minute interval, evaluate the pattern of member and worker communications by writing "m" each time a member speaks and "w" each time the worker speaks [for example, w m m w m m m m].

How would you characterize the member communication pattern in the group?

_____ Primarily member to member.

_____ About evenly mixed between members talking to each other and to the worker.

_____ Members talk primarily to worker.

12. How frequently are expressings of warmth or caring expressed by a member to a member?

_____ Frequently.

_____ Occassionally.

_____ Seldom.

_____ Never.

Goals

13. Have any members stated goals for themselves? (specify)

14. Has the group set any goals for itself? (specify)

Emergence of Group Structures

15. Which members seek to exert the most influence? Is that helpful or harmful to others?

16. Do members volunteer for tasks? What is the effect of this or other member roles on group development?

17. Are any members seen as deviant by other members? What is the effect on the member(s) in question?

Contract

18. What kinds of agreements have been reached on the following procedures and processes? (specify)

Attendance _____

_____

Punctuality _____

_____

Participation _____

_____

Helping each other _____

_____

Helping specific others in group   _____

_____

Expectations of worker _____

_____

Expectations of agency _____

_____

Chapter 5

ACHIEVING GROUP PURPOSES THROUGH CHANGES IN GROUP CONDITIONS

IN THE PREVIOUS CHAPTER, we considered how the worker interacts with individuals and the group-as-a-whole during the group's formation period. In this and the next two chapters, we shall consider how the worker assesses and works with the group, its members, and the environment during the "middle" phases of the group's life. We shall assume, therefore, that we are presenting material relevant to both a group and its members who have determined their purposes and selected their initial goals. The members have developed some attraction to each other, as well, and sufficient cohesiveness has been attained to choose and pursue activities to attain group and individual goals. An initial structure and some group rules regarding procedures to be followed have also been selected.

ACTIONS OF THE GROUP WORKER

Group work writers generally assert that the value of group experience, as contrasted with one-to-one helping, centers on the ways that group conditions can help members attain their goals. As we have discussed earlier, some workers seek to bring this about through specifying such benefits specifically and uniquely for each individual. Others seek the creation of a group which, by virtue of circumstances such as norms of honesty, broad participation, and democratic decision making, is assumed to be beneficial to members.

In any case, the worker will interact with individual members, several members, the entire group, and people and institutions outside the group on behalf of the group. All of these entities interact and affect one another. A worker, consequently, to achieve changes in the group-as-a-whole, may initiate this change process through transactions with any one or more of these four components, and, in fact, different workers may achieve the same ends with different approaches. Whether, in an empirical sense, one of these types of transactions is more appropriate or effective than the others has not been established. The "practice wisdom" is undoubtedly that it depends on the circumstances. The group worker must be able, therefore, to employ skills relevant to interacting with members, subgroups, groups, and group environments. In any group the worker is likely to do all of these. Sometimes this is a planned sequence such as in the following example.

Example. The group worker sought a volunteer from the group to describe a problem she was having in social relationships. Agnes volunteered and the worker asked her to describe an example (*interaction with an individual*).

Agnes later agreed to role play a family situation about which she was concerned. The worker and Agnes secured several volunteers to role play Agnes's family and she helped them to set up the role play (*interaction with a subgroup*).

After the role play, the worker asked the group to give feedback to Agnes on her handling of the situation (*interaction with the entire group*).

The worker, at Agnes's request, agreed to interview her husband to help him to deal with his concerns about her participation in the group (*interaction with person outside the group on behalf of a group member*).

At other times, the worker interacts first with one of the various systems related to a member's concern and then makes decisions about subsequent interactions based on the flow of events. This is seen in the next illustration.

Example. The worker discussed with the boys in the group home the destructive events that took place on "Devil's Night." Several of the boys had thrown an egg at an elderly man on the street near the home (*interaction with entire group*). Jim denied any part in the affair although the other boys said he had been with them. The worker, at one point in the discussion, asked Jim what his feelings would be if his participation in something like this were known (*interaction with individual*). Jim said that Bill always tried to put him on the spot and the worker encouraged Jim and Bill to discuss this (*interaction with subgroup*). The worker also told the group about his discussion with the man who had been assaulted when he had come to the home to complain (*interaction with person outside the group*).

The worker is aware, when he is talking with a member in the group, that this will have an effect on the other members. This effect can be on their own problem solving as well as on their interactions with each other. Thus, during a group meeting, in a sense, it is impossible to interact with only one member. Nevertheless, the worker may, at times, have a compelling reason to single a member out. The effect on other members may or may not be a major consideration.

At other times when the worker speaks to a member, he or she may desire an effect on other members. Still again, when effects on other members are anticipated and are undesirable, the worker will refrain from individual attention. Similarly, when workers intervene in processes of the group-as-a-whole, they must consider how the process affects each individual member. Sometimes this is predictable. At other times, workers do not know the effects of group processes on members until they have occurred. They then must quickly decide what to do next in view of such effects. An example of this occurred when a worker in a group of youngsters in a residential treatment center participated in a discussion of feelings about holidays. He did not realize, until the discussion was underway, that two of the members had been very depressed a few weeks previously, on Thanksgiving, because their parents had not visited them. When the discussion began, these two members became emotionally withdrawn. The worker asked them about this behavior and learned about their parents. The worker expressed his understanding of their feelings, thus shifting his attention from the group-as-a-whole to the individual members.

As the preceding shows, it is impossible to affect one level of the individual–group–environment set without affecting all levels. Workers do, nevertheless, frequently focus their attention on one aspect or another of the interacting systems network. Even though in practice the worker recognizes the interrelatedness of such parts, we shall consider separately in this and the following two chapters how the worker might use one or another system when the target at that time is the group, the individual, or the environment. In this chapter, we shall focus on the group.

This way of approaching the activities of the worker is similar to that of Pincus and Minahan who distinguish between action and target systems.[1] *Action systems* are those with which the worker directly interacts; *target systems* are those that are to be changed as a result of these interactions. These two systems can, of course, coincide, such as when the worker helps the group (*action system*) change its methods of problem solving (*target system*). These two systems can be different, as when the worker helps the group (*action system*) plan a strategy for changing an agency rule (*target system*).

MIDDLE PHASES OF GROUP DEVELOPMENT

A number of authors have summarized group events during the middle phases of group development.[2] Most of them agree that after group forma-

---

[1]Allen Pincus and Anne Minahan, *Social Work Practice: Model and Method* (Itasca, Illinois: F.E. Peacock, 1973).
[2]Our discussion of group formation draws on such portrayals of group development as

tion, the group initiates activities related to the purposes of the group. While doing this, many groups develop new or more complex structures related to leadership and group tasks. They also acquire processes for goal attainment such as how to approach problem solving, how to deal with differences of opinion, and how to respond to members who represent a minority on issues. By this time groups have also developed some spoken or unspoken rules regarding such behaviors as attendance at and behavior during meetings.

After an initial period of considerable agreement, however, groups usually enter into a period of conflict. Garland, Jones, and Kolodny refer to this as a "power and control" phase while Sarri and Galinsky term it a "revision" phase.[3] At this time, leadership (either indigenous or that of the worker) is challenged and goals and activities are questioned. This is due to a larger number of members who now feel free to express their sentiments as well as to an initial assumption of leadership by aggressive individuals. Early experiences with pursuing goals may also produce new information or disclose unknown barriers.

During this phase the worker must be supportive at times when cohesiveness may be less because of conflict in the group creating anxiety for the members. Hopefully, the worker and the members are able to resolve conflicts in such a way as to lead to leadership patterns and reformulated goals to which members are even more committed than before. The experience of resolving conflicts can also lead to a feeling of closeness among members as well as a conviction that conflicts can be constructively coped with in the group.

After "revision" phases, the group resumes its activities with even more cohesiveness, commitment to goals, and appropriateness of structure. The members, however, with increased feelings of closeness to each other may stress their commonalities rather than their differences. This can lead to a degree of dependency that is not as conducive to pursuing individual goals as might be desirable. The worker will then support efforts of members to stress their individuality as well as commonality, thus creating a phase referred to by Garland and his colleagues as "differentiation."[4] In this phase, members reinforce each other's uniqueness.

During these middle phase processes, the worker examines specific group conditions to determine if they enhance or hinder goal-directed activities. We shall turn, therefore, to a closer description of such group conditions as they emerge in the group's middle phases. Worker activities to

Rosemary C. Sarri and Maeda Galinsky, "A Conceptual Framework for Group Development," in *Individual Change Through Small Groups,* eds. Paul Glasser, Rosemary Sarri, and Robert Vinter (New York: Free Press, 1974), pp. 71–88; James A. Garland, Hubert E. Jones, and Ralph Kolodny, "A Model for Stages of Development in Social Work Groups," in *Explorations in Group Work,* ed. Saul Bernstein (Boston: Boston University School of Social Work, 1965), p. 113; and Irvin D. Yalom, *The Theory and Practice of Group Psychotherapy,* 2nd ed. (New York: Basic Books, 1975), pp. 301-75.

[3]Garland, Jones, and Kolodny, in *Explorations in Group Work,* pp. 30–34; Sarri and Galinsky, in *Individual Change,* p. 76.

[4]Garland, Jones, and Kolodny, in *Explorations in Group Work,* pp. 37–41.

modify group conditions shall then be described based on the reader's understanding of their nature. An exercise to help the reader learn to identify these conditions is included at the end of this chapter.

A discussion of group conditions may at first appear overwhelming. We do not propose that the practitioner consider all or even several of these dimensions at the height of interaction with the group. Rather, at least at first, a list of such dimensions can be used as a checklist to think about what has recently happened in the group and the kinds of plans the worker should make. In the long run, the experienced worker will "zero in" on those concepts and related processes that are relevant to the situation. These group conditions consist of group structures, group processes, and group belief systems.

Group Structures

In the previous chapter, concepts frequently used to characterize group structures were defined and illustrated for the period of group formation. In this chapter we shall use the same concepts to describe group conditions that occur during middle phases.

Communications Structure. During the formation period, members tend to direct many of their remarks to the worker. By the middle phases, the members have developed more familiarity with each other and they should have developed a commitment to helping one another. For these reasons, communication among members increases and between members and the worker decreases. Patterns of communication emerge that are characteristic of the way members communicate in their life situations; and these may also contribute to the problems that led to their seeking group services.

These patterns include dominating discussion, talking primarily to the worker, or withdrawing. Such patterns may vary with the content of the discussion; some members will only talk about certain topics to selected other members. This can relate to a desire to secure reinforcement for behavior, a perceived similarity of the other member to a significant figure in one's history, or a wish to evoke a particular emotional response. Members may be willing to participate in discussions on some topics but not others. The worker should try to identify communication issues such as these. Depending on the relationship to the member's problems, the worker will seek to change such communication patterns. Ways to do this shall be described later in this chapter.

Sociometric Structure. The worker should assess the nature of the subgroups formed in the group. This can be done by observing who chooses to interact with whom, who comes or leaves meetings with whom, and the expressions of caring and affection exchanged among members. Workers do not usually use sociometric questionnaires to ask members to whom they feel closest because such questionnaires are experienced by members as very threatening and the same end can usually be achieved through observation. Fears of being excluded or rejected often cause such anxieties.

Some of the problems in middle phases of groups that are illuminated through sociometric analysis include the existence of dyads in which members reinforce each other's problematic behaviors, subgroups that compete with each other in destructive ways for control of the group, isolates who may become scapegoats, and intermember conflicts that reduce the overall cohesiveness of the group.

Power Structure. In the middle phases of the group, various members often seek to have more influence on group decisions and processes than they possessed in the beginning. This can be desirable if members use this influence to make the group responsive to them and also to help one another. At times, this is not the case and members challenge the authority of the worker in destructive ways or seek to manipulate other members in directions that do not correspond to such members' goals. These actions may represent the types of uses of power outside of the group that have created the problems for which the members seek help.

Other kinds of power issues are: members' attempts to coerce others into deviant activity; worker's failure to limit behavior that is destructive to individuals or even the whole group; outsiders' (teacher, parents, spouses) use of power over the group members in a negative way.

Therefore, the worker analyzes the sources of power (that is, stemming from expertise, from control over resources, from the ability to punish, from being a role model) as possessed by the worker, the members, and the people outside the group. The ways power must be used to help accomplish individual and group tasks is determined. When detrimental uses of power exist, the worker must seek to change this.

Role Structure. A role consideration during middle phases of the group is whether the members possess the skills to carry out their responsibilities during this phase. If there is a formal leadership structure, members may not be able to perform leadership functions because of behavioral deficits related to leadership. In any group when problem solving occurs, members should be able to give and ask for information and suggestions as well as alternative solutions and they may not have these skills. The worker may then have to train members in such skills.

In later phases of the group, also, members can be locked into roles that are dysfunctional for them. The "clown" may wish to behave more seriously, the "mediator" to take sides, and passive people to function assertively. The worker, being cognizant of roles that are created out of group interactions, will attend to those that impede either the attainment of individual goals or the creation of an effective group. In any case, the middle phase of the group should provide many opportunities for members to experiment with new roles and to consider employing these outside of the group in their natural systems.

Group Processes

As commonly defined, "process" is a continuous action, operation, or series of changes taking place in a definite manner. A group, as it exists over time, continuously changes and the nature of these changes constitutes *group process*.[5] Group process is a more difficult concept to operationalize, than group structure, perhaps because it is easier to think about a phenomonen as if it were unchanging. Also, group workers have often thought of process as one or another single aspect of the range of variables that change in groups. When Yalom defines process as the "relationship implications of interpersonal transactions" (a process to which we shall refer frequently), he is discussing a very important aspect of group process but not the only one.[6]

For this reason, in an earlier discussion, we defined process as "those changes occurring in the activities and interactions of group members that are related to changes in goal attainment and group maintenance."[7] Thus, we refer to group process as changes in group conditions and then determine whether such conditions relate to task or maintenance states or both. Again, as with structure, one has to recognize that changes are in the *group as an entity* and that their subdivision is only a way of analyzing group process. In fact, there are many valid ways for workers and members to examine their group "process": one important way is to consider some dimension of process, such as stages in problem solving. Another is to take the exact sequence of events in a group session and examine how some event, coupled with the forces present in the situation, produces a subsequent event(s).

In reviewing the research articles on group process, we were able to classify them as to whether they were more relevant to task processes, maintenance processes, or both. The following two processes were seen as falling into the last category, relating to both task and maintenance phenomena.

Role Differentiation. The process of role differentiation occurs as new positions are created in the group and members are selected and prepared to occupy them. The process begins when members first learn the role of group member. It continues as the group becomes more structurally complex over time, changes in response to changing conditions, and moves into different types of activities or through problem-solving stages. Such roles can fulfill either task or maintenance functions in the group.

Role Integration. As positions emerge in the group and are filled, the members will communicate with one another and these communications will

---

[5]For an extended discussion of group process, see Charles D. Garvin, "Group Process: Usage and Uses in Social Work Practice," in *Individual Change Through Small Groups,* eds. Paul Glasser, Rosemary Sarri, and Robert Vinter (New York: Free Press, 1974), pp. 209–32.
[6]Irving D. Yalom, *The Theory and Practice of Group Psychotherapy,* 2nd ed. (New York: Basic Books, 1975), p. 122.
[7]Garvin, "Group Process," p. 211.

be influenced by their respective roles. These transactions may be either efforts of members to induce others to confirm their positions, or to facilitate their performances, or to "illuminate" (that is, to clarify) the nature of these transactions. We list role integration as a process that can relate to both task and maintenance elements as this process can be pertinent to communications about either sets of roles and activities.

The following are examples of the inducement efforts just described.

Example. John, who has frequently explained the behavior of other group members to the worker, asked if he should continue.

Example. Sally, who had been asked to find information about possible speakers for the group, asked for suggestions as to how she might go about this.

The second aspect, that of illuminating these transactions, is close to Yalom's and other group therapists' concept of process illumination. As Yalom states, "If the powerful curative factor of interpersonal learning is to be set into motion, the group must recognize, examine, and understand process. It must examine itself, it must study its own transactions, it must transcend pure experience and apply itself to the integration of that experience."[8] Thus, in the first example just given, John might be helped to understand why he took on the interpretive role in relationship to other group members and the other group members might be helped to understand why they had supported the creation of such a position.

Goal Determination. This process is one of two relevant to task states of the group. It takes place as members interact to determine the desired end state to be achieved by the group. This action often takes place in stages related to short and long-range goals. Thus a long-range group goal of helping members to achieve social skills might be coupled with shorter-range goals of achieving skills, approaching others, carrying on conversations, and acting assertively.

An example of the process of goal determination is a discussion of the kinds of personal difficulties to be dealt with in the group. Such discussion often includes a consideration of whether the group will seek to change some aspect of the member's environment or to change their responses to that environment. When goals for either changes in the individual or the environment are chosen, the subsequent goal is often to change the other.

Goal Pursuit. Thibaut and Kelley define the process of goal pursuit as the one "by which actions are chosen as means of attaining [the] goal."[9]

---

[8]Yalom, *Group Psychotherapy*, p. 122.
[9]John W. Thibaut and Harold H. Kelley, *The Social Psychology of Groups* (New York: John Wiley, 1959), p. 263.

Sometimes these actions are chosen through group discussion, and this is characterized as a *problem-solving* process. At other times, the actions have already been prescribed, as when a group plays a game, enacts a script or role play, or sings a song. In still other circumstances, this process unfolds in a creative manner that involves cognitive, affective, and even kinesthetic elements as in creating an artistic product—a picture or piece of music.

In traditional group work terminology, the group's activities to achieve its goals are termed *programs.* Konopka, for example, states, "By program is meant any activity which the group does in the presence of the group worker during the course of group meetings. These activities must not be planned according to the particular needs or interests of the group worker himself, but only with reference to the group members."[10]

From the earliest writings in group work, the topic of program has been considered. A good part of Wilson and Ryland's classic text on group work, for example, is devoted to the use of such activities as crafts, dramatics, and dance. [11] Actual analytic models for assessing programmatic conditions have been sparse, however, An important development was the work of Robert Vinter, which we shall summarize later in this chapter when discussing ways of modifying group conditions.[12]

Recent researches in social psychology that should be drawn upon by group workers in understanding programmatic processes refer to such goal pursuit activities as group "tasks." These investigations have generated useful categories of tasks. For example, tasks termed "production," "discussion," and "problem solving" have different effects on process.[13]

An understanding of group problem solving is essential to group work practice,[14] since so much of the group process consists of this activity. Bales described three phases of group problem solving, identified by the activity that predominates in each phase. In the first one, *orientation,* the predominant activity is seeking and offering information; in the second phase, *evaluation,* the emphasis is on opinion, evaluation, and analysis; the third phase, *control,* has an emphasis on activities such as suggesting and deciding action.[15]

These phases constitute a rational and logical progression from secur-

[10]Gisela Konopka, *Social Group Work: A Helping Process,* 2nd ed. (Englewood Cliffs, N.J.: Prentice-Hall, Inc., 1972), p. 129.

[11]Gertrude Wilson and Gladys Ryland, *Social Group Work Practice* (Boston: Houghton Mifflin, 1949).

[12]Robert D. Vinter, "Program Activities: An Analysis of these Effects on Participant Behavior," in *Individual Change Through Small Groups,* eds. Paul Glasser, Rosemary Sarri, and Robert Vinter (New York: Free Press, 1974), pp. 233-43.

[13]Marvin E. Shaw, *Group Dynamics: The Psychology of Small Group Behavior* (New York: McGraw-Hill, 1976), pp. 316-19.

[14]Harold H. Kelley and John W. Thibaut, "Group Problem Solving," in *The Handbook of Social Psychology,* 2nd ed. (Reading, Mass.: Addison-Wesley, 1969), Vol. IV, *Group Psychology and Phenomena of Interaction,* ed. Gardner Lindzey and Elliot Aronson, pp. 1–101.

[15]Robert F. Bales and Fred L. Strodbeck, "Phases in Group Problem Solving," in *Group Dynamics: Research and Theory,* 3rd ed., eds. Dorwin Cartwright and Alvin Zander (New York: Harper & Row, Pub., 1968), pp. 389-400.

ing relevant information, to consideration of value issues, to decision making. It appears, therefore, that groups operate dysfunctionally if they move too rapidly to evaluation with insufficient information or make decisions without regard to such information or without an inadequate evaluation of alternatives. There are research results to show that there is a tendency for groups to do just that, and, for this reason, as we shall discuss later, worker interventions in problem solving processes are usually necessary and helpful.[16]

The goal pursuit process in social work groups usually involves some combination of problem solving and other types of task activities. For example, a group in a prison began a group session by discussing how, when seeking employment, they could overcome the stigma of having been in jail. This discussion first involved the sharing of information about actual job-seeking experiences, availability of jobs, and the resources to help ex-offenders; out of this discussion, various suggestions were made for finding jobs and these were evaluated. Members then talked about which of these ideas they will implement.

During this problem-solving discussion, it was evident that the men were apprehensive about talking with potential employers. A "script" was drafted from some of the ideas offered during the discussion. Various members used the script to role play both applicants and employers. After each role play, members gave feedback to each other regarding how they had handled the "interview"; they also gave suggestions to each other as to how to improve their interviewing behavior. This second segment of the meeting represents the latter kind of goal pursuit activity that incorporates "prescribed" as well as "creative" dramatic elements.

Maintenance Processes. According to Mills,[17] maintenance processes take place on three levels: behavioral, emotional, and normative.

The first level, *behavioral,* consists of interactions directed at controlling behavior and resolving conflict. Some of the group maintenance processes at the behavioral level are: (1) struggles for power among members, (2) struggles for power between members and the group worker, and (3) efforts to control behavior that deviates from group norms. None of these events are intrinsically good or bad and the worker's judgments regarding them will depend on the purposes and the goals of the group. Thus some power struggles will be between those members who are committed to the goals of the group and those who are not.

At other times, power conflict may relate to problems some members have in finding an identity and role in the group. In a group of adolescents, for example, an influential member supported the goal of "making it" in school. Another member sought the recognition of others in the group and

[16]Theodore M. Mills, *The Sociology of Small Groups* (Englewood Cliffs, N.J.: Prentice-Hall, Inc., 1967).

[17]Ibid., p. 57.

thought the only way he could do this was to rebel against the idea that it is desirable to secure additional education. The worker's task was to help the members understand this process so that they could consider alternative means of gaining status that were consistent with the group's purpose to support educational attainment.

The second level of maintenance process, the *emotional* one, consists of the attractions among group members. Earlier we referred to the sociometric structure as the pattern of attraction in the group; here we refer to such attraction in terms of the process of changes in such an emotion over time.

One group event that characterizes this process is the way members ask for information from each other in first meetings when they search for commonality on which to form relationships. During this early period, also, members express emotions to the group worker to test the worker's acceptance and liking of them.

In later meetings, as members become more secure with one another, they will often be freer to express less socially acceptable emotions. As groups develop, they are likely to develop the norm that tensions resulting from such emotions should be discussed and resolved.

The third level of the maintenance processes, the *normative* one, pertains to the development of the norms that govern the behavior of group members as well as the sanctions for violating these norms. Typically in social work groups, members discuss behavior that occurs outside of the group such as stealing, sexual activity, conflict with relatives or peers. Considerable discussion also takes place regarding in-group behavior such as concern for other group members, responsibilities for others in the group, and obligations to the group itself. This latter issue includes performance of tasks for the group as well as attendance and promptness at meetings.

Shared Attributions

A third category of group conditions, that of shared attributions, is defined as understandings of events that are held by all or most of the group members and that have developed out of group processes. It is a well-established fact that groups are very powerful in defining reality for members.[18] These definitions are often maintained even after the members who originally introduced them into the group have departed.

In social work groups, these shared attributions may be problemmatic; for example, beliefs in the superiority of certain social classes or races, in the impossibility of succeeding in life, or in false ideas about the causes of one's problems. On the other hand, shared attributions in a group may enhance the members' achievement of goals; for example, members may learn together how to analyze the "antecedents" and "consequences" of behaviors they

[18]Shaw, *Group Dynamics*, pp. 201–5.

wish to change in themselves. They may learn to perceive everyone, including themselves, as potent and capable of modifying their individual destinies.

A number of approaches to work with groups present sets of concepts to use in analyzing interactions among members as well as between members and people in their environments. Examples of these include transactional analysis[19] and the "psychotherapy through the group process" approach.[20] The latter model of group events conceptualizes them as affected by a common overt conflict (*focal group conflict*) that consists of an impulse or wish (*disturbing motive*) and an associated fear (*reactive motive*).

An example of a focal group conflict is from a group of adolescent girls who wished to discuss some of their dilemmas regarding sexual behavior (*disturbing motive*). They feared that this discussion would cause them to be rejected by the worker (*reactive motive*). The conflict between this wish and this fear led the girls to attack the worker before "she could attack us." This behavior is a "solution" to the conflict that will *not* help the girls to reach their goal. The worker, therefore, helped the girls to understand the nature of this conflict and this solution so that a more therapeutic solution could be found.

Whitaker and Lieberman's approach to the focal group conflict is based on a view of members as participating in similar ways in focal group conflicts because members associate to one another's perceptions and emotions. The focal group conflict influences how members see and react to many group events and thus provides the worker with a tool for helping the members to understand some of the sources of their attributions, emotion and actions.

THE MODIFICATION OF GROUP CONDITIONS

The preceding discussion of group structures, group processes, and group attributions presents the way we assess group conditions. In a sense the stage of group development constitutes a group condition although we have analyzed this in terms of how structures, processes, and attributions may vary at different times in the group. We shall now turn to the ways group workers *act* so as to influence or to facilitate the members' influences on such group conditions.

The way we categorize influences on group conditions is related to the type of action system utilized. The worker can influence group conditions, therefore, by interacting with one member (in front of others or privately),

---

[19]Eric Berne, *Transactional Analysis in Psychotherapy* (New York: Grove Press, Inc., 1961).

[20]Dorothy Stock Whitaker and Morton A. Lieberman, *Psychotherapy Through the Group Process* (New York: Lieber-Atherton, Inc., 1964).

several members, the entire group, or people outside the group. Needless to say, this decision can be and is often made as a result of group discussion.

Modifying Group Conditions through Individuals

One way of influencing the group is for the worker to interact with one member of the group. Single members can have significant affects on group conditions when they (1) have tasks to perform for the group, (2) when they have considerable power in the group, or (3) when they fulfill critical functions in the group.

Some examples of the first category, *tasks to perform,* are: members who arrange for group activities, secure resources for the group (information, equipment), or fulfill roles such as observer, chairperson, secretary, or referee. The allocation of the tasks constitutes part of the structure of the group. The worker usually is active in decisions as to who will fulfill these roles. The worker, when necessary, will facilitate the way the members perform in these roles, thus contributing to the process of goal attainment.

One of the ways the worker facilitates role performance is by "coaching" the member. This term is analogous to coaching in athletics: the worker gives support to such members, feedback on their effectiveness, and "tips" on how to do the job.

The worker may use behavior modification techniques to help members with their roles, such as offering to tell or to show the member how to perform the role; the worker will also reinforce the member for his or her actions. Members may be anxious about the way they are carrying out group responsibilities and the worker can help the members to reduce some of their tension through relaxation techniques.[21]

In the second circumstance, when the member fulfills a leadership function for the group (for example, chairperson or committee member), in addition to the preceding techniques, the worker can also provide leadership training. This consists of sessions for some or all of the members on such leadership skills as moderating a discussion or facilitating participation.[22]

At times also the worker interacts with a member in relationship to the power structure of the group. This occurs most often when there is an imbalance of power that hinders the effective functioning of the group. For example, some members may dominate group decision making and exclude others from this process. The worker can involve the entire group in an examination of this problem but may interact instead with individuals. These individuals may be those who are powerless and who the worker seeks to empower by training in assertiveness or by appointment to roles in the group that carry power.

At other times, the worker helps more powerful individuals to relin-

[21]Douglas A. Bernstein and Thomas D. Borkovec, *Progressive Relaxation Training: A Manual for the Helping Professions* (Champaign, Ill.: Research Press, 1973).
[22]Harvey Bertcher, *Group Participation Techniques for Leaders and Members* (Beverly Hills, Calif.: Sage Publications, Inc., 1979).

quish power or to use it sparingly in the interests of other members as well as inter-member relationships. This can be done by helping to develop members' values of concern for other members as well as helping them to see the ways that domination of others can be destructive to oneself.

The third circumstance, when workers interact with individuals to modify group conditions, is when the individual's behavior has the function of maintaining problemmatic group structures or processes. Such circumstances are maintained *both* by the behavior of the individual concerned and by the responses of other group members. A good example of this is a scapegoating process. This occurs, according to Northen, when the members "turn their aggressions on to one who becomes a symbol of some tendency or characteristic they dislike in themselves and on whom they project their hostility, thus protecting themselves from recognition of their own unacceptable tendencies and freeing themselves from guilty feelings."[23]

The worker responds to scapegoating situations by calling the member's attention to his or her own behavior and also the other group members' attention to the reasons for their response to it. Both "parties" should examine their contribution to the maintenance of a scapegoating situation. Shulman warns the worker against "preempting" this encounter between member and group as both attempt to cope with the scapegoating process.[24] The worker can do this by too rapid a defense of the scapegoat or condemnation of the other members. As the worker helps the group members to take common responsibility for a scapegoating process, they may each then be supported in finding ways to behave differently.

Sometimes scapegoating is a dysfunctional response to stress or to a stigma placed on group membership. The worker will then help members to redirect their efforts so as to cope directly with these sources of tension.

Modifying Group Conditions through Subgroups

Group conditions are also changed by the worker's interactions with subgroups. The following are some examples of occasions when attention to a subgroup is an appropriate way of changing a group condition:

A subgroup may form and sabotage the whole group. The subgroup can do this by opposing group purposes or activities or by rebelling against the actions of the worker. The underlying cause of this process often is that the subgroup members seek a "place in the group" and recognition of their uniqueness that they cannot find through acceptable behavior when those roles have been preempted by other members. Members of such a subgroup also want an opportunity to influence the group and they may even experience the worker as undercutting this.

Based on the worker's assessment of such issues as these, he or she can

[23]Helen Northen, *Social Work With Groups* (New York: Columbia University Press, 1969), pp. 165–66.

[24]Lawrence Shulman, "Scapegoats, Group Workers, and Preemptive Intervention," *Social Work*, XII, no. 2 (1967), 37–43.

discuss legitimate desires for influence on the group with the subgroup members concerned. The worker can also act so as to create useful roles for members of such subgroups by helping them to accomplish tasks, thus attaining more influence in the group. Instead of responding to a tendency to "fight back," the worker looks for ways to "connect" with dissident subgroups and to demonstrate a concern for their wants.

In less complex situations, subgroups can be helped to take responsibility for plans affecting the entire group. Subgroups can gather information for the group, can plan group activities or exercises, and can observe other subgroups in a "fish-bowl" format. This latter procedure as we described previously involves one part of the group observing and giving feedback to another part that is holding a discussion or engaging in an exercise.

A subgroup may help a group to undergo changes that are necessary but that the full group is, for one reason or another, unable or unwilling to accomplish. This principle of utilizing systems to affect their "parts" or parts to affect the whole is an important one in group work.

Modifying Group Conditions through the Whole Group

How the worker can facilitate changes in group conditions or help the group to consider changes in itself shall now be considered.

Altering Member Cognitions. The group members can become aware of existing group conditions and plan a different way of structuring the group, a different process, and so forth. This can occur by examining group conditions and making a decision to change them, usually as a result of developing a new picture of the group through information collected as a part of a problem-solving effort. The data for such an effort can come from charting the structure (for example, communication structure) or subgroup patterns using the same devices as workers employ. Members can also identify poor problem solving such as too quick a progression into decision making without having examined enough alternatives or collected enough information.

Members have also been taught ways to examine other processes or the effects on process of emotions or attitudes, For example, Bion's concepts of basic assumption groups can be taught to members.[25] Members have also applied, as mentioned earlier, Berne's transactional terms to chart process.[26]

One device which has been used with such divergent groups as those of institutionalized adolescent delinquents and hospitalized mental patients is to assign the group to make important decisions affecting members, such as granting "passes."[27] "Poor" decisions can be rejected by the staff or ad-

[25]W.R. Bion, *Experiences in Groups* (New York: Basic Books, 1959).
[26]Berne, *Transactional Analysis*. pp. 90–97.
[27]See George W. Fairweather, ed., *Social Psychology in Treating Mental Illness: An Experimental Approach* (New York: John Wiley, 1964).

ministration. The group is expected, however, to examine the processes that led to its decisions.

Modifying Members' Behavior. In the preceding section, we noted that group conditions can sometimes be changed through modifying one member's behavior. It is also possible to change the group by modifying the interpersonal behavior of many members through a single procedure. The following are a series of examples of how this has been done in groups.

Example. A group of boys had a low rate of participation in group discussions. When the worker gave each boy a peanut every time he spoke, the overall rate increased. Subsequently, to increase the amount of conversation devoted to the group's purpose, peanuts were only awarded for that type of contribution. The boys, in this case, were not only affected by being given rewards but by observing the entire process and by vicariously experiencing each other's rewards. This type of procedure can be used to change any class of behavior in the group such as statements about feelings, personal statements, and so forth.[28]

Example. As we stated earlier, Rose reported on changing a pattern in which some members talked too much and others too little. Low participants were reinforced by people on their right whenever they spoke, while high participants received a restraining hand on their shoulders whenever they spoke.[29]

Example. Another example provided by Rose was of a group in which members spoke more frequently to the worker than they did to each other, thus limiting many of the ways they could help one another. This pattern was shown to exist by the input of an observer who recorded the sequence of member and worker contributions in a simple manner: L M L M M L M L. The group discussed this pattern and decided that the person sitting next to the worker will remind him of his behavior by holding a card up to him which read "pause."[30]

Example. One group, also reported by Rose, was composed of mothers. Their problem—frequent deviation from their planned agenda—was dealt with in the following manner:

> ...the trainer showed a video tape of a segment of the previous week's meeting. She pointed out how the off-task discussion prevented the members from achieving the agreed upon goals. However, she noted that social contact with each other was an important part of coming to the group. She wondered how the members could meet both aims—the achievement of the task goals and the

[28]For an extensive discussion of such procedures, see Rose, *Group Therapy*, pp. 86–102.
[29]Ibid., p. 137.
[30]Ibid., p. 139.

satisfaction of informal discussion. One member suggested that they plan to stay a few minutes longer after the formal session to discuss their children. The trainer agreed to increase the break between the first and second hours to 15 minutes. The group members then tried to define task-oriented discussion. They decided that it referred to any verbal contribution related to the agenda item being handled at any given point in time. If it was not related, it was off-task. One member agreed to review the tapes with the trainer to monitor the off-task behavior. They then decided that each person would remind her buddy if she were off-task. The trainer suggested that if the agenda items were finished early, the meeting could be ended early, which would give them more time for socializing.[31]

Example. A final behavioral technique, also reported by Rose, was used in a group where members made too many critical and unpleasant remarks to one another. Each time members felt abused, they placed a white poker chip in a large can in the center of the group; a red chip signified a feeling of reinforcement. This simple procedure immediately led to a modification of the type of comments made in the direction of more reinforcement.[32]

Utilizing Tasks and Activities. Group workers have made a major contribution to practice with groups through the examination of the effect of program activities on both group conditions and member goal attainment. Virtually every group work text describes the use of such media as crafts, games, dramatics, cooking, nature study, and dance. Perhaps the best of these types of efforts was the work of Wilson and Ryland; these authors went into great detail to describe each of these media and the way it is used in group work.

A further conceptualization of program was developed by Robert Vinter, who identified a series of variables that can be used to characterize any group activity.[33] The value of this system is that it can be used in advance of a group session to plan the activity for that session. It can also be used to predict some of the effects of any activity that has been introduced and, on the basis of this, to seek to change some activity dimension in order to enhance the usefulness of the "program."

An exercise in the application of this approach may be found at the end of this chapter.

Vinter's analysis begins with the idea that all activities take place in a *physical field* that "refers to the physical space and terrain, and the physical and social objects characteristic of each activity." Group workers learn to predict the positive and negative effects of items in the physical field. It does not take much experience, for example, to forecast what happens when a person of the opposite sex enters the meeting room of a group of adolescents. Group workers interacting with children, also, never forget such experiences as bringing a group of hyperactive boys into a room with lumps of clay on the

[31]Ibid., p. 141.
[32]Ibid., p. 142.
[33]Vinter, in *Individual Change*, pp. 209–32.

table—the clay soon flies. A positive example is that of a worker who wished to stimulate a group of youths to consider occupational career issues and, therefore, placed a number of colorful career pamphlets around the meeting room.

All activities also consist of *constituent performances* which are "behaviors that are essential to the activity and thus are required of participants." For example, a discussion requires members to listen to each other and to respond appropriately and a baseball game requires participants to learn a set of rules and to follow them in accomplishing such actions as running bases, catching the ball, and batting.

Vinter states that the physical field and the constituent performances constitute the *activity-setting*. The activity-setting produces the *respondent behaviors,* which are "individual participant actions evoked by, but not essential to, participation in the activity." Thus, in a game, group members may cheer, express feelings of disappointment on losing, or embrace each other. These are respondent behaviors occurring through that activity. Group workers will choose or help the members to choose activities that require constituent performances or elicit respondent behaviors that are relevant to the member's individual goals.

An example of this type of planning is a group worker who introduced a simple craft project into a group of mildly retarded children. The project necessitated that the children learn some construction skills and cooperate with each other (constituent performances). The worker's conviction was that these skills would be useful to the children; however, cooperative behavior was also a treatment goal. In the process of accomplishing the activity, the members struck up conversations with one another (respondent behaviors) which also were consistent with the worker's goals of helping the members to acquire social skills.

The worker who is planning an activity or predicting the effect of an activity on the group can utilize Vinter's scheme for assessment of the dimensions of activity-settings. These dimensions consist of six factors.

The first factor, the *prescriptiveness of the pattern of constituent performances,* denotes "the degree and range of rules or other guides for conduct." Thus baseball is more prescriptive than tag and painting a portrait that is an accurate likeness is more prescriptive than creating an abstract drawing.

The second factor, the *institutionalized controls governing participant activity,* consists of the "form and source or agent of controls that are exercised over participants during the activity." The controls might be exerted by the group worker or by members of the group on each other or might stem from norms that have been internalized by the members. A group discussion or project in which the rules or procedures are maintained by the worker through the use of rewards places the worker as the source of controls. In many activities chosen by the members and known to them, such as a basketball game selected by adolescents, the members will enforce the rules on each other and the group will be the source of controls. If the activity has been engaged in frequently by members, they are likely to have internalized the rules to such an extent that very little control is exerted actively by either the worker or other members.

The source of controls has great implications for the power structure of the group. Workers should be aware that activities that force them to exert most of the controls are likely to produce hostility toward the worker. Thus workers will choose or support activities, particularly in early stages of the group, that produce controls from within the group and even within each member. A worker, for example, who was planning a first meeting with a group of aggressive, hyperactive youngsters included a tag game that they all knew. The game had the dual function of releasing energy and drawing on rules members were likely to follow without external pressure.

The *provision for physical movement,* the third factor, involves "the extent to which participants are required or permitted to move their bodies in the activity-setting." A discussion is obviously more restricted in movement than a ball game. Even within a discussion, however, members may have opportunities to move around or may be restrained from such movement. These physical movement options will have such effects on the members as allowing or limiting discharge of tension, encouraging or discouraging interactions, or increasing or decreasing the ability of the worker or the members to exert controls.

Fourth, the *competence required for performance,* is "the minimum level of ability required to participate in the activity." The level of ability is usually determined by the worker and/or the members and is not primarily a product of impersonal and remote decisions of "authorities." Thus the members of a group or the worker will decide whether a person is "good enough" to play ball or take part in discussions or join in a song.

Norms regarding competence will also have many effects on group conditions: they will determine whether a member is regarded as deviant because he or she is much more or much less competent than others; whether a member has much or little power because of degrees of expertise; and whether subgroups will form because of similarities and differences in competence for group activities.

Provision for participant interactiveness is the fifth factor. The definition of this dimension is "the way the activity-setting locates and engages participants so that interaction among them is required or provoked." A group discussion, for example, in which members direct most comments to the worker is less interactive than one in which members are reinforced for responding to each other. An art project involving a group mural is likely to be more interactive than an art project in which each member makes a separate drawing. Thus this dimension has many implications for the kinds of group structures and processes that emerge.

The final dimension, the *reward structure,* consists of "the types of rewards available, their abundance or scarcity, and the manner in which they are distributed." Some aspects of the reward structure are easier to assess than others because a full assessment of rewards must include the intrinsic gratifications that members receive from participation (for example, feelings of worth, release of emotions) as well as the extrinsic ones such as tokens, food, or being a "winner." The importance of the reward structure is severalfold: whether or not members will enter the activity at all or stay with it; whether members will tolerate a large number of rules, a restriction in movement, or a demand to increase competence; and whether members will modify previously acquired structures or processes are all affected by the availability of rewards. Within limits, therefore, a change in any dimension can be enhanced by appropriate rewards.

Vinter's approach to analyzing program activities and their effects has been used to generate many hypotheses about differential use of programs. Vinter, himself, indicated the likely effects on respondent behaviors of variations in each of the activity-setting dimensions.[34] For example, he predicted that high prescriptiveness is associated with high fatigue, high physical movement with aggressiveness, and scarcity of rewards with competiveness.

Whitaker, utilizing Vinter's format, makes highly specific recommendations for programs that might meet the needs of various kinds of children as group members.[35] He utilizes the member variables of skill, motivation, and internal controls to define eight categories of children out of the various permutations possible for high or low ratings on these three attributes. Thus one child may have high skills, motivation, and control; another may be low on all three of these; a third may have high control but have low skill and motivation, and so on.

His example of the latter child who is low on skill and motivation but high on control is stated as follows: "This child is poorly motivated and unskilled but presents no great control problem. He is probably a shy, withdrawing youngster who feels rebuffed by his peers and has a very low self-image. He too needs immediate successes and uncomplicated games and projects. Lots of help and praise will enhance his development; the rest of the group could help in this respect."[36] Whitaker proceeds to indicate the kinds of activity-setting dimensions that each of these types of children will require. He selects "programs" such as swimming, finger painting, copper enameling, kickball, and Simon Says and rates them with regard to such dimensions. This then leads to specific prescriptions of such activities for each type of child.

Such an analysis has not been made for programs used primarily in adult groups but Whitaker's approach could be extended in this way. This is an important area: one which could easily be researched and to which more attention should be paid. Even without research validation, however, the

---

[34]Ibid., p. 239–41.

[35]James K. Whitaker, "Program Activities: Their Selection and Use in a Therapeutic Milieu," in *Individual Change Through Small Groups*, eds. Paul Glasser, Rosemary Sarri, and Robert Vinter (New York: Free Press, 1974), pp. 244–57.

[36]Ibid., p. 249.

knowledge of how to analyze the dimensions of programs is very useful to practititioners.

Social-psychological research regarding program dimensions has also been advancing and is generating the kinds of findings that will be applied by group workers..The term used in this literature, relevant to our understanding of program, is "group task." As noted above, a subdivision of group tasks into production tasks, discussion tasks, and problem-solving tasks is often made.[37] Production tasks require "the production and presentation of ideas or images." (Examples of these are creating stories or works of art). Discussion tasks require an "evaluation of issues." (An example is discussing changes taking place in contemporary families). Finally, problem-solving tasks require "specification of a course of action to be followed to resolve some problem." (An example is deciding how to discipline children in the face of changes in families).

Considerable research has been done utilizing this task typology. The results are sometimes difficult to interpret, probably because of the complexity of task phenomena,yet they have heuristic value for group workers. For example, problem-solving tasks "were characterized by high action orientation," production tasks by "high originality," and discussion tasks by "high issue involvement."[38] There are many occasions when workers and members will wish, for example, to secure a commitment to action. These occasions occur when members believe they have their problems well identified; the worker will then try to have these problems portrayed as occasions for decision and action.

At other times in groups, interest will lag and members will not be sufficiently involved. A discussion task in which the members' opinions are solicited around an issue of importance to all of them is then the most appropriate one. At still other times, the worker will be concerned about the degree of creativity which is being manifested in the group and will wish to stimulate a greater degree of originality. Some type of production task related to the purposes of the group is then the best one. This last proposition is consistent with techniques often suggested in transactional-analysis-oriented groups to free the "creative-child" present in all of us.

Altering Group Norms. Group conditions are, in part, maintained by group norms. These are beliefs about what such conditions ought to be. Group workers will use a number of approaches to help members alter their norms in order to modify group conditions.

One set of techniques for altering group norms is *value clarification exercises,* which can be used to help members identify and change their individual beliefs and can be used to alter beliefs that are collectively held by all or most group members and which serve, therefore, to maintain group condi-

---

[37]Shaw, *Group Dynamics,* pp. 316-19.
[38]Ibid., p. 318.

tions. Value clarification exercises usually help members to become aware of values they hold in specified situations or on specified topics. The following are a few examples of such value clarification experiences.

Example: A Values Auction. In a value auction, members are given a set amount of play money. An "auction" is then held for such "values" as friendship, health, a guarantee of a good job, and a good marriage. Members keep an account of how much they bid on each of these items. On the basis of this, a discussion is held in the group as to how and why values differ. Members discover others in the group who hold similar as well as different values and they seek these people out to discuss how they wish to realize their values.

Example: Alligator River. The group worker reads the group a story about a woman who wishes to cross a river to meet her lover. She consulted one friend who refused to be involved. A boatman then agreed to take her across at the price of sexual relations. When she had thus crossed, her lover found out the "price she paid" and deserted her. She told another friend about this and he did harm to the lover. The story thus ends. The members of the group are asked to rank these characters in terms of the most harmful and the most harmed individuals. Afterwards members share and discuss their ratings. The exercise illuminates values associated with sex roles and loyalties. Members, as in the first example, seek others in the group for further clarification of similarities and differences on these issues.

Because group workers will have a great deal of emotional meaning to group members, staements of their own values can affect the values of group members. Workers can express their points of view on what constitutes respect, how human beings ought to treat one another, what constitutes a "good" society, or what are desirable norms on sexuality, economic honesty, or cheating on examinations. Workers will avoid stating their values when this will interfere with members' exploration of their own values or when worker statements will be regarded as "preachy" by members. Another important set of norms has to do with openness among group members and the kinds of self-disclosure that might take place.

For many normative statements, the worker will be careful to indicate what his or her beliefs are and that members must examine and take responsibility for their own beliefs. Some workers take the position, in addition, that some beliefs are so essential to human dignity that the workers should present these vigorously and conclusively. These include, for example, nonuse of violence (for example, sexual assault) to achieve one's objectives.

Some values are relevant immediately to group processes, such as requiring full consensus on some issues and at least majority rule on others. The full consensus rule is employed for discussion of issues or decisions that could bring harm to a member; an agreement not to discuss sensitive issues without full agreement in a group of very anxious persons is an example of this. These kinds of decisional roles are included in what Vinter calls "operating and governing procedures." Such procedures can also include standardized ways of opening and closing meetings, expressing opinions on topics, serving refreshments, notifying the group about absences or tardinesses, and so on. These procedures, then, are supported by group norms. They also serve to provide members with a sense of structure which, for many, is associated with security. It also serves to define the group as different from others, a fact that can also enhance the members' sense of the group as an entity with which they can identify themselves.

Another norm related to group processes is that a member should not be pressured to give personal information or to take part in an exercise. The worker should assess the need for all of these kinds of norms as part of creating a safe group atmosphere.

The worker also has the responsibility to set limits in the group. This is more often required in some groups, such as children's groups, than in others. The worker, in these groups, may be required to restrain members from physical attacks on one another and this can extend also to destructive use of property. Children may run in and out of the room disturbing other activities in the agency or they may use obscene language which, at times, is anxiety provoking to themselves or others.

The worker faced with behavior as just described has several options. A statement regarding permissible behavior and group discussion and support of such rules will help to prevent some antisocial behavior. Additional prevention is possible when workers are aware of and respond to tensions that are building in groups before they reach the point where the members with the poorest controls begin to act aggressively. The major tool the worker will use is *program* which can help to discharge tension or to control behavior because the rules intrinsic to the activity lead to rewards which are also part of it.

Fritz Redl and David Wineman have described a number of techniques that are useful in group situations to control behavior.[39] These include "planned ignoring," "tension decontamination through humor," "direct appeal," "antiseptic bouncing," "physical restraint," and "permission and authoritative verbot."

Control issues can also be present in adult groups. They arise more frequently in groups of adults who are psychotic or seriously retarded. However, in any adult group in which interpersonal relationship issues are intensively examined, strong emotions may be aroused. Emotions such as crying or expressions of caring and affection are not usually inhibited by the worker but aggressive expressions likely to lead to physical attack will be. In this latter case, in some encounter-type groups, members are encouraged to express physical competition in such controlled ways as arm wrestling.

[39]Fritz Redl and David Wineman, *Controls From Within* (New York: Free Press, 1956). pp. 153–45.

Even minor physical encounters are seen as controversial as a group therapeutic device although some therapists have written favorably about personal issues that have been brought to awareness and dealt with in this manner.[40] The determining criterion should be that no actual physical harm is likely and that no psychological harm befalls participants or observers. This certainly places a heavy burden of proof on the worker.

Altering Group Emotional States. A final set of techniques for modifying group conditions through direct interactions with the group are those directed at the emotions of group members. One set of techniques is employed when the group climate is tense because of the anxiety of all or many group members. Under these circumstances, workers may simply discuss the fact that members are tense and then explore the sources of such tension. An example from one group was a discussion of an untrue rumor that the agency would close.

Group workers, to reduce tensions, also introduce procedures to enhance coping with a common issue such as the termination of the group. The ability of the worker to be a model of relaxation in the face of such stresses is useful in this process.

At still other times, the worker will choose to deal with the group members' tension level through a relaxation procedure. This can range from encouraging members to be more conscious of their breathing to a progressive relaxation exercise. The latter requires that the worker develop skills in the use of relaxation training. One way of providing this training involves, according to Rose, "the alternation of tension of the muscles in each large muscle group, with the release of that tension...."[41] The member must receive feedback on the appropriate actions and Rose accomplishes this through pairing the members, with one member being the coach and the other the relaxer. The coach can call the worker over when uncertainties as to the proper instruction arise. Rose cautions the worker to bring members out of a relaxation procedure gradually by slow movements of various body segments. He also warns that the procedure is not to be rushed and that part of several sessions should be used to learn the entire procedure. Members must also try, if possible, to practice relaxation outside of group sessions.[42]

Another technique for relaxation involves the use of fantasy. Each member is encouraged to imagine a peaceful scene. Some members have chosen listening to music or sitting by a slowly moving river. The members picture themselves as present at such scenes. Members are then gradually encouraged to "return" to the group.

Sometimes the emotional condition that the worker seeks to alter is the lack of positive emotional expression among the members when members feel it but do not communicate it. Lange and Jakubowski describe an exercise they call "giving and receiving compliments" that helps to instill more skill in

[40]William C. Schutz, *Here Comes Everybody* (New York: Harper and Row, Pub., 1971).
[41]Rose, *Group Therapy*, p. 121.
[42]Ibid., p. 122.

expressing and receiving this sentiment.[43] The exercise involves pointing out behavior that discourages compliments, such as denying their validity or behavior that is a negative way of giving a compliment, such as depreciating one's self in the process. A demonstration and practice of brief, unqualified compliments follows. In the experiential part of the exercise, members stand in a circle, give a compliment to the person to their right, and receive an appropriate response. In a second "go round" each "giver" expresses to the receiver—something which he or she specifically *liked* about how the "receiver" responded to his or her compliment.

A host of other emotional conditions arise in groups and may be idiosyncratic to some members or widely shared. These include competitiveness, sadness, jealousy, and elation. The worker on occasion desires members to become more aware of these affects and to examine their effects on behavior. This can often be secured through process illumination, that is asking members to discuss the implications of their communications to one another. At other times workers will introduce an exercise to elicit already present emotions. Thus a game might reveal some competitive feelings, an art project, feelings of elation or depression, and a discussion of positives members see in each other, feelings of jealousy.

Modifying Group Conditions through Influences from the Environment

The Agency. In Chapter 2, we discussed the ways that the agency can affect group work. Several of these can be utilized by the worker who wishes to use the agency to change some internal condition of the group. The worker can do this either through making the agency's input more visible or by approaching others in the agency in an effort to *change* the organizational input.

One of the agency conditions that can be made more visible is the agency's purpose for the group. A group that avoids working on members' problems can be reminded of this purpose by the worker or the agency can act, for instance, by asking the group to evaluate how it is responding to its purposes.

The agency can also affect group conditions by referring more members to the group, thus modifying composition. Some of the occasions when the worker might ask the agency to do this are when the group is overloaded with antisocial members, when the group members lack expertise to carry out the group's purposes, or when some members of the group have become isolated because of the ways they differ from other members.

Another way the agency can modify the group is through the resources

[43]Arthur J. Lange and Patricia Jakubowski, *Responsible Assertive Behavior* (Champaign, Ill.: Research Press, 1976, pp. 74-76.

allocated to the group. The room in which the group meets can be changed to another more conducive to desired activities; equipment can be supplied to the group for prescribed programs; expertise, in addition to that of the worker, can also be made available so as to affect group conditions. Examples of this latter were a speaker on contraception for an adolescent group, a "process observer" for a social skills group, and an expert on value clarification for a group of probationers.

The agency can also affect the group through interacting with indigenous leaders or other group members. Some agencies will form either a council of representatives of groups or will include group members and other consumers of services on advisory committees or boards, where issues of importance to the agency will be reported to the group and discussed. This may have effects on the group's goals, activities, and values. An example of this was a discussion an agency had with such an advisory committee regarding the fact that the agency, a settlement house, was underused by the Chicano members of the community. Following this discussion, several of the youth groups in the agency sought out Chicanos and invited them to join their groups.

Agencies have a major effect on group conditions through their preferences for the techniques workers should employ in working with groups. One agency, for example, wished to facilitate the use of behavior modification. It solicited items that could be offered to members in exchange for tokens, made various counting devices available for determining the frequency of behaviors, and issued brochures to members explaining a behavioral approach to group work. This had a major influence on the discussions and approaches that were utilized by these members.

Lastly, it is important to remember that groups are likely to interact with other staff and other clients of the agency. The agency, therefore, can use these actions purposefully to modify group conditions. Groups can be brought together in the agency when the interaction between them can prove beneficial; members of one group can visit another to describe to the host group how their own group dealt with selected issues; a few members from each of several groups can be brought together around a common issue and still return to their "own" group; group members may receive one-to-one services from staff members other than their group worker and this may have influences on the group.

In all of these examples of how an agency might affect conditions within the group, the group worker should have had a role in initiating the agency input or in approving it. The worker's subsequent role within the group then becomes a different one than when he or she sought the change by interventions within the group. The worker can become the person who helps the group members to consider their response to the agency input. This places the worker in a mediating rather than directive role and this can be important in work with some resistant groups.

The Family. Group conditions can also be modified by other forces in the environment outside of the agency and the worker may decide to utilize these. The families of the group members are one important possibility. Workers who form groups of children in agencies such as child guidance clinics will usually meet with the parents, often in a group. Joint meetings can also be arranged between the parents' and the children's groups. The parents can discuss such issues as how to reinforce the children's progress and commitment to their group and how to deal with issues that the children might bring home about their group. The parents can also encourage the children to raise their concerns in their own group.

Another example of the impact of relatives on a group was presented in a report of work done with a group of husbands who assaulted their wives.[44] The agency was one that provided a shelter for abused wives and it continued to provide a range of services to these women. It supported the husbands in moving toward meeting with the wives present and helped the wives make use of this meeting. Ultimately the agency helped form a new group in which both the husbands and wives were members.

The Community. Workers may also seek to influence group conditions through the impact of other agencies in the community. For example, a group service agency formed groups of children who were referred by the local school because of difficulties they were having in the classroom. The worker acted to set goals with each child concerning what the child hoped to achieve through group participation. In many cases this involved securing better classroom grades. The grading period, however, was too far off to provide the kind of immediate reinforcement each child needed. The worker, therefore, secured agreements from the teachers to give more immediate feedback and encouragement to the children than might otherwise have been the case.

Workers also seek the cooperation of indigenous community groups because of their impact on group conditions. Spergel, for example, presents an extended discussion of work with adolescent gangs.[45] An intrinsic part of his approach is the worker's activity with community groups because of their impact on the adolescents. This type of effort can include helping the group members find jobs, cope with the restrictions of probation, and learn new skills.

A very important part, also, of the environmental impact on the group relates to culture and ethnicity. One of the ways that this is manifested, for example, is on the structuring of group meetings. In some cultures, group meetings begin and end with a prayer or a song. Quaker groups are accustomed to silent periods in which members reflect quietly before speaking.

[44]Janet A. Geller, "Reaching the Battering Husband," *Social Work With Groups* I (Spring, 1978), pp. 27-38.

[45]Irving Spergel, *Street Gang Work: Theory and Practice* (Reading, Mass.: Addison-Wesley, 1966).

Cultures also have values regarding what may be addressed in public gatherings and what must be restricted to intrafamilial deliberations.

The worker can utilize knowledge of cultural inputs into the group in several other ways. A group's utilization of cultural forms can enhance its cohesiveness through the members awareness of their common heritage. The worker can also help the larger cultural system interpret its values to group members. A case of the latter was when a worker suggested the group invite members of the Southern Christian Leadership Conference (SCLC) to speak about the SCLC and its goals for social change in reference to black people. This presentation provided inspiration to group members when they discussed their personal goals.

At times the worker will target cultural conditions that have negative impacts on group processes for change. In one ethnic community, there was little encouragement for higher education yet many members of a group meeting in a community center wished to consider this career option. The worker held several meetings with parents and other community leaders to discuss and try to change their antipathy to education. She felt that only in this way might the youths in the group secure the support or at least acceptance they needed.

SUMMARY

In this chapter we analyzed the group conditions that affect practice with groups during middle phases. These included group structures, group processes, and shared member attributions. We described how these conditions change during this period and the varying manifestations of each condition. Following this, we indicated how these conditions may be modified by worker and member activities to create group circumstances conducive to member goal attainment. Ways of modifying group conditions were subsumed under work with individual members, subgroups, the group as an entity, and systems in the environment.

In the next chapter, we shall focus our attention on changing the behavior of the individual member. We shall describe the types of goals that members seek to achieve through group experience. These, also, may be attained through the worker's interactions with the group members themselves, the group-as-a-whole, and people outside the group.

GROUP DEVELOPMENT EXERCISE

Goals

1. To be able to identify the stage of development of the group.

2. To understand the means of helping a group achieve group conditions conducive to accomplishing group purposes.

Procedure

1. Prior to the exercise, trainees read about and discuss the nature of group conditions during its middle phases and means for modifying such group conditions.

2. One of the problems in experiential learning around middle phases is that role plays and simulations, however characterized, are "new experiences" and participants usually respond in ways appropriate to formation processes. The accompanying observation questions should be used with a genuine middle phase. Several options are available to the trainee to accomplish this.

(a) Have observers respond to a discussion in the classroom itself, as the group. This can be the discussion called for in step (1).

(b) Have a student bring in a tape of an actual group that has completed the process of formation.

(c) Have a group of students, for whatever purpose, agree early in the course to meet several times outside of the class and to hold a "later" meeting in a "fishbowl" format in the class. This can be a brief meeting (about fifteen minutes).

(d) Have the trainees "as a last resort" attempt to role play a group in its middle phases. The best way to do this is to have a class member describe to the role players the behaviors at a meeting of a group he or she has participated in that was in its middle phases. The players try, as much as possible, to simulate that meeting.

Assessment of Phase

1. Is the group "in fact" post formation? (The answer is probably "no" if several of the following items below are not present.)

_____ Group is more invested in carrying out an activity (including discussion) than in deciding what activities are relevant. If an activity or discussion topic is picked, this occurs easily and with considerable consensus.

_____ If there is disagreement about choosing or carrying out the activity, there exists considerable consensus among at least one set of group members and this is opposed by another subgroup or a member or members. (This may be true in a so called "revision" or "power and control" phase.)

_____ References are made to agreed-upon group norms or rules.

_____ Members talk as much or more to each other than they do to group worker or indigenous leader.

_____ A pattern exists as to who talks to whom, and/or where persons sit and/or who has most influence and/or who carries out which tasks.

_____ Group purposes and/or goals are clear.

Group Structure Observation

2. Using a "sociogram" format, [for example,] sketch who seems to be most attracted to whom.

Is this conducive to attainment of group goals?

3. Who appears to have the most influence on members?

Is this conducive to attainment of group goals?

Group Process Observation

Select some comments members' made to others in the meeting.

4. What implications did these comments have for the relationship among the members concerned?

5. What kinds of discussion, if any, took place regarding the relationship implications of these interactions?

6. What was the impact of the discussion referred to in Question 5 on the achievement of group goals?

For any problem-solving discussion(s) during the session, use the following scale.

7. By the end of the problem-solving discussion, what was the staus of the problem?

_____ Completely resolved: all aspects of the situation were decided on to the complete satisfaction of the group [and the member(s) concerned] so that no further work was necessary in this area.

_____ There has been movement on the direction of resolution but the group [and member(s) concerned] could have moved further toward resolution, given the time and resources available.

_____ No change took place toward resolving the problem yet the problem was not worsened in the process.

_____ There has been movement away from resolution during this episode in that greater verbal differences were produced and/or more "friction" occurred.

_____ The movement was completely away from the problem in that the issue was abandoned either due to frustration or the immediate attraction of an alternate issue.

8. Did a member or members speak or act in any way that was substantially different from most others in the group?

How did other members respond to this?

After a group response, did the member change his or her "deviant" behavior?

Shared Attribution Observation

9. Indicate an example in which the members appeared to agree on the "causes" of a situation.

Was this shared perception of cause facilitative or hindering of the group achieving its goal?

Worker's Effects to Change Structures, Processes, or Attributions
Choose one of the preceding group conditions that the worker sought to modify.

10. Which of the following ways characterized the worker's intervention to change the group condition:

Modifying group conditions through individuals.

_____ Assigning an individual a task.

_____ Assigning an individual a role.

_____ Coaching or training an individual.

_____ Reinforcing an individual.

_____ Modifying the influence of an individual.

_____ Other (specify).

Modifying group conditions through subgroups

_____ Modifying the influence of a subgroup.

_____ Assigning the subgroup a task.

_____ Helping a subgroup to study its process.

_____ Other (specify).

Modifying group conditions through interacting with the group-as-a-whole

_____ Altering member cognitions of these group conditions.

_____ Modifying the behavior of many members.

_____ Use of program (task, activity).

_____ Altering norms.

_____ Altering group emotional states.

_____ Other (specify).

Modifying group conditions through the environment

_____ Use of agency purpose for group.

_____ Secure change in agency allocation of resources.

_____ Establishing or changing linkage between some group members and external people or systems.

_____ Change interactions between group or group members and people or systems outside of agency.

_____ Use norms and traditions coming from a reference group of the members (for example, ethnic groups).

_____ Other (specify).

PROGRAM EXERCISE

(Adapted from an exercise originally developed by Harvey Bertcher for classroom use.)

Goals

1. To be able to analyze a "program" in terms of its physical field, constituent performances, respondent behaviors, and activity dimensions.

2. To be able to plan a modification in the activity dimensions of a "program" in order to better attain the group's purposes.

Procedures

1. Prior to the exercise, trainees read about and discuss ways of analyzing a "program."

2. Trainees are divided into three groups. Each group is assigned one of the accompanying program problems. The group will follow the instructions for choosing, role playing, and analyzing a "program" to solve the problem.

3. After completion of the entire exercise, trainees can discuss program problems from their own practice as a way of learning more about this approach to programming.

The Program Problems

Group A. The Mental Health Association has decided to sponsor the formation of a social club for ex-psychiatric hospital patients, and has employed you on a part-time basis to direct its activities. The purpose of this club is to assist members with reality problems such as finding employment, developing friendships, becoming involved in community activities with people who are not ex-patients and so forth, rather than treatment of their psychological problems. You have had three meetings with the group and are still having trouble helping the members interact. You have to use a game for this purpose.

1. Select one game and *demonstrate* your use of it with such a group. (Read the General Instructions before proceeding.)

Group B. You have been assigned to work with a group in one ward of a psychiatric hospital. Most of the patients on this ward have been in the hospital for several years and are extremely withdrawn. While a long-range goal is to help patients improve sufficiently so that they can leave the hospital, you are primarily concerned at this time with getting them to communicate with one another—something they generally avoid. Since several of the members seem to enjoy music, you have decided to introduce a *musical activity*.

2. Select a musical activity and demonstrate your use of it with such a group. (Read the General Instructions before proceeding.)

Group C. You are working with a group of college students who are having difficulty focusing on their reason for attending the group which is that they are having difficulties in interpersonal relationships. You have decided that an exercise involving *fantasy* might help them with this avoidance of facing the reason they have joined the group. The group is meeting in the Counseling Services of the University.

3. Select an activity involving fantasy and *demonstrate* your use of it with such a group. (Read the General Instructions before proceeding.)

General Instructions—All Groups

You will be expected to present an analysis of the activity or task you have been assigned with regard to the following, using Vinter's "Program" paper as a guide:

A. *Identify*

1. The physical field
2. The constituent peformance
3. The respondent behaviors

B. Rate the activity according to Vinter's six "activity-setting dimensions."

C. Select a particular respondent behavior you might like to have seen increased or decreased. Indicate which of the activity's dimensions can be altered or decreased. Indicate which of the activity's dimensions can be altered to secure the desired change. Also indicate how this alteration would affect all of the other dimensions. (Obviously, this will be based on the respondent behaviors observed in class during your presentation.)

Chapter 6

ACHIEVING INDIVIDUAL CHANGE
THROUGH GROUPS

SOME GROUP WORKERS may assume that creating a set of desirable conditions in a group will benefit all or most members. There is no strong evidence to support this proposition that conditions such as democratic processes, maximum participation, norms of self-disclosure, or any combination of such group events will inevitably lead to an achievement of the goals members have set for themselves. These conditions may be sought by members and may even be necessary to achieving individual change but they are not sufficient. For this reason, in this chapter we shall consider a variety of approaches and procedures which may be required, in addition to creating a supportive group, for members to attain their goals. An application of these approaches is available to the reader through an individual change exercise at the end of the chapter.

In a manner parallel to that of the previous chapter, we shall present ways of bringing about individual change that are directed at various systemic levels. Thus, we shall demonstrate that individual change may be brought about by the worker addressing a member on a one-to-one basis, often in the presence of other group members; by the worker affecting group processes; and by the worker and/or the group interacting with people and systems outside of the group. These activities should be derived from an assessment of the problems of the group members thus leading to individualized goals and plans.

ONE-TO-ONE INTERACTIONS

A central issue for some group workers is whether or not there should even be any significant amount of one-to-one interaction between the worker and an individual member. Some group workers believe that this can undermine the contract that members should help one another and that they should receive what they need through participation in group processes. We believe that this is an extreme position and one based more on ideology than research.

In contrast, we believe that the decision to help a member through a one-to-one transaction or through affecting a group process that, in turn, will benefit the member is a question to be decided through an examination of the specific situation. The following are criteria that should be used in making a decision on this issue:

1. Is the group ready to act in ways that will benefit the member? The group may be preoccupied with initial organizational tasks; the number of members requiring individual attention at a particular meeting may be too great; the group may have an attitude toward the member that will not be therapeutic, as in the case of members seen as deviant by others. In these situations, the worker will often interact directly with the member.

2. Is the member's problem of such a crisis nature that a lack of immediate help will have serious consequences? The worker can try to change some of the group conditions mentioned in criterion 1 if the member can wait for help. The worker, therefore, is frequently in the position of weighing the costs of waiting until the group is ready to help against the costs of "jumping in" instead of relying on the group. Such an issue can be discussed with some groups as a way of helping the group to become more aware of the changes it should make in itself in order to be more helpful to members. Such a discussion may even aid the group to move more quickly to help members.

3. Will there be negative consequences, in the long run, for members helped on a one-to-one basis? We are all familiar with the "teacher's pet" phenomenon. This is only one of several negative consequences of giving attention to one person in a group that is not given to others. The members may become hostile to the person the worker helps the most or, in contrast, may join in helping this person to such a degree that he or she is permanently labeled as needy and maintained always in a dependent position in the group.

4. Will there be negative consequences, in the long run, for the group when the worker helps members on a one-to-one basis? As described in the preceding chapter, the rationale for group work is that the group does provide resources that are not available in one-to-one approaches. The objective of the worker, therefore, should be to help the group to help the members and, whenever possible, to strengthen the group's commitment to this. One-to-one helping by group workers should be used but not as the preferred mode. Too frequent use of it will create the expectation that the only or major help to individuals is from the worker, a perception that often exists early in the group's life and can be hard to overcome. Group workers have always been highly critical of practitioners who establish communication structures in which members speak primarily to the worker rather than to each other and this has been disparaged as "casework in the group."

5. Will the group's help to one member harm other members? A member may have a problem that, if dealt with in or by the group, may be

harmful to another member. An example of this occurred in a group of patients in a mental hospital. A member had a great deal of anxiety about sexual fantasies. The worker believed that the group's discussion of sexual problems would provoke anxiety in other members that they could not handle at that time. He, therefore, offered to talk with the member outside of the group.

6. Are there legitimate reasons for one-to-one confidentiality? A member's presentation of an issue may require the member to reveal information to the group that violates commitments made to others. On the other hand, members do illegitimately confide in the worker rather than the group. Their desire may be to occupy a special position vis-a-vis the worker, or they may be avoiding efforts to develop more trust between themselves and other members. These latter problems will be discussed with the member in terms of the implicit or covert intent of the member so that appropriate solutions may be found.

7. Which form of help—individual or group—will be the most potent for solving the problem? In most cases, when the group is prepared to consider the problem, the influence of other members will be greater than the influence of the worker alone. Exceptions may be when the group has a great deal of dissension or conflict regarding the ends sought by the member (and the member is made insecure by this), when the group has little or no expertise or experience with the issue, or when the member is an isolate in the group. Thus, when an analysis of all other factors is not conclusive for the worker's decision as to how to help, the most effective and efficient approach should be used. Even in the examples just given, however, if the situation is not an emergency, the worker may rely on the group's processes. Helping the member in areas in which the group lacks knowledge may lead to all members acquiring more information. Seeking to help an isolate may lead to less isolation for the individual.

After considering the preceding criteria, the worker must still decide whether an interaction with the member should take place outside of the group meeting or in the presence of other group members. When interaction takes place other than in group sessions, workers will employ the same techniques as those used in individual sessions. These include problem-solving approaches, interpretation, confrontation, support, and offering advice.[1] We shall not elaborate on these because this book's primary emphasis is on group work activities. Nevertheless, all group workers must be skillful in individual interviewing and must be able to engage effectively in this activity during intake periods, in an auxiliary way after the group is formed, and for follow-up and transfer of learning purposes after the group has terminated.

Several of the preceding criteria are also relevant to the choice of either talking with the member during or after a meeting: the first when there is no time to deal with a crisis issue during a meeting, the fifth when the discussion

---

[1]For a discussion of these techniques, see Beulah Roberts Compton and Burt Galaway, eds., *Social Work Processes,* rev. ed. (Homewood, Ill.: Dorsey Press, 1979),pp. 367–78.

will harm another, and the sixth when confidentiality is essential. These are the main reasons for extra-group sessions with individuals. The other criteria suggests reasons for employing group processes or worker–member communications *during* a meeting.

In addition to these criteria, there are some additional considerations when a one-to-one session is to occur outside of a meeting. The worker must consider whether the one-to-one session afterward will diminish the member's investment in the group and this should be discussed with the member. The worker should also assume that the member may make reference to the session, and even its content, to other group members publicly and privately and this will affect group processes.

An example of the latter was a discussion a worker had when a member approached her after the meeting of a group formed to help socially isolated adolescents. The worker held this discussion because the member was very anxious about an invitation to a party to take place prior to the next group meeting. At the meeting, the member told of his party experience and of the suggestions the worker had made. Because of the other members' envy of the social success of their peer, they deprecated the worker's suggestions as well as the value of the member's experience. The worker recognized the necessity of discussing their reasons for this response with the members.

Another consideration is that the member's concern may involve relationships with other group members. In this case, the worker should postpone the discussion until all relevant members are present. At the very least, a report of the content of the discussion to the other members may be necessary as they may resent the fact that the worker discussed material relevant to them when they were absent.

Robert Vinter termed worker interventions with the members to effect change in them as "direct means of influence."[2] In a group work context, he identified four types of such influence.[3]

1. The worker as central person–object of identification and drives. Worker actions in this category are encouragement, relating to feelings, modeling a behavior for a member, and reinforcing a member's behavior. The worker, by virtue of assuming the worker role takes on importance and emotional significance to the members which is the source of such influence.

2. The worker as symbol and spokesperson–agent of legitimate norms and values. Worker actions in this category are describing rules and policies as they affect the member and warning the member of the negative consequences of some actions. The distinction between these actions and the

[2]Robert D. Vinter, "The Essential Components of Social Group Work Practice," in *Individual Change Through Small Groups,* eds. Paul Glasser, Rosemary Sarri, and Robert Vinter (New York: Free Press, 1974), p. 17.

[3]In this discussion, we present a further explication of Vinter's direct means of influence which we developed in Charles D. Garvin and Paul H. Glasser, "Social Group Work: The Preventive and Rehabilitative Approach," in *Individual Change Through Small Groups,* eds. Paul Glasser, Rosemary Sarri, and Robert Vinter (New York: Free Press, 1974), pp. 42–43.

worker's role in creating group norms is that in the former the intent is to affect the behavior of a specific member. The effect, of course, may be on any member who is aware of the worker's action. There may also be subsequent effects on *group* norms.

3. *The worker as motivator–stimulator–definer of individual goals.* Worker actions in this category include exhorting, interpreting the psychological causes of the member's behavior, and behavioral assignments. The intent of each of these actions is to create the conditions for "unfreezing" the member's current behavior so that change is possible or securing the member's commitment to and involvement in an individual change process.

4. *The worker as executive–controller of membership roles.* Worker actions in this category include orienting a member to the group (role induction), training a member to perform a function in the group (for example, secretary) and assigning a member to a role in an activity (for example, scorekeeper in a game, character in a play). The worker is often the one who prepares individuals for the group although, in some groups, members share responsibility for this. The worker, in addition, bears in mind the goals members have for their participation in the group as roles emerge in group activities and exercises as well as in other group processes. The worker helps to bring about a "fit" between member needs and group "positions."

Example: Worker's Direct Means of Influence. In a group of ten- and eleven-year-old boys in a child guidance clinic, the activity at one session included a project in which the boys worked on decorative plaques to take home. Jim, who was of low status in the group, complained that he did not have the skill. The worker said that he would teach him to do the things he did not know how to do. The worker also expressed his understanding that Jim was worried about how his plaque would look (*worker as central person*). As Jim worked on his plaque, Bob made some critical remarks about it. The worker reminded Bob about the group's rule that when a boy said something about another, it should be with an effort to be helpful (*worker as symbol and spokesperson*). A little later on, Jim appeared to be discouraged about his work even though it was clearly as good as that of the other boys. The worker reminded Jim of discussions they had had about how heavily Jim criticized himself and the reasons for this (*worker as motivator–stimulator*). Toward the end of the session, Bill said that he did not know how to apply shellac and the worker asked Jim to show him as Jim had done this very well (*worker as executive–controller of membership roles*).

In each of these interventions, the worker could have turned to the group. He did not do so in this series of events primarily because he thought the group was not ready and the consequences of inaction might be costly for the boys. The worker planned, as the group continued, to help the group members to take these kinds of responsibilities for each other.

Several criticisms have been leveled at Vinter's conceptions. Some workers are uncomfortable with the concept of "means of influence" because of its suggestion of an all-powerful or overly controlling worker. We do not envision a worker seeking an unreasonable amount of power but we do recognize the worker's influence on individual and group processes and, therefore, use such terminology in recognition of this reality. Another criticism is leveled at such terms as "controller of membership roles," as implying that all control is from the worker. We do not mean that *all* member roles are determined by the worker but rather that the worker has influence and, depending on the situation, either will exercise it or will encourage the members to do so. Ethical issues related to self-determination and respect for individuals must always be in the forefront.

When the worker communicates with an individual during a group session, the effect on others must be assessed. For purposes of analysis, this can be sequentially divided into events prior to, during, and subsequent to the worker's action.

Prior to such one-to-one encounters in a group, the worker considers the following:

1. Are other members likely to act with similar intent to the worker's? If not, can they be helped to do so?

2. Should the entire group be asked to discuss the issue?

3. Does the member in question prefer the worker to help, other members to help, or no one to interfere?

4. Will the worker's action facilitate or hinder subsequent helping behavior by others in the group?

5. How will the worker's action affect other group conditions such as group cohesiveness, group norms, or group attributions?

During the worker's interaction with a single member, he or she observes the immediate effects on other members. Some of these effects may be as follows:

1. Other members observe the worker's intent and join in to support it by imitating the worker's actions, agreeing with them, or praising them.

2. Other members react negatively to the worker's actions and seek to sabotage them by disagreement and ridicule.

3. The worker's actions initiate a group process in which the actions, their intent, or their content are discussed or reacted to in some other way. For example, in the group of ten- and eleven-year-old boys just described, some members reacted to the worker's discussions with Jim by stating that the important thing was not whether anyone else thought your work was good but how you felt about it yourself. As the boys worked on their project, they continued to discuss times when others had criticized work that they liked.

After the worker interacts with a member, he or she observes the subsequent and longer-term effects on others. These can include the following:

1. Members continue efforts to help the member initially helped by the worker.

2. Members utilize the worker as a model and seek to help others in ways demonstrated by the worker.

3. Members withdraw from or react to the member in negative ways.

4. Members become more dependent on the worker for help.

5. The worker's words and actions have an effect on group norms, group structures, group processes, or group attributions.

THE INDIVIDUAL AS TARGET OF GROUP INTERVENTIONS

In the previous chapter, we described ways in which the worker seeks to modify group conditions so as to create a group beneficial to all members as well as a group conducive to facilitating individual goal attainment. At this point, we shall describe how the worker intervenes in group processes to benefit *specific individuals.*

Factors Affecting Use of Group

Time. In this discussion of enhancing individual change through group processes, we must elaborate on several factors affecting the worker's intervention plan. The first of these is the time frame, that is, whether the worker asks the group to allocate a substantial amount of time to a member or whether the attention paid to the member by the group is brief. The second is the specific approach used in the group to help the individual (for example, problem solving, role allocation, feedback). The third is the intent of the group's attention to the member, whether it is to help the member to understand himself or herself or the situation, to set personal goals, to change some aspect of self or situation, or to evaluate and maintain a change. In regard to each of these issues, we shall discuss the worker's actions and the criteria for employing them.

An issue, when the group is focusing on a member, is how much time it is possible for the group to invest in this activity. The range can be from briefly commenting on a member's problem or behavior to devoting an entire meeting to the problem. Brief comments on a member's behavior by other group members are appropriate under several circumstances. One is when the group has a good understanding of the goals of a member and how the member hopes to achieve them. Such brief attention is then for giving praise or feedback, or even for confronting the member with some aspect of behavior. The following is an example from a weight reduction group.

Example: When members reported on their progress the preceding week, one member said that she had attended a dinner party and had not asked for second helpings; she was praised by several members. Another member briefly illustrated how she had refused an offer of food and, in this case, it was pointed out to her that she did not sound very convincing. Another member told of an effort she had made to find a job and she was confronted with the fact that, in her reports, she avoided telling of her efforts to diet. The worker had previously discussed with the group the usefulness of these types of comments.

Brief comments made by group members to one another do not present as many issues for the group worker as spending most or all of a meeting on the problem of one member. Obviously, under those circumstances, the worker must seriously consider how this attention will affect other members. If their concerns are very similar, they may learn vicariously from this and, therefore, will not grow impatient or uninterested. In any case, a group should not be expected to use its time in this way during group formation, except under crisis conditions for one member. Afterward, when members have developed concern for one another and have learned that each person's needs for group attention will be met, such use of a meeting will be more acceptable.

Size. The size of the group will be a major factor in how much time a group can comfortably give a member. A small group, of five to seven members, will usually be willing to spend time in this way because in a few meetings all who desire this experience can receive it. A larger group will usually not tolerate an entire meeting devoted to one member but may accept considerable focus on one member's problems if several persons receive such help at each meeting. This type of group usually has two or two and a half hour sessions also.

Theoretical Issues. There are major differences of opinion as to the validity, at all, of focusing extensively on one member. Yalom, for example, in his emphasis on group process has the group focus on relationships among members rather than on one member as such.[4] Members who seek to spend a great deal of time on their "story" are described in Yalom's chapter on problem patients as "monopolists."[5]

Several approaches do focus on individuals. In one gestalt technique, the "hot seat," the worker directs attention to one individual, often asking that person to take roles representing parts of self, significant individuals, or people and objects in a dream.[6] The rest of the group remains passive during this procedure unless called on to give the member feedback or to provide the person with an opportunity to experience some emotion or thought by

---

[4]Irving D. Yalom, *The Theory and Practice of Group Psychotherapy,* 2nd ed.(New York: Basic Books, 1975), pp. 121–63.

[5]Ibid., pp. 376–81.

[6]F. S. Perls, R. F. Hefferline, and P. Goodman, *Gestalt Therapy* (New York: Julian Press, 1965), pp. 146–61.

repeating it to others. Several people, but not everyone, take the hot seat at a session. The exception is a marathon session, often of several days' duration, in which each person is likely to "work" in this way.

In gestalt groups also— and increasingly in any group—members may do a "round." The procedure is for members, usually in rotation, to speak for a few minutes about their current state; for example, their thoughts and their feelings. This may be used to open a meeting, at points when the meeting has reached some impasse or plateau, and at the end. Members are not expected to react to each other's statements; however, content that emerges may be used either for "hot seat" work or general group discussion and new and important material is often uncovered in this way.

Another example of focusing on one individual is from positive peer culture groups utilized to help delinquent adolescents. Members will declare problems they have had since the last session using agreed upon terms to characterize such problems. Members then state whether or not they wish to be "awarded the meeting." The group decides this based on a consensus as to who most needs help that day.[7]

Many group workers will not use the gestalt and positive peer culture approaches because of their emphasis on one individual receiving help for such a sustained period and, in traditional gestalt groups, more from the worker than from other members. The emphasis in group work is on helping members to help one another through group discussions and other activities. In the latter, one member may, in view of the circumstances, become the focus of attention for most or all of a meeting but this is not standard practice.

We agree with this group work practice and do not recommend, as a group work procedure, the standard "hot seat" technique or even an award of an entire meeting to a member. These remove attention from the current interactions among members and what is learned from these. Nevertheless, there are occasions when only such sustained attention can affect strong yet maladaptive defenses and workers and members can allocate their meeting time in these situations accordingly.

More research should be done on such issues. The effects of sustained attention to one member should be compared to briefer process comments to the same or other members. The immediate and long-range effects of such interventions should be examined both in terms of the actual behavior in question as well as on group cohesiveness, the indiviual's attitude to the group, and the ways the individual is perceived by others.

An important distinction is whether the group's change strategy is *active* or *passive*. By "active" we mean that the group, with intent and planning, participates in the change effort; for example, the members of one group agreed to praise Don for assertive behaviors. By "passive" we recognize that

----

[7]Harry H. Vorrath and Larry K. Brendtro, *Positive Peer Culture* (Chicago: Aldine, 1974), pp. 100–1.

a group may modify the behavior of a member without intentionally seeking to do so; for example, Don observed assertive behaviors of other group members and sought to emulate them. The passive effects are very important and powerful and constitute one of the main reasons for referring people to groups. Other reasons are opportunities to imitate other members, to learn vicariously from the efforts of others, to identify with group norms, and to behave in such a way as to secure status in the group. Nevertheless, these influences are more nebulous than the active and so we shall give the latter the most attention here.

Active efforts that the worker helps the group to mobilize include those to (1) change the perceptions, cognitions, effects, and actions, and (2) to facilitate the problem solving of the member. These efforts can take place through interactional processes between the member and the group and through the ways the member's role is structured by the group. The worker's role in each of these efforts will now be described.

Techniques for Changing Individual Perceptions

One of the best-established propositions about groups is that they are influential in modifying a member's perception of reality.[8] This principle, of course, can work in opposite ways: either to move the individual's perceptions closer to "reality" or away from it. Nevertheless, the idea of reliability rests on the argument that when several people see the same thing, it is more likely to be so. The group worker operates on this principle in several ways: When there is some question as to the accuracy of the member's views, the worker will ask others to give information to a member on their perceptions of the member's behavior and also of other people's actions toward the member.

Example. A group of socially inadequate young adults had recently taken an outing to a restaurant. A member was convinced that she had been singled out by the waitress for poor service. She attributed this to her lack of attractiveness. The other group members, when asked by the worker, had all noticed that the waitress was very busy and she had not given any of the members enough attention.

Another example, related to the same member, occurred at a meeting when she again referred to her physical appearance. The worker suggested that members report to her what they "saw." One commented on her attractive eyes, another on her pleasant smile, and a third on the way she managed to convey a sense of personal energy in her movements. These comments were very helpful in changing this woman's image of herself.

---

[8]M. A. Deutsch and A. B. Gerard, "A Study of Normative and Informational Social Influences upon Individual Judgment." *Journal of Abnormal and Social Psychology* 51 (1955), 629-36.

Techniques for Changing Individual Cognitions

Members' problems are often related to what they think about as well as what they perceive about their situations. One crucial type of cognition is attributions; namely, what members believe about the causes of their behavior or that of others.[9] The reason for the importance of attributions is the proposition that people will strive to change circumstances they believe cause their difficulties. Some people are likely to attribute their difficulties to the environment and others to themselves. Others can, of course, attribute problems to both.

The group can affect attributions in several ways. As Strong states in reference to clients in general, "if the client believes his behavior is due to a specific circumstance, event, or person, showing him a consistent pattern of similar actions over a wide spectrum of other persons or events would free the act for stable personal attribution." When the opposite occurs and the individual in some inappropriate way attributes something to self, "information that suggests he responds in that way only to a particular individual or circumstance, or that he has never behaved that way before or since, leads to external or circumstantial attribution."[10]

The group is a situation where the process of determining attributions, as described by Strong, is very likely to occur. Members are in a better position to observe the circumstances under which each person's behaviors take place than a single worker with a single client. In order for the worker to help the client to establish suitable change targets, whether internally, in the environment, or both, the member must make appropriate attributions. The worker, consequently, will help the members to identify the circumstances under which the member in question has acted in some problemmatic manner.

When the behavior has occurred in a great variety of circumstances and this is pointed out to the member, the member is likely to attribute negative outcomes to self. The member is then likely to seek to change his or her behavior so as to secure better outcomes in those situations. When the behavior, on the other hand, as pointed out by the group, typically occurs only in one situation, the member is likely to attribute problemmatic outcomes to that situation and consequently will try to change the situation.

Example. In a group of adult parolees, one of the members complained that his employer did not listen to "his side" of an argument. The worker asked the group if they recalled other similar complaints from this member. Several members pointed out that he had made such complaints about his wife and even about other members of the group. The member then moved to

[9]For some important clinical applications of attributional concepts, see S. R. Strong and R. P. Matross, "A Study of Attribution Techniques in the Interview," *Office for Student Affairs Research Bulletin, University of Minnesota* 15, No. 2 (1974).

[10]Stanley R. Strong, "Social Psychological Approach to Psychotherapy Research," in *Handbook of Psychotherapy of Behavior Change: An Empirical Analysis,* 2nd ed., eds. Sol L. Garfield and Allen E. Bergin (New York: John Wiley, 1978), p. 126.

a personal attribution of the causes of the problem and was open to the worker's observation that it may have something to do with how he presented his "side."

Example. In contrast, in a group composed of couples working on marital problems, a wife stated that she believed her problem was due to the fact that she was not as intelligent or articulate as her husband. The members pointed out to her the many occasions in the group when she had made well-stated and insightful comments. This led to a change in her attributions in the direction of considering her husband's attitude to her rather than her sense of personal inadequacy. She and her husband became more open to considering the sexist roots of their troubles rather than blame them on the wife.

Techniques for Changing Individual Affects

This section could be more appropriately labeled "expressing affects" as, aside from learning to be relaxed rather than tense in some situations, a major effect of the group on member feelings is to help the member to become more aware of or more able to express them. This can be facilitated by the worker in several ways. One way is to ask the members to provide information to the individual as to the kind of emotion he or she communicates, verbally and nonverbally.

Example. In a group of recently divorced people, one member, Jack, denied that he was angry when another member criticized him. Several members then told him that he had said this with clenched teeth, loudly, and while "jabbing his finger" at the group. Jack smiled and said that "I guess I have a hard time admitting what I felt."

A technique the worker can use to help members to express feelings is to set up practice opportunities in the group.

Example. Sarah, a member of an assertiveness group, said that she had difficulty letting people know that she felt good about them or what they did. The worker asked her to pick out another member who had done something that she liked and to tell her about it. Sarah told Jane that she liked the way she accepted the ideas of others about becoming defensive. The worker asked Jane to give Sarah some feedback on Sarah's compliment. Jane said that Sarah looked very sincere when she said this and that it was also said in a warm manner.

Techniques for Changing Individual Actions

Members can have direct effects on each other's actions as well as their thoughts, perceptions, and feelings. As discussed in this book, members, by plan, can increase or decrease behaviors by applying reinforcement principles. This can be in the form of a reward for desirable actions or an aversive stimulus for undesirable ones. The reward can be in a verbal form (for example, praise) or a nonverbal one (for example, tokens, candy, money). The aversive stimulus can also be in either form. The verbal one can range from extended criticism to a simple "no." Nonverbal can include a token whose color is designated as "criticism" (red for criticism, blue for reward) or can consist of taking back tokens that already have been awarded. In any of these cases, the worker will help the member to contract with some or all of the other members to provide these stimuli.

Example. In a group of school-age boys in a child guidance clinic, Bob frequently hit other boys in the group when he felt angry with them. He indicated that he wanted to decrease this behavior and instead tell the other boy what was bothering him. A contract was established, with the agreement of all concerned, that Bob would receive a token each time he initiated a conversation about his feelings and would relinquish one each time he threatened to or actually hit another. The tokens were exchangeable for items in the group's "store."

Another way members can influence each other's behavior is by various forms of modeling. A verbal form of modeling is for one member to describe to another member how he or she could act in a given circumstance. The member can either try this out as a role play in the group, with appropriate coaching and feedback, or in the real life situation. In the latter case, the member will report back to the group.

A behavioral form of modeling involves one member demonstrating to another member how the latter might act in a specified situation. As with verbal modeling, the member can rehearse the behavior in the group, execute it in the environment, or both.

A "trial-and-error" approach can also be used when the members do not have behavioral suggestions or when the member does not want them. The member, under this procedure, tries out a behavior in a role play or describes a potential behavior and other members join the member in evaluating the effects of the behavior.

In all these ways of affecting an individual's behavior, the group is analogous to a rich "smorgasbord." Members usually possess a great variety of experience among them and they each can draw on this to broaden their behavioral options and to become more socially adequate and effective.

Techniques for Helping Individuals Solve Problems

The ways just described in which the group can help the members are, in a sense, forms of problem solving in that changes are sought in order to solve problems. When we use the term *problem solving,* however, we specifically mean a rational, cognitive, process of identifying, evaluating, choosing, and implementing a solution from among a range of alternatives. Problem solving can be used to determine a course of action for the group, a solution to a problem affecting several members, or a solution to the problem of one member.

Subject to the considerations regarding the amount of time consumed by one member, the group may agree to engage in a process of finding a solution to one member's problem. A major difference between this and problem solving in respect to a group problem is in whose hands the final decision rests. In the former case, the decision ultimately is made either under a consensus or a majority rule. In the latter, since it is the individual's "life," he or she must be the final arbiter. This can be frustrating to the group if the individual rejects the solution that the other members support. This is not likely to happen, however, when the individual is part of the process of problem solving rather than a bystander. When it does occur, it may be an example of a game transactional analysts call "yes, but."

Under the right circumstances, a group problem-solving process related to a member's problem can be a very valuable experience for the member and can employ all of the procedures previously discussed in this chapter. The member's perception of what the problem is can become clearer as various members describe the problem as they see it or ask the member questions about it. Sometimes members, even more than the worker, can be helpful in assessing the problem because of the similarity between them and the person presenting the problem—a similarity that often extends to common problems, ages, social backgrounds, and environmental circumstances.

Similarly, the members will use their life experience to help the individual evaluate solutions to the problem. Again, they may know better than the worker does which suggestions are feasible in terms of both the capacities of the member as well as the responses of the environment. When the individual, with the help of the group, has determined a course of action, the members can reinforce the member's behavior as well as engage in further problem solving as new problems arise.

A form of problem solving is involved in "process comments" to the member. These include raising issues with the member as to the intent and effects of his or her acts in the group. The member uses this to identify problems in interpersonal behaviors. Solutions to these can then be sought through interactions with other members.

Techniques for Structuring the Member's Role

The preceding group procedures are all based on the idea that the members may affect each other through direct interactions among themselves. In addition, the group, as facilitated by the worker, can seek to change a member through assigning the member particular roles in the group. The expectations of the member as he or she seeks to perform the role are then instrumental in producing the changes the member desires. The worker can, with the concurrence of the group, make such role assignments or the group can, with the help of the worker, make its own decisions in this respect.

One set of roles about which the group makes decisions are "officers" in groups which are structured in this way. Whatever type of role is being considered, the group should be helped by the worker to assess both the needs of the group and the needs of the members considered for various positions.

Example. In a group of teenagers meeting in a community center, the group selected as its treasurer a boy who felt that he was not accepted by the others because he was the only Chicano. The boys said that they wanted to show Carlos that they liked him and wanted him to feel part of the group. The worker had been active in helping the boys and Carlos to discuss how they felt about their cultural differences and the decision was an outcome of this discussion.

Some roles are specific to particular activities. Thus there are playing positions in a baseball game, "teacher" of a song, "designer" of an art project, and "creator" of a fantasy to be acted out by the group. The people who perform each of these roles will have their behavior affected by that performance. No "cook book" exists regarding this use of roles but even beginning workers, out of their own experience, can analyze such positional effects. These effects include following sets of rules, expressing repressed aspects of one's self, developing skills, learning to control impulsive behavior, and changing a self-image.

A third set of roles grows out of the interactions among members. These roles are very informal, sometimes to the degree that they exist but are not recognized. These roles may sometimes be harmful to the member, such as the group scapegoat or deviant. Others can be constructive, if consistent with the individual's goals, such as the group "mediator," "tension breaker," or "most objective" of the group members.

The existence of such "interactive" roles can be identified by the worker when one member is consistently called on by the group to perform the same task or to be the recipient of either negative or positive emotions. When the role is beneficial to the member, the worker can reinforce the members for responding in the way they do. When the role is not beneficial, it usually takes many discussions with the member and the whole group to get the member "off the hook."

The worker can even create such roles. Thus, in a difficult situation for the group, the worker might say, "Let's see what Sue thinks about this. She's usually pretty sound in her ideas on this subject." Or, when the group is in need of some tension release, the worker can turn to a member who has provided the appropriate light touch before and even with a nod communicate an expectation that this type of help from the member will be useful at that point.

PHASES OF INDIVIDUAL CHANGE

Many changes that individuals achieve through group participation take place in ways that are not specifically planned. We do not wish to minimize the sudden insight, the accidental discovery of a skill or an interest, or a leap that may take place in a member's sense of self. Nevertheless, many changes can be and should be the result of a process moving through problem identification, assessment, goal determination, creation and implementation of a change plan, and assessment and stabilization of change. This sequence, in more or less orderly fashion, can take place through group experience as well as one-to-one counseling. The ways that groups, with the help of the worker, facilitate individual change are employed in one or more of these phases of change. Each, however, is more pertinent to some change tasks than others.

Problem identification can be enhanced through expansion of the member's perception of the situation. As previously described, this can be accomplished through other members sharing their perceptions of the member, particularly the member's behavior in the group. Assessment is affected by the member's attributions regarding the problem and these attributions are determined, in part, by the way the group helps the member to identify the occasions when he or she behaves in specified ways. Goals are determined by the member in terms of what is realistic, given the member's capacities and the environmental opportunities. Other members' perceptions of these realities are useful information. In addition, the individual must be aware of and be able to express his or her feelings about the problem and the individuals related to the problem—and the group, as we have shown, facilitates this.

The change plan, under some circumstances, is a matter of choosing the right change procedure. Depending on the nature of the problem, this may be a choice to change a perception, feeling, attribution, or action. The group can help the member to do this in any of the ways described in this chapter. Under some circumstances, the change plan must be chosen from a range of alternatives whose appropriateness can only be determined as a result of a problem-solving process. The group can help the individual to identify various actions, evaluate them on the basis of appropriateness and effectiveness, and choose one for application to the problem.

The group, subsequently, can help the member in a variety of ways to implement the change plan. The members can rehearse various parts of the plan by either discussing or role playing their behaviors in the group. The members reinforce with praise, for example, the member's efforts. They can provide him or her with feedback on how well the plan is being carried out. They can suggest modifications of the plan to take new information into consideration. A buddy "system" can be employed in which the member calls others in the group for support when the group is not in session.

When the change involves the member acting differently, this new behavior must be stabilized and maintained in the member's actual environment. The group can help with this in the following ways:[11]

1. The group can afford the member a continuing opportunity to practice the behavior, so as to strengthen it.

2. The group can provide the member with an opportunity to practice the behavior under a variety of circumstances. This principle also contributes to the member's ability to behave in the desired way. This variety can be provided by role playing the behavior as it may occur in many different circumstances. It can also be provided through the program of the group. For example, a group of adult mental patients in a half-way house were taken on weekly trips by the worker. The members had been learning effective ways of making requests. The trips were to a restaurant, a vocational training program, a department store, and a community center. In regard to each of these institutions, the members planned ways of expressing requests. The worker helped the group to list how to make effective requests such as knowing what you want, describing what you want specifically, deciding what alternatives you will settle for, and so on. Members then evaluated each other's behavior on the trips in terms of these criteria.

3. The group can help the member to think of "natural reinforcers." This means that some sort of gratification, reward, or support must be found in the member's environment to help to maintain the change. Because members are likely to be familiar with each other's life circumstances, they are in good positions to suggest realistic natural reinforcers to each other. These may include encouragement from a friend or family member or membership in a "support group." Members may have to learn how to ask for encouragement and this behavior can also be practiced in the group.

4. It is difficult to think of an example of a change sought through group experience, either in one's self or others, that will continue without problems or "setbacks." The worker initiates a discussion for this for several reasons: Members will be less likely to become discouraged when this occurs; they can also be prepared with coping strategies for at least some contingencies. The worker can help the members to help each other, particularly around the latter issue. Members, again because of the frequently found similarity in their circumstances, can predict some of the setbacks for each other. Some may have struggled already with these setbacks and can describe what they did and how this worked for them.

Rose gives a number of very specific suggestions for dealing with setbacks:[12]

1. Members can be helped to create lists of what they can and cannot control in relationship to maintaining their progress. Members can then help

---

[11]This section draws on a similar discussion in Sheldon D. Rose, *Group Therapy: A Behavioral Approach* (Englewood Cliffs, N.J.: Prentice-Hall, Inc., 1977), pp. 154–63.

[12]Ibid., pp. 158–59.

each other to work out plans for influencing those situations that can be modified. For others that cannot be influenced, the members can at least discuss ways of dealing with the resulting feelings of inadequacy and frustration.

2. Members can help each other to create lists of potential resources, particularly social service agencies, together with notations on the types of services rendered and the way one applies for service. Members may discuss their previous experiences with these resources so that members can approach them with concrete knowledge rather than the abstract information that is provided in informational bulletins.

3. Members, with suggestions from the worker, can role play some situations where setbacks are likely to take place. Rose suggests that an element of surprise can be introduced by the workers out of their knowledge of previous occasions for setback. Members will then give feedback to each other on how members coped with these unexpected occasions.

A generalized reason for setbacks is what Rose refers to as an "unsympathetic environment."[13] Anyone who has been in or worked with groups oriented to the personal growth of their members has experienced the kind of almost utopian group atmosphere that can emerge. The group, hopefully, is a place in which members are accepting and supportive and in which they can take risks through sharing personal experiences and experimenting with new behaviors. This leads to two types of stress. One is that others in the environment must adapt to changes that have taken place in the member and this can be a major source of setback. It is, in fact, the major argument for a "systems" perspective in which others are involved in one way or another in the change process rather than having to adapt to its "results." Second, group members sometimes experience a "halo effect" in which they "expect" people outside the group to be as understanding and supportive as the group has been. Members should discuss this with each other so that they can cope with the transition between group and environment; they may also seek to make their families and work places and other immediate environments more like the group, that is, more honest and supportive.

ENVIRONMENTAL INTERACTIONS

In this chapter we have considered how people may be helped to change and to cope more effectively with their environments through the worker's one-to-one interactions with each member and through the worker's facilitation of the group's attention to members as individuals. Effective individual help may require, however, a third level of worker intervention: the worker's activity in the environment on behalf of individual members. In the next

[13]Ibid., pp. 159–60.

chapter, we shall elaborate on how individuals and groups attempt to change their environment. At this point we shall consider how and when the worker acts *on behalf of* members to change the environment so as to promote individual change.

The term "environment" is a very nonspecific one. Operationally, in group work, the aspects of the environment that are targeted for change are likely to be the agency itself, the members' families, other social institutions (schools, welfare departments, and various social agencies), law enforcement and criminal justice agencies, and voluntary affiliations (peer groups).

Examples of worker interventions in this category are a worker's actions to have the agency obtain a Big Brother for a member of a boys' group; a discussion with a child's parents as to how they can support the behavioral changes sought in the group; a conference with a probation officer to ask for reinforcement for a probationer's participation in the group; and a meeting with a public assistance worker to back a group member's appeal for additional funds because of the cost of attending the group.

The worker will target the environment as part of the plan to help the members attain their goals. Such plans almost always include modifying some aspect of one's self as well as of the environment. The worker will directly intervene in the member's environment under the following circumstances:

1. The environmental change is a prerequisite to individual change and the member lacks the skill or the power to accomplish the change. Workers will try to help members to acquire such skill and power, and this shall be discussed in the next chapter. Sometimes this is not possible within the time frame of the group, or the consequences of waiting until the member can acquire these resources may be too great. In the previous example in which the worker consulted with the member's parents, the member was a retarded youngster, whose parents overprotected him. The member in this case will not be able to point this out to them until much more work is done both in the group as well as in other training environments.

2. The members should be fully appraised of the choice between changing their own environments or having the worker do so. Their wishes in this matter will be the main factor in the worker's decision. The worker, however, should seek to understand the members' reasons for this preference. Some members are too dependent and may seek inappropriately to have the worker act in their behalf outside the group as well as in. Other members may equally inappropriately tell the worker to refrain from acting in their behalf in the environment. This may be due to a dsyfunctional desire to avoid seeking any help from others; it may also be due to fears that the worker's actions will lead to punishment of the member.

3. When the members cannot act in their own behalf, the worker must also determine that the appropriate agency of change is the worker and not the group. The group, as we shall see in the next chapter, can also take actions in the environment on behalf of individual members. This is most likely to be

appropriate when the "environment" that is targetted is a large system, such as the service agency itself or another institution or agency. The group may represent more power by virtue of its numbers and, therefore, may be more potent than the worker acting alone. The other members might also have had similar problems with the organization in question.

On the other hand, the worker will be more likely to act alone with smaller systems such as the family and the peer group. In these cases, group action might be overwhelming. Confidentiality can also be a concern in these situations.

Example. In a group formed to help mothers receiving Aid to Families of Dependent Children Grants, the members had concerns about helping their children achieve in school. One of the mothers was concerned with the rules of the school that made it impossible for her child to receive extra help that he needed. The entire group composed a petition and asked to meet with the principal as a way of seeking a change in the rule. Their reason was that several of their children had had trouble with the same rule in the past (*group takes action for change on behalf of individual*). The group was successful in having the rule changed. The son was reluctant to take advantage of the new rule as he was embarrassed by the group's action. The worker met with him on a one-to-one basis to help him to overcome this feeling. In this instance, the boy represented part of the "environment" of the mother in the group.

Worker's Roles

When the worker intervenes in the environment in order to accomplish a change in group member behavior, the worker takes on one of four roles and each role is associated with specific techniques. We shall not give extensive detail on these roles here as they are generic skills of all social workers, not only group workers, and they are dealt with extensively in most practice texts.[14] We shall, however, briefly describe them.

Advocate. The first worker role is that of the *advocate*. As Grosser points out, the social work client is often in conflict with social institutions.[15] When workers function as advocates, they become partisans in such conflict. They will "argue, debate, bargain, negotiate, and manipulate the environment on behalf of the client."[16]

The role of advocate is appropriate in many circumstances to group workers. Examples of these include a group worker urging a judge to grant probation to a member of an adolescent group; pressuring a housing agency

[14]See Compton and Galaway, *Social Work Processes,* pp. 337–44; Ruth R. Middleman and Gale Goldberg, *Social Service Delivery: A Structural Approach to Social Work Practice* (New York: Columbia University Press, 1974), pp. 54–82.

[15]Charles F. Grosser, "Community Development Programs Serving the Urban Poor," in *Social Work Processes,* rev. ed., eds. B.R. Compton and B. Galaway (Homewood, Ill.: Dorsey Press, 1979), p. 348.

[16]Compton and Galaway, *Social Work Processes,* p. 342.

to grant a priority to a member of a group of welfare recipients; requesting a manpower training program to respond better to the career aspirations of a member of a rehabilitation group; insisting that the agency reevaluate the basis for calculating the service fee that the worker believed was too high for a member of a therapy group.

Several cautions have been raised regarding fulfillment of the advocacy role. One is that some workers serve as the client's advocate when a clear agreement with the client is lacking. The other is that the client may suffer retribution for having used the worker as an advocate; a consensus on this should clearly be sought as part of the member–worker contract.

Mediator. The second role is that of *mediator.* In this role the worker seeks to resolve disputes between members and others. This includes helping the parties to negotiate together and to find the common ground for their respective interests. The worker's techniques include facilitating listening and communication, maintaining engagement, focusing on the issue at hand, persuading, and conciliating.

Examples of group workers using mediation include a worker mediating between some members of an abused wives' group and their husbands, between some members of a foster childrens' group and their foster parents, and between some members of a school group and their teachers.

The caution to be observed in fulfilling this role is to avoid taking sides inappropriately. The group members must not perceive the group worker as turning against them. The people in the environment must, on the other hand, also perceive the worker as empathizing with their feelings and concerns.

Broker. The third role is that of *broker.* In this role the worker focuses on helping members to define social resources that they require and then helping them use the necessary resources. The environmental change aspect of this is to help the environmental component to provide information to the client and facilitate the client's entry. Worker techniques include information gathering, clarification of organizational requirements, communicating how intake procedures should change to meet the needs of particular clients, and securing support from the agency for the client's entry.

Some examples of this from group work include securing marital counseling for a member of a job training support group, tutoring for a member of a child guidance group and medical care for a member of a group of older persons.

The caution that the worker must observe is to be well enough acquainted with the services offered in the community to be sure that the referral is an appropriate one. The intake procedures of those agencies must also be familiar to the worker; frequently these are problematic to group members and this can lead to either an advocacy or a mediation role for the worker.

Conferee. The final role is that of *conferee.* Middleman and Goldberg describe this role as fulfilled when "two or more persons consult together, compare opinions, deliberate, and devise actions to be taken after the conference."[17] Unlike the advocacy role, there is no assumption that the worker and client have determined in advance their expectations of the system in question. Rather, the assumption is that something is amiss in service to the client and this will be worked out in a collaborative way, usually involving the client in the process. The primary skills in this activity are problem solving and enhancing communication. An example of this role was a meeting held with a member of a hospital group and her doctor.

Group workers who have assumed the role of conferee have been those in agencies offering a variety of services to the group member and those in which several agencies have agreed to cooperate in service to the group member and to seek a concensus on compatible ways of offering services.

The major caution here is for the worker to refrain from placing agency needs for conflict-free service ahead of client needs. Another concern is to prevent major decisions from being made without client involvement in decision making.

SUMMARY

This chapter has been devoted to presenting ways the group worker acts so as to facilitate change in individual group members. The worker's activity can be with the member in question, the group, and the environment. The worker must decide which of these, singly or in combination, should be utilized for such facilitation. The complexity present in groups is that such decisions must be made in ways that consider the effects on other group members as individuals as well as the group-as-a-whole. This is difficult and often all the worker can do is to monitor such effects rather than to know and to consider them prior to an intervention.

The worker's activity on behalf of individuals can draw from many techniques, depending on whether the action system is the individual, the group, or people outside of the group. The special skills of the group worker, when interacting with individuals in the groups, is related to knowledge of the effects on other individuals and how this will also affect the member in question. The group worker also possesses skills in applying knowledge as to the many ways groups impact individuals differentially. Finally, the group worker, along with all social workers, must be skillful in affecting the environment on behalf of clients. These environmental techniques were summarized in terms of the roles of advocate, broker, mediator, and conferee.

Chapters 5 and 6 have considered the activities of the worker when the target system is the group and the individual. In the next chapter, we shall consider the activities of the worker when the target system is the environment.

[17]Middleman and Goldberg, *Social Service Delivery,* p. 73.

INDIVIDUAL CHANGE THROUGH GROUPS EXERCISES

EXERCISE I

Objective

1. To identify group effects on individual behavior.

Procedure

1. Trainees read and discuss the section of chapter VI which represents group effects on individual behavior [pp. 150 to pp. 153].

2. Trainees observe a group for fifteen to thirty minutes while taking notes of the effects on individual behavior utilizing the accompanying observation form.

3. The trainer leads the discussion utilizing feedback from the Group Effects On Individual Members Observation Form.

EXERCISE II

Objective

1. To identify worker's efforts to facilitate change in a member.

Procedure

1. Trainees read and discuss the sections of chapter VI in which worker's actions to change members' behavior (through one-to-one, group, and extra group interventions) are presented [pp. 153 to pp. 158].

2. Trainees observe a group (or read a group record).

3. Each trainee selects a behavior of a member in the group that the member wishes or would be likely to wish to change.

4. Trainees complete the accompanying Planning and Assessment Form.

5. The trainer leads the discussion based on this form.

GROUP EFFECTS ON INDIVIDUAL MEMBERS
OBSERVATION FORM

Select one member in the group and observe the following:

Name _____ Sex _____ Age _____

Passive Effects

In which of the following is this member like other members? Describe.

1. Style of dress.

2. Posture (erect, slumped, and so on).

3. Use of language (slang, repeats terms, and so on).

4. Expresses support of goal, value, or activity as stated by others.

5. Acts towards another member in ways similar to acts of others in group.

Active Effects

Describe each of the following, including the effects on the member observed.

6. Do others tell this member how they expect him or her to perceive something?

7. Do others give an explanation of an event to this member and expect him or her to accept this?

8. Do members ask or tell this person how he or she feels or seek to change his or her affects?

9. Do members seek to reward or punish this member's behavior?

10. Do members seek to instruct this member in how to perform tasks?

11. Do members seek to help this member go through a problem-solving process in relation to his or her "own issue"?

12. Do members assign this person to a "role"?

13. Do members seek to secure a commitment in this member to change himself or herself?

INDIVIDUAL CHANGE PLANNING AND ASSESSMENT FORM

1. Describe the behavior of an individual in the group as *it occurs in a specific situation* and what the target of change might be.

2. Describe the behavior as it should occur at the end of a planned intervention.

3. To change this behavior, check any of the following worker (with member) interventions which would be likely to help achieve the change as described in 2.

_____ Encouragement/reinforcement.

_____ Relating to feelings.

_____ Modeling behavior.

_____ Describe a rule, policy, or value.

_____ Warn of consequences of behavior.

_____ Interpret behavior.

_____ Homework, task, behavioral, assignment.

_____ Orient and assign member to role.

4. Check any of the following worker (with group) interventions which would be likely to help achieve the change as described in 2.

_____ Help the group discuss their perceptions of the nature of the member's behavior.

_____ Help the group discuss their perceptions of the causes of the member's behavior.

_____ Help the group to discuss the member's feelings.

_____ Help other members to reward the member's behavior.

_____ Help other members to criticize the member's behavior.

_____ Help other members to model the behavior for the member.

5. Check any of the following worker (with environment) roles which would be likely to help achieve the change as described in 2.

[First indicate the person or system in the environment to be contacted:

_____]

____ Broker.
____ Advocate.
____ Mediator.
____ Conferee.

6. Which of the preceding approaches that you have checked will be the most appropriate given the member's attitudes and capacities, group conditions, and environmental realities?

Chapter 7

GROUP WORK AND ENVIRONMENTAL CHANGE

THROUGHOUT THIS BOOK we have asserted the principle that all social work activity should be directed at understanding the impact on individuals of their own behavior, their environments, and the interactions between the two. Worker interventions can be directed, as required, at changes in any one of these. In this chapter, our focus shall be on occasions requiring changes in the environment and ways of achieving these changes through group services. Such changes may be sought and achieved by the individual (often with the help of the group), by the group (on behalf of one or all members) or by the worker. The worker's activities in the environment were dealt with in the last chapter; the way workers help members to change their own environments shall be presented now.

We shall begin with a discussion of the rationale for environmental change. This shall be followed by an analysis of ways in which the "environment" can be assessed so as to facilitate the development of effective plans for environmental change. Actual procedures for changing the environment as employed by members, as individuals, and by the group-as-a-whole shall comprise the final section of the chapter. An environmental change exercise follows the chapter also.

RATIONALE FOR ENVIRONMENTAL CHANGE

Interaction with Environment

The proposition that the individual's behavior is a consequence of his or her interaction with the environment is the first reason for the group worker's attention to environmental change. Vinter has termed this type of analysis "an interactional view of deviance," which he clarifies as follows:

All behavior amenable to change is regarded as socially induced, acquired through learning and related processes; it is exhibited, evoked, or constrained within the context of specific social situations. The sources of behavior lie both within the individual (in terms of his enduring attributes and acquired capabilities) and within the social situation (in terms of opportunities, demands, and inducements). Behavior, moreover, is judged, encouraged or sanctioned by others within the person's immediate social situation. These actions between persons constitute a series of interactions which shape and sustain behavioral patterns. The judgments and responses of others must be regarded as crucial features of all behavioral patterns. Social definitions of deviance are necessarily relative, and those who define behavior as problemmatic often refer to specialized standards of conduct. In this view, therefore, the targets of intervention include not only the individual whose behavior is judged to be inadequate or deviant, but also the judgments and interactional responses of individuals and groups whom he contacts regularly or frequently at the time.[1]

The "interactional view of deviance," therefore, means that those environmental transactions and forces that maintain problems of group members must be identified and changed. One controversy springing from this contention is the degree to which environmental forces that initially created such problems must be understood when these existed in the past but not the present.

Those who argue for some historical reconstruction believe that the members' understanding of such forces is necessary for individual change, particularly as they may be unable to free themselves from their memories of the past. Furthermore, an uncovering of the history and initial causes of problems may provide clues to forces that my be operating in the current situation. Those who oppose attention to history believe that this may obstruct a focus on current conditions and that it is the current conditions that must be understood and changed; furthermore, behavior *can* be changed through modification in the current situation with little or no attention to historical causes.

Our position is the moderate one. We do not find that attention to history is always required and such attention can obstruct efforts to change the contemporary situation. Nevertheless, the individual sometimes must be freed from "unfinished business" in the form of an obsession with the past; the past also provides clues to present patterns in functioning. The worker must help the members to assess, then, in the group how their reflections on the past are used.

Labeling Process

Another reason for attention to the environment is that, as Vinter also suggested in the preceding quotation, it is the environment that has "ob-

---

[1]Robert D. Vinter, "An Approach to Group Work Practice," in *Individual Change Through Social Groups,* eds. Paul Glasser, Rosemary Sarri, and Robert Vinter (New York: Free Press, 1974), pp. 4–5.

served, evaluated, and officially labeled the behavior."[2] Changes in this evaluation and labeling process are often required for the group member to be able to function in desired ways.

Example. In a group of boys with problems in associating with peers, one member, John, fought a great deal with other children. The initial causes of his behavior stemmed from the abusive ways his parents had disciplined him. Currently, however, he is labeled as a "bad" boy by the neighbors who keep their children away from him. He also was under the frequent scrutiny of the police who had been contacted by a neighbor; the police often made remarks to John to "stay out of trouble" and this served to lead John to feel stigmatized and rejected. The worker concluded that it was necessary, consequently, to target the neighbors and the police for change.

Choosing New Environments and Transactions

A third reason for attention to the environment is that, as a solution to their problems, members may wish to function in new environments or in different ways in the environment. The environment may not provide opportunities for this, thus requiring an analysis of and change in environmental opportunity structures.[3]

Example. A deficient opportunity structure was observed relevant to group work in an elementary school. The group worker recognized that several members of the group needed tutoring in order to compensate for educational deficits. This service was not available; the worker, therefore, joined with a group of parents to lobby for it.

Example. In a group of welfare recipients, most of the members were from black and Chicano groups. They experienced discrimination in employment from several of the employers in the area. In this case, necessary opportunity structures were closed to them because of racism. They decided, with the aid of the worker, to seek the help of a union to challenge this discrimination.

One issue raised by some workers is the appropriateness of any environmental targets at all. These workers argue that focusing on the environment can be a type of member "projection" and abdication of personal responsibility for one's life. These workers, furthermore, are only willing to contract with members to facilitate individual change. We are strongly op-

---

[2]Robert D. Vinter with Malda J. Galinsky, "Extragroup Relations and Approaches," in *Individual Change Through Small Groups,* eds. Paul Glasser, Rosemary Sarri, and Robert Vinter (New York: Free Press, 1974), p. 283.

[3]A more extended discussion of the importance of opportunity structures is found in Richard A. Cloward and Lloyd E. Ohlin, *Delinquency and Opportunity* (Glencoe, Ill.: Free Press, 1969).

posed to this position as many of the problems brought by members to social work groups are maintained by dysfunctional environments and can only be solved by changes in those social conditions.

Furthermore, we have found that even when the member's behavior constitutes a major component of the problem, many members would not accept help if a recognition of this were demanded prematurely. A good example of this principle is found in a report of group work with husbands who physically abused their wives.[4] In the first sessions of the group, the men blamed their wives for "making them do it." After they had developed sufficient trust and cohesiveness, they were able to look at their own contributions to the violence in their marriages. In addition, when a member states that something is entirely the fault of other people or systems, the worker can ask "what do you want to do about it?" This immediately involves the members in examining their own behavior as well as that of others.

SELECTION OF ENVIRONMENTAL TARGETS

Choosing the System

The first task confronting workers and members is the selection of those systems in which change is necessary in order for members to achieve their goals. The following are some examples of the major types of targets that are likely to be chosen.

Family Targets. In a group of adolescents, the members discussed such issues as the rules established by their parents. the kinds of support they received in their families for achievement, and conflicts between their parents that were deflected on to them. They discussed strategies for helping their parents to change, including joint meetings with the parents.

Peer Targets. A group of men preparing themselves for discharge from a prison discussed many ways that peers had influenced them, thus contributing to their lack of adjustment prior to committing their offenses. This included pressures to go to bars as well as to join in illegal activities. The men discussed ways of being more assertive in rejecting such pressures as well as, on occasion, seeking to change the behavior of friends with regard to such destructive acts.

Organizational Targets. A group of youths in a residential treatment center discussed the rules of the institution. They believed that some of these rules were arbitrary and were more for the convenience of the staff than for the benefit of the youths. This point of view was reinforced by thoughtful

[4]Janet A. Geller, "Reaching the Battering Husband," *Social Work with Groups* 1 (Spring, 1978), 27-38.

discussion in the group. The members began to explore ways in which they have input into consideration of agency rules. The youths also attended a local public high school. Their discussion of rules turned to the ways the high school maintained discipline that they thought were overly harsh. The members thought that some of the ways they will use to affect their agency's rules could also be used by them in the high school to change the school's rules.

Societal Targets. A group worker met with a group of welfare recipients who were also enrolled in the Work Incentive Program, a program for training and employment. They learned that new legislation was being considered by the Congress to restrict the amount of training the program could offer. The members resolved to contact the local welfare rights organization to see if they could do anything to oppose this legislation.

Choosing the "Level"

The second task for the group and the worker is to consider the "level" of the chosen environmental system that should be targeted. The levels include one individual within the system (for example, mother in the family, teacher in the school, co-worker in the factory); a set of people with similar roles in the system (for example, all teachers, both parents, all fellow employees); the entire system (for example, all members of the family, the entire school, the business or factory); or finally the system's authority structure (for example, the board of directors of the agency).

The following criteria will help the worker and the group decide which level to target:[5]

1. The members must decide the degree to which the behavior of some individual external to the group is determined by idiosyncratic factors or organizational ones. For example, is the individual following "orders" or creating them? This is sometimes a difficult assessment to make because people can perform in ways condoned by the "system" but not part of its official rules. Thus a teacher might discriminate against some group of students when this is unofficially supported by the school yet is not part of its "official rules."

When the behavior of the individual is idiosyncratic, the member should seek to have an effect on that individual's behavior. An exception to this is when the individual is intransigent; the member may then seek to have the larger organization exert influence on this person or remove him or her. Thus a teacher who was prejudiced against members of a minority group and who would not change was replaced after an appeal to school authorities.

[5]For a more extended discussion or organizational change in social work, see Edward J. Pawlak, "Organization Tinkering," in *Social Work Processes,* rev. eds. Beulah Roberts Compton and Burt Galaway (Homewood, Ill.: Dorsey Press, 1979), pp. 498-504.

2. The members should also assess the aspects of the external system that are most amenable to change. In some school situations, for example, the teacher concerned might be most responsive; in others it may be the principal, the teacher's union, or the superintendent. As a general rule, it may be easier to change an individual or a few individuals than the whole system, unless such individuals are acting in clear conformity with the rules and procedures of their organization.

When seeking to change a system, rather than a few individuals within it, consideration should be given to which aspect of the system to change. The following concepts are useful in this respect:

1. *The rules of the system.* A youth group sought to change the rules regarding smoking in the high school so that areas are designated where smoking will be allowed.

2. *The way the system is structured.* One group sought to change the channels of communication in a school system so that they will be permitted to express their grievances to the Board of Education without first consulting the principal; another group wanted to alter the decisional structure in a hospital through the establishment of an advisory group of patients; another group wanted to modify the division of labor in a residential treatment center so that paraprofessional workers, with whom they felt secure, will be allowed to sponsor "support" groups.

3. *The allocation of resources in the system.* In a residential treatment center, some rooms that were appropriate for group meetings were reserved, even after school hours, for the use of the agency's school. The members of a group sought to change this allocation of space.

STRATEGIES FOR ENVIRONMENTAL CHANGE

Before a specific strategy is chosen, a decision must be made as to whether the major instrument of change is the individual, the group, or the worker. Since the choice of the latter was described in the preceding chapter, the decision regarding individual or group shall be presented here. As we stated elsewhere, "clients should be maximally involved in securing changes in the environments which affect them, so that ultimately they will be able to act on their own behalf without professsional help."[6] Constraints on this are suggested by an evaluation of the following factors:

[6]Paul Glasser and others, "Group Work Intervention in the Social Environment," in *Individual Change Through Small Groups,* eds. Paul Glasser, Rosemary Sarri, and Robert Vinter (New York: Free Press, 1974), p. 297. The discussion that follows draws extensively from this work.

1. *Member Motivation.* The member must have a desire to act to attain environmental change. This desire will be a product of previous experiences with efforts to change the environment. Such experiences may have met with reinforcement either in terms of actual success or other rewards for having made the effort. On the other hand, the member may have experienced failure or may have been otherwise punished for such activity. The members may also have identified other reasons for anticipating their success or failure in modifying social conditions and situations such as knowledge of the experiences of others and assessments of the actual situation.

2. *Member Capacity.* The member's willingness to seek environmental change or the worker's judgment that this is appropriate will be related to the skills the member possesses. These skills, as we have stated elsewhere, include the member's ability "to understand the intent of the change effort, perform the actions required, and withstand the anxiety and stress which may be engendered by the effort."[7] We concluded in that discussion that young children, psychotics, or the retarded will not be able to contribute a great deal to environmental change but that public welfare recipients, inmates of correctional institutions, and parents of school children will have capacity for such activity.

In our previous discussion of factors to be considered in deciding the agent for environmental change, we also listed the likely effectiveness of any strategy, the risks to which the group member will be exposed, the effect of the effort on such group conditions as cohesiveness and group structure, and its relationship to the members' goals.

Based on the preceding criteria, the individual and the group should consider whether the group will help the individual to plan his or her own strategy for environmental change or whether the entire group will take action on behalf of one or more members. The following are some examples of such decisions.

Example. In a group of high school students experiencing school difficulties, one member complained about the impatience of one of his teachers. The teacher did not give him adequate explanations when he asked questions. The member discussed with the group ways of explaining his needs to the teacher and he was helped to role play appropriate assertive responses that will make his needs known and will not be experienced by the teacher as an attack. In this case, an individual change effort was appropriate because it was likely to be effective, the client wished to take responsibility and it was consistent with the members' goals to become more assertive with people in authority.

In the same group, several members concluded that they received less help from their teachers than other students because they were not judged to

---

[7]Ibid., p. 297.

be "college material." In this case, the members planned to invite their teachers to a group meeting in which they would discuss their own ambitions and the role of a high school education in achieving these. This was deemed more appropriate by the worker than individual appeals because the worker and group believed this would be the most effective strategy. Also the members collectively were better able (*capacity*) to present their case. They were not as highly motivated to act individually as the student in the previous case and they needed the group's reinforcement to present their case. Moreover, they were still acting on their own behalf and this was a step in developing motivation and capacity to act individually when this became a necessity.

We shall now present the strategies that can be employed for environmental change.[8] Some of these are most appropriately used by individuals, others by the group, still others by either entity. In any case, our assumption is that the choice of strategy should be a product of group problem-solving activity.

One important consideration in selecting an environmental change strategy is the level of conflict induced with the system being changed. In some cases, the environment can be changed in ways that are regarded as benign; that is, the environmental system may regard the change as also in its own best interests; in other cases, the environmental system is only amenable to change when forced to do so in ways that it regards as unpleasant or punitive. We propose that the best strategy is the least conflictual one that can attain the desired objective. This is usually the least costly in terms of energy and resources; it has the fewest side effects in terms of future retaliation; and it still permits an escalation of conflict when this is deemed necessary. Finally, the least conflictual approach is also viewed by observers as a just one. There are many other related value issues that are difficult to enumerate without describing specific situations. We shall, however, present and rank strategies in an ascending order of conflict.

A second consideration underlying any environmental change is that such efforts require the members to be assertive. An extensive literature exists on means of acquiring assertive behavior.[9] Such behavior is defined as acts that secure a person his or her rights without denying the rights of others. It is distinguished from *nonassertive* behavior which fails to assert one's rights and *aggressive* behavior which attains one's rights while denying those of others. Assertiveness is related also to a philosophy that leads people to value themselves and to believe that they have the right to actualize themselves and to prevent others from infringing on this right.

Assertive responses can be increased through training. Such training,

[8]These categories of environmental change activities are a modification of one presented in Glasser and others, in *Individual Change*, pp. 299–305.

[9]See, for example, Arthur J. Lange and Patricia Jakubowski, *Responsible Assertive Behavior* (Champaign, Illinois: Research Press, 1976).

usually done in groups, begins with helping members to understand and apply an assertive philosophy. Members then are taught the differences among assertive, nonassertive, and aggressive behaviors. Situations are subsequently identified in which members have not behaved assertively. With the facilitation of the worker, the members help each other to identify the nonassertive or aggressive components of their responses and how these can be made assertive. Members practice such assertive responses through role playing them in the group with other members. The members try these responses out in the environment and report back to the group on the result. This may require further modification of member responses if the member's objectives have not been adequately achieved, because the response was inadequately assertive. An escalation in the degree of conflict may also be justifiable when the member's rights are still denied.

Environmental Change Activities Solely for Individuals

Some environmental change activities can only be employed by the group members as individuals because they involve immediate ways of interacting with environments.

Avoidance. In the avoidance approach, the member changes the environment *as it affects him or her* by staying away from it. An example of this is adolescents who avoid peers who elicit behavior that will get them into trouble. The group can help the youth to find alternative peer groups as well as resist invitations to associate with the problematic group.

Alternate Reactions. In employing alternate reactions, the member changes his or her own behavior without making any overt demand on the other person. This change, however, is presumed to lead to a change in the other. An example of this is a husband who resolves to respond to his wife's aggressive responses with assertive ones although he had been aggressive before. He hopes that his wife will use his newly acquired behaviors as a model for her own behavior.

Manipulation of the Social and/or Physical Situation. An example of manipulation occurred in a group meeting in a children's residential treatment center. A member of the group lived in a cottage consisting of several bedrooms. The other boys in his room were older than he and tended to reinforce his dependence on others. With the help of the other members of the group, he resolved to ask for a change to a room with younger boys.

Environmental Change Activities Employed by Individuals and Groups

Interpretation. One action that can be used either by members in their own interests or by the group on behalf of members is *interpretation;* that is, to explain to others the causes or consequences of either the member's behavior or their own. One example is of a group that helped a member to explain to his teacher that his sleepiness in class was due to a new medication he was trying out to prevent seizures. In another youth group, the members decided to explain to an agency that assigning them the meeting room occupied by the Alcoholics Anonymous program was leading to ridicule from other groups.

Education. Another approach is *education,* as the actions of others may be due to incorrect or missing knowledge. A group of former prisoners, for example, discussed their difficulties in securing employment. They realized that many employers were unaware of the excellent work performance of rehabilitated offenders. The group drew up a fact book indicating research findings on this that members will use to better inform themselves as well as prospective employers.

Evaluation. The action involved in evaluation is to gather information on the behavior of individuals or organizations. Such data may relate to either the extent of the behavior itself or its effects. A wife, for example, complained that her husband seldom showed her affection. The group suggested to her that she talk to her husband about keeping a chart of the frequency of this behavior. She later reported to the group that his demonstrations of affection increased when he became aware of their low frequency. In another group, the sponsoring agency decided to raise the fees for service, arguing that increased revenues were necessary and this raise would not have an effect on members' use of the agency. The group members discussed this and suggested that the agency keep a record of attendance and continuance. After three months, this information was compared to the experience during the three months prior to the new policy. The agency discovered that the members who were of the lowest income began to use services less; this led the agency to reexamine the policy.

Use of Influentials. The strategy of using influentials is one in which the member or the group asks a person with power to change a person or system. A group of patients in a hospital, for example, were concerned about some of the actions of the nursing staff. They had originally tried interpretive and educational approaches without success and now believed that an escalation in the use of power was legitimate even if this led to the possiblity of conflict. They invited the director of nursing to meet with them so they could try to convince her of the justice of their cause. They hoped she would use her influence to change the actions of the nurses. In another example a college student in a group sponsored by the university's counseling services complained about unfair grading policies of an instructor. He had been helped previously by the group to explain to the instructor the results of his policies (*interpretation*). He had also urged the instructor to ask for feedback from the students on the policy (*evaluation*). Since neither approach was acceptable to the instructor, the student was helped by the group to plan how to present his case to the department chairperson.

Bargaining. Either the member or the group can use *bargaining.* This means that either can do something in exchange for a desired environmental modification. A group wanted a meeting room of its own. It agreed to clean out a room, now used for storage, if it was made available to the group. The woman in the previous illustration who did not receive the affection she wished from her husband considered the possiblity of offering to cook his favorite meals more frequently for him in exchange for more attention.

Confrontation. The strategy of confrontation can lead to more conflict than the other strategies as "the client forces the other to face the ways in which his behavior or attitudes are problemmatic for him and demands some change."[10] This type of action can also be taken by the group. A member of an adolescent group was concerned about the fact that he was usually the one singled out for blame whenever the classroom become noisy or was disrupted in any other way. The group, many of whose members were in the same classroom, confirmed his perception that he was a scapegoat in that situation. The member was supported in his plan to tell the teacher to stop scapegoating him and to find a better way of affixing the blame. In another group of welfare recipients, several of the members had the same Assistance Payments Worker. This worker, they believed, was lax in submitting legitimate requests for more funds for his clients. The group members drew up a list of occasions when the worker had been negligent and submitted this to him. He was told that his actions would be reviewed in a month and if better service were not received, charges against him would be filed with the director of the agency.

Mass Media. Groups will also resort, on occasion, to uses of the *mass media,* such as the newspapers. Individuals in the group, as well as the group-as-a-whole, can submit documentation to the mass media on injustice. For this purpose members have used the "letters to the editor" column as well as contacts with feature reporters. Members of an adolescent group in a residential treatment center asked a reporter to investigate charges that the agency overlooked drug use in the agency and failed to protect members who were suicidal. This process induces a great deal of conflict with the agency because of the repercussions the agency faces from legislators and other funding sources.

Resistance. The two most extreme strategies for change are *passive* and *active resistance.* Both have the intent of causing a major disruption in the system at which they are directed. The former accomplishes this through non-cooperation with key authorities. Members engaging in passive resistance

---

[10]Ibid., p. 301.

will refuse to perform tasks or, in a more extreme way, will obstruct other activities by "sit-ins." People in groups that use this device have refused to do homework that was regarded as excessive or "make work" chores in residential centers or at places of employment. Members, operating singly, have been reluctant to use this strategy because they usually perceive themselves as powerless and likely to lose more than they gain when confronting the full power of social institutions. Nevertheless, constant frustration of legitimate demands often leaves few other choices when the demands are serious enough.

Passive resistance must be part of a long-term, complex strategy with structures for maintaining such a strategy when the immediate retaliation, likely to ensue, erupts. For example, a group of welfare mothers who "sat in" in a local welfare department to demand clothing allowances were arrested and jailed. The group was so demoralized by this experience that it was completely destroyed.

Admittedly, these forms of resistance are more often used when the group is viewed as part of a community organization effort. Nevertheless, with poor or otherwise oppressed people it is difficult to separate the need for personal change from social change efforts as both are so interwoven and necessary to improve their lot. Some agencies, such as the Mobilization for Youth program in New York, in the 1960s, employed teams of treatment-oriented as well as community-oriented workers to work with individuals and groups.[11] This method of service, while at its peak in the 1960s, may yet have its day again.

Active resistance involves taking an action that is likely to be unpleasant or disruptive to a system. Actions that fall in this category are picketing and marching. More extreme forms include destruction of property or depriving people, even temporarily, of their freedom. The more extreme forms are not considered by most social workers to be professionally acceptable.[12] Nevertheless, social workers should be cognizant of the extremely cruel conditions that have led some clients to engage in prison riots, university disruptions, or industrial actions. In these circumstances, attention should clearly be drawn also to the systems that are inhumane and self-seeking.

Whenever any escalation of conflict is contemplated, even short of active and passive resistance, group members must be helped to consider whether lesser strategies are likely to be effective as well as the other factors affecting such choices. Some people, because of the kinds of neglect and abuse they have suffered in their lives, believe that they are justified in responding in destructive ways throughout their lives. This type of characterological problem requires expert and sensitive handling by workers

---

[11]For a case study of this combination of individual, group, and community services see Francis P. Purcell and Harry Specht, "The House on Sixth Street," *Social Work* 10, no. 4 (October, 1965), 69-76.

[12]For an extended discussion of the ethical issues involved, see Harry Specht, "Disruptive Tactics,", *Social Work* 14 (April, 1969), 5-15.

so that members do not persist in ultimately self-destructive responses. Some such members are found in groups meeting in correctional settings where confronting this behavior is not easy because of the support it may receive from other clients as well as the reality support it encounters whenever injustices reoccur in such settings.

Environmental Change Activities Employed by Groups

The preceding list is composed of strategies that may be used by individuals or groups; there are also two procedures that require a group for execution.

Cooptation. Cooptation involves the interaction with the group of the people to be influenced. This is accomoplished in such a way that the group becomes a reference group for the person, helping to define his or her values and perceptions. An example of this is provided by Klein in his discussion of a youth group's efforts to cope with police officers who harrassed the members when they used the local park. The members' strategy included inviting members of the police force to visit some of their meetings to become better acquainted with them and their activities.[13]

Alliance. In the alliance strategy the group joins together with other groups to attain a common environmental change goal. An example provided by Glasser and co-workers is stated as follows: "A psychiatric orderly consistently brings the ward patients to the dining room late. As a result they must eat hurriedly and sometimes do not get a full meal. Treatment group patients may enlist the support of the other groups on the ward or organize other patients into a larger group, to put pressure on the attendant to change his pattern."[14]

SUMMARY

In accomplishing group work goals, the targets of change at any given time may be the individual, the group, or some aspect of the environment. This chapter was devoted to procedures used when the latter is the target. The instrument of such change can be the individual member, as influenced by the worker and/or the group, the group itself, or the worker. When the worker tries to change the member's environment, it is usually to affect some subsequent change in the member and, therefore, we dealt with worker efforts to change the environment in the previous chapter.

This chapter presented a rationale for environmental change followed

[13]Alan Klein, *Society, Democracy and the Group* (New York: Woman's Press and William Morrow, 1953), pp. 329-330.
[14]Glasser and others, in *Individual Change*, p. 302.

by procedures to accomplish this as used by members acting alone, by either members as individuals or the group-as-a-whole, and finally by group action. Each procedure was defined and examples from group work practice were provided.

ENVIRONMENTAL CHANGE EXERCISE

Goals

    1. To identify occasions for environmental changes.

    2. To discriminate among occasions when the members, the worker, or the members and worker together seek to change the environment.

    3. To choose the appropriate strategy for environmental change.

Procedure

    1. Prior to the exercise, trainees read about and discuss reasons for environmental change and strategies for accomplishing this.

    2. Five trainees are asked to volunteer to form a group which will hold a short meeting in front of the class. The topic of the meeting is to be "Concerns I have about learning to be a group worker." One member is chosen as worker for the group.

    3. After the meeting, the entire training group or class uses the environmental change planning form as a means of analyzing the group meeting.

ENVIRONMENTAL CHANGE PLANNING FORM

1. Briefly describe a problem one or more members have in attaining a goal.

2. Will a person or persons outside of the group hinder the member from attaining the goal? If so, describe.

3. Is this hindrance a product of one of the following? (check any that apply):

    _____ rules presented

    _____ the structure of the situation

_____ the way the person(s) allocate resources

_____ other (specify) _____

_____

4. Describe motivation of member(s) to seek changes in the environment through his or her own efforts.

5. Describe capacity of member(s) to seek changes in the environment.

6. What risks will the member(s) incur by seeking changes in the environment?

7. In view of 4, 5, and 6, should the member be helped to plan to achieve changes in the environment alone or with the help of the worker, or should the worker become the main instrument of change?

8. Which of the following change strategies will be used:

   _____ avoidance

   _____ alternative reactions

   _____ manipulation of situation

   _____ interpretation

   _____ education

   _____ evaluation

   _____ use of influentials

   _____ bargaining

   _____ confrontation

   _____ mass media

   _____ passive resistance

9. Describe in detail the way the strategy will be used.

10. How will the effectiveness of the strategy be evaluated (Trainees can consult Chapter 8, Evaluation of Environmental Changes, for help in answering this question.)

Chapter 8

THE EVALUATION OF
GROUP WORK PRACTICE

A GROWING CONCEPT in social work is that the "practitioner" should become a "practitioner–researcher." One reason for this is political—the current emphasis on accountability. Funding sources and legislative bodies have raised questions about whether the funds for social programs are well spent, which has led to the requirement that workers collect and report data on the outcomes of their activities. While the purpose of this is to ensure that funds are routed to activities that are the most effective, thus benefiting more people, this is unfortunately not always the result of evaluative efforts.

A reason for difficulties in performing an evaluation is the current state of knowledge regarding measurement of the outcomes of social work intervention. An exception is the rapid development of the field of behavior modification; one that has led to many reliable devices for the measurement of behavioral change. However, not all intervention goals are conceptualized as changes in discrete behaviors. Goals are sometimes described in terms of emotions, attitudes, self-evaluations, the qualities of decisions that one may make, as well as institutional changes. While practitioners and researchers are working to create valid and reliable measures of *all* phenomena related to social work objectives, there are still weaknesses in their products as well as disagreements among practitioners as to appropriate types of measurement.

Another problem with the current approach to accountability is that the type of data to be collected is often imposed by the agency upon the worker, at times with little regard for the worker's concerns regarding the types of variations that exist among clients. Workers, therefore, do not always take data collection for purposes of program evaluation seriously. Many group workers known to the author record data on agency forms with little thought because of their lack of identification with the purposes and methods of evaluation required by the agency.

Group workers, like all social workers, experience the difficulties with current evaluative technologies that we have described. This does not militate against our conviction that workers' evaluation of their practice should be an essential component of their activity and that all workers must struggle to overcome some of the barriers to such practice that exist through inadequacies in evaluative technology and approaches inappropriately imposed by the agency. The reasons for such evaluation go beyond, also, the concern that resources should be allocated to programs that are effective. The worker also has an obligation to the group members. They have a right to examine whether or not their investment in the group work process has attained the goals they have established for themselves.

Furthermore, the worker has a responsibility to practice in ways that are effective. Workers, consequently, must know which of the procedures they employ to facilitate individual change are the most effective and efficient. When workers apply procedures to change group and environmental conditions to attain individual goals, they must also know whether those "work." Thus the requirement we place on workers, as professionals, is that they must modify their practice to employ the interventions that are the most likely to help members with the least investment of time and energy.

In the term "practitioner–researcher," we have purposely placed the word "practitioner" first. The interests of practitioners must be in serving the members of the group. If taking responsibility for the effectiveness of that service leads to a better understanding of the procedures employed—and in some instances to insights into human behavior—that is valuable but secondary to offering service in a responsible and accountable way. Thus the practitioner should not employ questionnaires or other instruments or subject members to any stresses unless these are required to serve those members. When practitioners desire to do research, as such, members should be informed about this as a separate issue which they can accept or reject on its own merits.

It follows from these comments that all relevant parties should be involved in determining the nature and extent of an evaluative procedure. First and foremost the group members should be helped to determine what they wish to know about the effects of group services. Secondly, the workers themselves should consider what kinds of information will help them to be responsible to the members as well as lead to better practice. Agency requests for information from workers or even members should not conflict with or impede these requirements.

In determining how to evaluate group work practice, the worker must decide (with proper involvement of members and significant others) on the design of the evaluation and on the instruments to be used. Furthermore, the worker must gather evaluative information not only in relationship to the members but to the group and to the environment when these systems are targets of intervention. We will, therefore, separately consider issues of design and measurement as these apply to individual members, the group, and systems outside of the group.

EVALUATION OF INDIVIDUAL CHANGE OF GROUP MEMBERS

Evaluation Design

The design of an evaluation consists of plans as to when and from whom information will be collected as well as the type of information that will be sought. These plans, in turn, are based on the way in which the information will be analyzed to determine the effects of service.

To identify whether individuals have benefited from group work service, a measurement must be made of their relevant circumstances and behaviors prior to the group work experience and after it. In addition, depending on the situation, additional measurements must be made during the group work process as well as some time after it has terminated.

The measurement of the status of a member's problems or concerns prior to group work service is referred to as a *baseline*. The member, then, seeks an improvement in this measure as a result of group participation. An appropriate baseline requires a process in which members decide what they wish to change as a result of group experience and what their change goals are. Examples of some ways used by group members to establish individual baselines are as follows.

Example. A member of a group of college students measured, for three classes, how anxious he felt when he spoke out. He used a scale in which zero represented complete calm and 100 the most anxiety he has felt.[1]

Example. A member of a parents' group counted for three consecutive days how many times a day she criticized her son.

Example. A member of an assertiveness group measured his degree of assertiveness using the Rathus scale.[2]

Example. A member of a career decision group indicated that he had twice previously thought he had made the right career decsion but had withdrawn from training programs because of his doubts about his decision before they started.

Example. A member of a gay "coming-out" group said that he had gone home twice in the past month to tell his parents about his "gayness" and left without accomplishing this.

[1]This is referred to as a "subjective units of disturbance scale." For details, see Joseph Wolpe, *The Practice of Behavior Therapy*, 2nd ed. (Elmsford, N.Y.: Pergamon Press, 1973), p. 120.

[2]S.A. Rathus, "A 30-item Schedule for Assessing Assertive Behavior," *Behavior Research and Therapy* 11 (1973), 398–406.

Many technical issues regarding baseline measurements are beyond the scope of this text. A major one relates to the number of baseline measurements that should be made in order to ensure that the measure represents the *typical* behavior of the group member. The reader can consult a number of texts that explain, in detail, the criteria for an appropriate baseline.[3]

In addition to a decision as to the frequency of measurements, another must be made as to whether effectiveness will be evaluated in terms of each individual separately or whether it will be evaluated for a number of individuals. There is a long tradition of evaluating group and individual treatments by examining their effects on individuals. The presentation of case studies are instances of this. In such case studies, the practitioner asserts the value of his or her approach by showing that it has helped specific persons. This method, without a doubt, advanced knowledge about many techniques and will continue to do so. The measures were qualitative in that they described the situation of the person before and after treatment.

One of the newest designs for evaluating change efforts is also focused on the individual case but quanitative rather than qualitative measures are employed. These are usually referred to as "single subject designs" and include a baseline measure as well as subsequent measurements. Because of the quantitative nature of the measurements, statistical procedures are usually employed to rule out some of the causes of the change that must have been brought about by events other than the group experience. For example, an anxious member may, without treatment, experience a gradual lessening of anxiety. During treatment, this progress may occur more rapidly. Relatively simple statistical procedures can be used to determine the likelihood that a change in the rate of progress is due to something other than the group intervention.[4]

There are a number of different kinds of single case designs, each with a rationale for its use.[5] One of the most common designs is the AB design in which a baseline measurement is made followed by a measurement after (and sometimes during) the intervention. Another is a multiple baseline design in which baseline measures are made on some behaviors while treatments occur on others. Variations of this latter design include measuring baselines and changes that involve different members in the group or different situations for the same member. Another common design involves obtaining a baseline followed by several types of interventions with measurements secured after

[3]See, for example, D. M. Gottman and S. R. Leiblum, *How to do Psychotherapy and How to Evaluate It* (New York: Holt, Rinehart & Winston, 1974), pp. 38–41.

[4]For a discussion of statistical procedures that can be applied by practitioners with little knowledge of statistics, see S. Jayaratne, "Analytic Procedures for Single Subject Designs," *Social Work Research and Abstracts* 14 (Fall, 1978), 30–40. For an analysis of technical issues in the use of such designs in social work, see Joel Fischer, *Effective Casework Practice* (New York: McGraw-Hill, 1978), pp. 88–102. The same author also discusses what he terms "objectified case studies," on pages 102 to 108.

[5]For a comprehensive presentation of single case designs, see M. Hersen and D. H. Barlow, *Single Case Experimental Designs* (Elmsford, N.Y.: Pergamon Press, 1976).

each intervention. This last design helps to identify the relative potency of different interventions especially, if one utilizes them with different members and in different sequences.

A problem for group workers with some of the designs is that what is done with one member will affect others. It is, therefore, difficult to separate the effects of an intervention in the group from the effects members have on each other. Nevertheless, it is still valuable to know if members are making progress, even when the variable responsible for the progress cannot be determined with certainty.

A major issue for group workers who utilize a variety of techniques or who do not primarily use behavioral ones is how to measure baselines and changes that are not thought of in terms of specific behaviors that can be counted. These include the quality of one's communications, decisions, satisfactions with self, and perceptions of self. Measures exist for all of these phenomona and new ones are now being created. The lack of measures, therefore, cannot be a reason for failing to evaluate individual progress.[6] Rose provides a number of examples of measurements of changes in members in groups that were examined in single subject designs. These included leadership behaviors, emotional responses, and information-giving responses.[7]

Practitioners will occasionally use control group designs,[8] in which the worker compares a number of members who received a particular form of service with those who received an alternative form or no service at all. The value of this approach is that reasons for change, other than the specific intervention, can be ruled out. The practitioner's problem with such designs is that they require procedures that are time consuming and sometimes difficult to achieve, such as random assignment of members to experimental and control group. In addition, data analysis problems are caused by premature termination of members from groups and the influences of members on each other.

In rating individual behaviors to evaluate the effects of group work, the worker has a number of different data sources that can be utilized. One is the member's *self report.* In this instance, the members count their own behaviors or rate their own feelings or attitudes or indicate the situations in which they experience some form of difficulty. Another is the *worker's observation* or *judgment.* The worker can count how often the member speaks, rate the degree of assertiveness of the member's statements, or whether the

[6]For a recent and authoritative discussion of the measurement of individual change as a result of treatment, see Allen E. Bergin and Michael J. Lambert, "The Evaluation of Therapeutic Outcomes," in *Handbook of Psychotherapy and Behavior Change,* 2nd ed., eds. Sol L. Garfield and Allen E. Bergin (New York: John Wiley, 1978), pp. 139-89.

[7]Sheldon Rose, *Group Therapy: A Behavioral Approach* (Englewood Cliffs, N.J.: Prentice-Hall, Inc. 1977), pp. 66–72.

[8]Readers interested in applying such designs should consult texts on the subject such as D. T. Campbell and J. C. Stanley, *Experimental and Quasi-Experimental Designs for Research* (Skokie, Ill.: Rand McNally, 1963).

member speaks of personal material in the group. *Outside observers'* ratings can also be employed for the same purpose and these observers, with the permission of the members, can either sit in on meetings or review tape recordings. The worker can also use records kept by others such as school teachers, parents, or employers, with permission of the member.

Measurement Techniques

Workers must be familiar with a variety of measures. The following are some of the approaches with which workers should become familiar.[9]

Behavioral Counts. Behavioral counts include the number of times a member engages in a desired act such as completion of homework assignments, absences from school, initiation of conversation with acquaintances, or expressions of affection. Many devices have been developed to facilitate counts such as mechanical counters and charts.[10]

Goal Attainment Scaling. Goal attainment scaling is a procedure for measuring clients' progress in attaining goals.[11] As can be seen in the completed form in Table 8-1, a scale is developed for all goals of each client. The scale consists of five levels ranging from the most favorable to the most unfavorable outcome with relationship to the goal. The midpoint of the scale represents the "expected" level of success. When this approach is used in groups, the group members can help each other to define each level and to rate outcomes in terms of these levels.

Kiresuk and Garwick have developed statistical procedures that create goal attainment scores for clients.[12] These scores can be used to help the group worker to identify which groups are the most helpful to their members. Workers can then examine the conditions found in successful and unsuccessful groups as a way of developing a better understanding of the most effective types of group experience.

Self Ratings on Emotional States. One of the emotions for which members often seek help is anxiety. This type of discomfort is experienced by members with problems such as phobias or when performing such tasks as asking a person for a date or answering questions posed by a teacher. As we reported, practitioners have found considerable reliability in asking members

[9]For an excellent discussion of the training of practitioners who can utilize appropriate outcome measures, see Martin Bloom, "Incorporating Objective Outcome Measures into Competency Training," in *The Pursuit of Competence in Social Work*, eds. Frank W. Clark and others (San Francisco: Jossey-Bass, 1979), pp. 111-22.

[10]For a comprehensive discussion of counts used in group work, see Rose, *Group Therapy*, pp. 43-46.

[11]For further details on this approach, see Thomas J. Kiresuk and Geoffrey Garwick, "Basic Goal Attainment Procedures," in *Social Work Processes*, 2nd ed., eds. Beulah Roberts Compton and Burt Galaway (Homewood, Ill.: Dorsey Press, 1979), pp. 412-21.

[12]Ibid.

Table 8-1

GOAL ATTAINMENT FOLLOW-UP GRID[a]

Program using GAS Intercity Head Start
Client Mrs. B

Date of scale construction 8-1-73
Follow-up date 9-1-73

Levels of Predicted Attainments	Scale Headings And Scale Weights			
	Scale 1	Scale 2	Scale 3	Scale 4
Most unfavorable outcome thought likely.	Mrs. B. reports angrily yelling at Jimmy daily or oftener during last week in August.	No action on or discussion of Mrs. B's loneliness.	No discussion or action about returning to clinic.	
Less than expected success.	Mrs. B reports angrily yelling at Jimmy more than three times but less than daily during last week in August.	Mrs. B discusses her loneliness but cannot make plans to deal with it.	Mrs. B is discussing her reaction to the clinic but has not formulated plans to return.	

191

Table 8-1 (continued)

Levels of Predicted Attainments	Scale 1	Scale 2	Scale 3	Scale 4
Expected level of success.	Mrs. B reports angrily yelling at Jimmy no more than three times during last week in August.	Mrs. B. is discussing her loneliness and making plans to join a group.	Mrs. B has discussed her reaction to the clinic and plans to secure a return appointment.	
More than expected success.	Mrs. B has discontinued angrily yelling at Jimmy but has not discovered another way to discipline him.	Mrs. B has initiated contacts with a group.	Mrs. B has telephoned the clinic for a return appointment.	
Most favorable outcome thought likely.	Above, and Mrs. B is using another form of discipline before becoming angry with Jimmy.	Mrs. B has attended one group meeting.	Mrs. B has been into the clinic for a return appointment.	

[a]These are examples of scales that might have been developed with Mrs. B. Taken from Beulah R. Compton and Burt Galaway, *Social Work Processes*, rev. ed. (Homewood, Illinois: The Dorsey Press, 1979), p. 410. © 1979 by The Dorsey Press.

to rate their own degress of anxiety on a scale of 0 to 100.[13] Such objective scales have also been used for irritation, anger, and congeniality.[14]

Value Clarification Ratings. Members often seek to clarify and affirm their values as a result of group experience. Some of the instruments utilized for value clarification exercises can also be used to determine baselines as well as changes in the values of members. One example of this is the "values grid" (see Table 8-2). The members place in the issue column, the value issues relevant to them. For example, in one adolescent group, the members listed "declaring pride in being black," "what it means to be a man or woman," and "how honest I should be with people I am close to." Members check the seven columns in terms of the following questions:

1. Are you *proud* of (do you prize or cherish) your position?
2. Have you *publicly affirmed* your position?
3. Have you chosen your position from *alternatives?*
4. Have you chosen your position after *thoughtful consideration* of the pros and cons and consequences?
5. Have you chosen your position *freely?*

[13]Wolpe, *The Practice of Behavior Therapy*, p. 100.

[14]T. M. Sherman and W. H. Cormier, "The Use of Subjective Scales for Measuring Interpersonal Reactions," *Journal of Behavior Therapy and Experimental Psychiatry* 3 (1972), 279–80.

Table 8-2

VALUE GRID[a]

Issue	1	2	3	4	5	6	7
1							
2							
3							
4							
5							

[a]Taken from Sydney B. Simon, Leland W. Howe, and Howard Kirschenbaum, *Values Clarification: A Handbook of Practical Strategies for Students and Teachers* (New York: Hart Publishing Company, Inc., 1972), p. 35.

6. Have you *acted* on or done anything about your beliefs?
7. Have you acted with *repetition,* pattern, or consistency on this issue?[15]

Ratings on Skills in Understanding Self and Situation. A goal of group services for members may be to help them to learn how to understand and make rational decisions regarding behavior or situations. After the group experience is over, the improved ability to analyze situations and make decisions will help these members to cope better with problem situations. A number of approaches previously discussed present the members with ways of accomplishing this, including problem solving, behavioral analysis, and transactional analysis. Scales can be used to evaluate the ability of the member to use any of these approaches. The member can apply the scale to his or her own process or other members can use it as a basis for interviewing the members to assess their cognitive effort. Some questions, for example, that can be used to assess members' skills in problem solving are the following:

1. Has the member sought information relevant to the problem? For example, if the problem is finding a job, has the member found out about the types of jobs most available for persons with his or her training and abilities?
2. Has the member identified the alternatives available to him or her? Do these alternatives include all the most important or relevant ones? Has the individual used the information generated in question 1 to identify alternatives?
3. Has the member evaluated the alternatives using criteria such as the following?

- the alternative with the most likelihood of helping the member achieve his or her goal to the optimum degree
- the alternative with the fewest disadvantages or costs
- the alternative most consistent with the member's values

4. Has the member chosen the alternative which he or she evaluated most favorably?
5. Has the member developed or begun to develop a plan to implement the alternative?

These questions can be answered either with a "yes" or "no" or they can be rated on a zero to five scale with zero standing for absence of the behavior and five representing its presence to the fullest degree. Admittedly such a scale does not represent the kind of specificity that is used in formal research but it does present information that will help the members and the worker to

---

[15]For many such instruments, see Sidney B. Simon, Leland W. Howe, and Howard Kirschenbaum, *Values Clarification: A Handbook of Practical Strategies for Teachers and Students* (New York: Hart Publishing Co., Inc., 1972).

judge whether a rational approach to problem solving has been utilized and is, therefore, likely to be a part of the way members will now approach problems.

Psychological Instruments. Many instruments developed by psychologists and other behavioral scientists, as well as social workers, can be used by social work practitioners and their use does not require highly specialized training. Increasingly, in fact, social workers themselves are developing evaluation and assessment instruments that are compatible with social work objectives and methods. The Rathus scale for measuring assertiveness, referred to previously, can be used when social workers seek to help members become more assertive. Examples of other instruments of similar availability are Thomas's[16] and Hops and co-workers'[17] for assessing marital communication, Rose's and co-workers' for interpersonal competence,[18] Derogatis's and co-workers' for psychiatric symptoms,[19] Fitts's for self concept,[20] McNair's and co-workers' for moods,[21] and Hudson's for marital satisfaction, generalized contentment, self-esteem, sexual satisfaction, parent attitudes toward children, and child's attitude to either mother or father.[22]

EVALUATION OF CHANGES IN GROUP CONDITIONS

As discussed in Chapter 5, the group worker seeks to modify group conditions and to help the members to do so also in order to create a group conducive to attaining members' goals. A variety of procedures were presented for the worker to accomplish this. Workers, therefore, should seek to evaluate whether their activities lead to desired changes in the group. Often these group changes will be self-evident. At other times, the worker will seek a reliable means of measuring group changes so as to evaluate the effectiveness of group work techniques and to reinforce members for cooperating in their use.

Measurement Techniques

We shall now discuss some of the approaches that should become familiar to group workers for measuring changes in group conditions.

[16]Edwin Thomas, *Marital Communication and Decision Making: Analysis, Assessment and Change* (New York: Free Press, 1977).

[17]H. Hops, T. Wills, G. R. Patterson, and R. L. Weiss, *The Marital Interaction Coding System* (unpublished manuscript, University of Oregon and Oregon Research Institute, 1972).

[18]S. D. Rose, J. J. Gayner, and J. L. Edleson, "Measuring Interpersonal Competence," *Social Work* 22 (1977), 125–29.

[19]L. R. Derogatis, R. S. Lipman and L. Covi, "SCL-90: An Outpatient Psychiatric Rating Scale (Preliminary Report)," *Psychopharmacology Bulletin* 9 (1973), 13-27.

[20]W.F. Fitts, *Tennessee Self-Concept Scale Manual* (Nashville, Tenn.: Counsellor Recordings and Tests, 1965).

[21]D. M. McNair, M. Lorr, and L. F. Dopplemen, *Manual for the Profile of Mood States* (San Diego: Educational and Industrial Testing Service, 1971).

[22]All these scales are printed in Fischer, *Effective Casework Practice,* pp. 110-15.

Behavioral Counts. We began our discussion on evaluating individual changes with behavioral counts, largely because of the simplicity of this form of measurement. For similar reasons, such counts can also often be used to assess changes in group conditions. Many changes that group workers seek to achieve in groups are manifested in specific behaviors of members that can be defined and counted on a tally sheet. For example, the worker and the group may seek to increase certain classes of member behaviors for all members such as expressions of feelings, self-disclosure statements, requests for help from others, arrivals on time to the meetings, declarations regarding one's values, or verbal reinforcements to others. Either the worker, an outside observer, or a member can keep a record of all such acts and can report the results to the group. This represents a group condition in that such behaviors are partially under the control of group norms that call for either expressing or inhibiting them. Group members and workers, when evaluating their groups, will often seek to change the frequency with which certain behaviors are expressed so that the effectiveness of the group will be enhanced.

Measurements of Group Structures. Since the basic tool in group work is the communication among members and between members and the worker, the communication structure—who talks to whom about what—is often the target of change. In Chapter 5 we presented a number of examples of ways to assess communications structures and these can be used to evaluate whether efforts to change such structures are effective. One of the simplest techniques, which was described in that chapter, was a tabulation of the sequence of member and worker statements (M M M W M W M M M W). This can be used to indicate whether there is an increase in member-to-member as compared to member-to-worker interactions simply by dividing the number of Ms by the number of Ws.

Some devices that are used to change group conditions can also be used to measure changes. Rose, for example, described a procedure to help a group become more aware of its pattern of offering reinforcement as compared to aversive remarks.[23] Members placed poker chips in a can using one color to indicate feeling reinforced and another to indicate feeling punished. While the chips were used to signal subjective experience, they can be counted to evaluate a change in this type of communication in the group.

Rose has also developed a system for assessing content expressed by one member to another. He developed the following content categories: suggestion–opinion-giving response; questions; responses to questions; self-suggestion responses; negative affect; positive affect; and information giving.[24] The observer coded each remark in terms of who said it, who it was directed to, and the category into which it fit. This allowed the worker to

---

[23]Rose, *Group Therapy*, p. 142.
[24]Ibid., pp. 50–51. These categories are similar to those used by Bales to study group interactions; see Robert F. Bales, *Interaction Process Analysis: A Method for the Study of Small Groups* (Reading, Mass.: Addison-Wesley, 1950).

tabulate who spoke most frequently, who was spoken to most often, and the most frequent types of comments. Depending on member and worker concerns, any one of these as well as other potential tabulations might be used to select goals for changes in group conditions and then to monitor changes.

To assess changes in a group's sociometric structure, some workers rely on observations of subgroups while others have used standard sociometric questionnaires, in which members are asked with whom they chose to work with or to whom they felt closest. Such questionnaires can provoke a great deal of anxiety, however. Yalom reports, nevertheless, asking each member to rate all members of the group in popularity, apparently without serious harm to the members.[25] These approaches can be used to assess changes in the number of isolates and the composition of subgroups.

Workers may also wish to monitor changes in the power structure of the group, particularly when members are influenced by others in the group in dysfunctional ways. Some members, also, may have had little influence on the group and this has damaged their self-esteem as well as hindered their integration into group activities. One way to assess changes in this pattern is to record responses to members' ideas or suggestions. These reponses can be coded as (1) support or agreement; (2) disagreement; or (3) not relevant (for example, change in subject or ignores statement). All responses are not coded; only those that are made in relationship to directions, suggestions, or new ideas. Some members do not contribute any of these and, at least by this measure, are low in this manifestation of power.

Measurement of Group Processes. One of the most important group processes is problem solving and workers will seek to assess changes in the group's problem-solving capacity. We previously presented a means of evaluating the group's handling of problem-solving incidents as an exercise (see exercise at end of Chapter 5). The instrument presented there was utilized as follows: tape recordings were made of group meetings and were replayed in order to identify problem-solving episodes. The scale was used to rate each problem-solving episode. Changes in problem-solving processes were examined both within meetings and over several meetings. Occasionally, a group which engages in effective problem solving regresses to a less effective one. The worker in these situations will examine the content of the problem as well as other events in the group in order to diagnose the source of the difficulty.

Another crucial type of process, also a form of problem solving, is the process illumination activity discussed in Chapter 5. Although this is an essential part of most approaches to group psychotherapy, we have not found any literature regarding an evaluation of its impact as a specific and discrete tool. We do have several suggestions, however, for an evaluation of this procedure. Members whose interpersonal processes have been examined in this

---

[25]Irvin D. Yalom, *The Theory and Practice of Group Psychotherapy*, 2nd ed. (New York: Basic Books, 1975), p. 51.

way can be asked, after the procedure has been utilized, to note in a personal journal what they have learned about their responses to the other person and about the other's responses also. Subsequent "processing" of their interactions can also be noted in the journal. The worker or an observer can also make notes on the types of learning they assumed took place. Periodically workers can examine the log, with the permission of the member, to assess the kind of learning that was accomplished. Hopefully, this kind of exploratory work might help workers to develop more systematic ways of studying the effects of process illumination.

The process of changes in attraction of members to each other and to the group, a major component of cohesiveness, is a very essential one. A successful group depends on the members' attendance and investment. The worker should, therefore, obtain feedback from members as to their reactions to specific meetings as well as to the group over longer periods of time. A two- or three-question instrument can be completed just before members leave in which they record how strongly they desire to return (for example, on a 7-point scale from "not at all" to "very much") and the activities or discussions during the meeting they found most and least useful. Yalom describes a cohesiveness scale that he and his colleagues used on which members rated the following items (on five-point scales):[26]

1. How often do you think your group should meet?

2. How well do you like the group you are in?

3. If most of the members of your group decided to disssolve the group by leaving, how would you like an opportunity to dissuade them?

4. Do you feel that working with the group you are in will enable you to attain most of the goals in therapy?

5. If you could replace members of your group with other "ideal group members," how many would you exchange (exclusive of group therapists)?

6. To what degree do you feel you are included by the group in the group's activities?

7. How do you feel about your participation in, and contribution to, the group work?

8. How do you feel about the length of the group meeting?

9. How do you feel about the group therapists?

10. Are you ashamed of being in group therapy?

11. Compared to other therapy groups, how well would you imagine your group works together?

This scale can then be totaled for each person and a group average computed. The worker should calculate the group median rather than mean so that the statistic is not strongly affected by a small number of members who

---

[26]Yalom, *Group Psychotherapy*, p. 51.

may be extremely positive or negative. Changes in group cohesiveness over time can be examined to identify the need for or the consequences of interventions aimed at this phenomena.

Workers should also assess the phase of development of the group. This is usually done through examining one's impressions of a variety of group conditions. We previously presented an instrument for collecting data about group development. It can be used by workers to confirm their impressions as well as to identify aspects of the group that are impeding development such as ambiguity of purpose, antagonisms among members, dysfunctional structures, or inappropriate choices of activities.

Measurement of Shared Attributions. As discussed in Chapter 5, the group affects the way members view events. The worker cannot assume, however, that a group discussion of the cause of some event accurately reflects how each individual views it. A number of members, for example, may have remained out of the conversation. Do they agree with what is being said? Are they afraid to voice disagreement? Are they suspending judgment to hear what others think? Consequently, workers will sometimes ask members privately to write their perceptions of the causes of an event or their values regarding it. If the worker has previously or subsequently asked the group to discuss its understanding of the event, this can be compared to members' individual responses. Similarities and differences in what individuals say privately and in the presence of others will tell a great deal about group conditions, such as willingness of members to honestly share opinions and ability of some members to control the opinions held by others.

Social-Psychological Instruments. Instruments that have been developed by social scientists can also be used, with some adaptation, for evaluation of group changes by practitioners. The practitioner who desires to measure change in some group dimension can usually locate such instruments by consulting one of the standard texts on the sociology of groups.[27] Some examples of instruments that can be used are Bales' for observing interactions,[28] Byrne's for assessing member's similarity of activity preferences,[29] and Crosbie's for charting members' statuses (for example, power and prestige).[30]

EVALUATION OF ENVIRONMENTAL CHANGES

The data for evaluating an environmental change, when the aspect of the environment that is targeted is some specific policy or resource, may be self-

[27]See, for example, Howard L. Nixon II, *The Small Group* (Englewood Cliffs, N.J.: Prentice-Hall, Inc., 1979): and Stephen Wilson, *Informal Groups: An Introduction* (Englewood Cliffs, N.J.: Prentice-Hall, Inc., 1978).

[28]Bales, *Interaction Process Analysis.*

[29]D. Byrne, *The Attraction Paradigm* (New York: Academic Press, 1971.)

[30]Paul V. Crosbie, "Effects of Status Inconsistency: Negative Evidence From Small Groups," *Social Psychological Quarterly* no. 2 (June, 1979), 110–25.

evident. Evidence can easily be secured that the policy has been changed, for example, the member has had a welfare grant increased, or a school has established a new curriculum. At other times, the environmental change that is sought may be a more complex or less overt one.

Measurement Techniques

We present some suggestions of ways of assessing types of environmental targets.

Documentation. A first consideration is the source of information on the environmental change. One is written documents. These will be useful if the change is to be in a policy of an organization embodied in official rules. A second is a compendium of each member's experience. This is appropriate if the change is in a reaction to the members, such as a teacher providing reinforcement or an agency offering services.

Several group members or the entire group can collect information. One group in a hospital, for example, sought more courteous attention from the nursing staff. Members agreed to keep a record of responses from staff members after assurances from the hospital administration that they would do something about the situation, if it was as the member alleged.

Interviews. As we previously described, another environmental problem that can harm group members is the imposition of labels that contribute to stereotypes of the member. These labels are often subtle and a series of sensitive interviews by trained observers is required to determine changes in the labeling process. Another occasion requiring skilled interviews in order to assess change is when the actions of individuals in the environment are problematic and these are not idiosyncratic, as they are supported by the unofficial reinforcements of peers and superiors. In these cases, the interviewer, once rapport has been established, should inquire as to who else in the system shared or supported the behavior in question and whether this has changed. Actual interviews with others in the organization may be required to support the conclusions.

Measurement Scales. Finally, the group, the worker, or both might choose to use a more formal instrument to evaluate changes in complex situations. For example, Moos has developed a number of scales to measure variables in environments that have impact on participants in those environments. The variables include such dimensions as the degree of structure, the freedom to express one's beliefs, and the presence of conflict. Members of a group can complete a questionnaire in order to evaluate changes in such environments as school rooms, hospital wards, residential treatment milieux, or even communities.[31]

[31]Rudolf H. Moos, *Evaluating Treatment Environments: A Social Ecological Approach* (New York: John Wiley, 1974).

Guerney, for a training program that can be used in groups to enhance relationships, developed a number of scales to measure changes in relationships such as an "interpersonal relationship scale" and a "relationship change scale."[32] Items in these scales can be used to assess changes in the quality of relationships, even when the specific procedure developed by Guerney is not utilized. These changes, because they are interactional, reflect not only the behavior of the group member, but the responses of significant others. Such measures may be used when these others are part of the group work process as in couples' groups or when a member of the group is working on relationship issues that involve people not in the group.

Example. In a group of high school students, the members were being helped to stay in school and to be more successful. For baseline data, the worker utilized the school grades of the members during the previous semester; responses to a brief questionnaire developed by the worker regarding their attitudes toward school; and the proportion of homework assignments they had completed the first two weeks the group met. During these first weeks, the worker helped the members to become more acquainted with each other and did not attempt any actions to modify the members' school behaviors. The worker asked the members to record their assignments on a daily basis and to check those that were finished. These same measures were utilized when the group had met for two months and when the group terminated at the end of four months. Several group process issues emerged during these four months. One was the attendance of members during the first meetings. Several times during these months the worker distributed a modification of the cohesiveness scale previously described. The worker discovered an increase in cohesiveness as the members became more committed to the group's goals and as changes were made in the group's program to make the group more attractive. At one point, also, some members who were less committed to the group's goals heavily influenced others. The worker asked the members separately to list the members of the group who most influenced them. The results of the survey were presented to the group and this led to a very thoughtful discussion on how and why members were influenced by peers. The same questionnaire submitted later showed a number of changes in who influenced whom that the worker believed were conducive to the member's attaining their goals. The means of helping the members included securing the teachers' support. A few teachers had negatively labeled the members and their lack of encouragement was demoralizing. The group invited these teachers to sit in on several meetings in order to learn about members' efforts. Afterward members who encountered these teachers in classes kept a "log" of these transactions. The logs were presented in group meetings to help the members to assess changes brought about by these interventions with the teachers.

[32]Bernard G. Guerney, Jr., *Relationship Enhancement* (San Francisco: Jossey-Bass, 1977).

RECORDING OF GROUP SESSIONS

Group workers will also keep a record of each group session. These records provide additional information that can help the worker to evaluate work with the group. They can also provide material that can help explain other kinds of evaluative data. Records can be used to describe what happened in the group so that ways of working with groups that are effective can be replicated. In keeping a record, the worker is forced to examine his or her own activity and to become more self-aware. Finally, records are essential in the workers' conferences with supervisors to enable the supervisors to interact with the workers around specific situations and ways of handling them.

Throughout much of the history of group work, practitioners, particularly students, maintained what were known as "process records." In these records, the students summarized as much as they remembered of the interactions among the members and between the worker and the members. The writer usually omitted behaviors that were deemed to be minor and irrelevant to the major issues confronting the group or its members, individually. Such process records still have their place in the training of new workers and in examining the events that occur in meetings that appear to have been critical for the future of the group.

Workers, with the current simplicity in the operation of audio and even audio-visual equipment, have electronically recorded meetings with the permission of members. Members have even viewed these recordings in order to study their own processes. Such recordings also have great value as workers, often with the help of supervisors, study their interventions as well as the group interactions that elicited them.

However, as tools, for the basic collection of data about a group, electronic recordings have disadvantages precisely because of the large volume of data they present. For this reason, we suggest simplified recording forms for all group sessions. These can be supplemented by process records or tapes. The accompanying form we present includes a planning item, a session assessment scale, a record of major topics and techniques, and the critical incidents occurring during the meeting. It, and forms like it, have been used to summarize the experience of the group, identify troublesome issues, facilitate supervision, and provide data for studying such group processes as the sequence of topics and events. An exercise in the use of the form is presented at the end of this chapter.

GROUP WORK RECORDING FORM

Practitioner's Name:_____Group Name:_____Session#:____

Date of Meeting:_____ Time of Meeting: From_____ To_____

Members Present:

1. Practitioner's goals for group session (Comment as to whether these are acknowledged by members):

2. Practitioner's goals for individuals during session (Comment as to whether these are acknowledged by members):

3. Practitioner's agenda for session (Comment on how this relates to members' agenda):

4. Process

Codes[a]	Episode 1 Time:	Episode 2 Time:	Episode 3 Time:	Episode 4 Time:	Episode 5 Time:
Content Code					
Intervention Codes					
Type of Process Code					

[a]Codes will be created by the agency; the following are illustrative; content = individual's problem behavior, group condition, group planning, nonverbal program; interventions = interpretations, facilitate problem solving, reinforcement, modeling; type of process = discussion, presentation, game, creative project, exercise, problem solving, role play.

Place in space below, by briefly describing incidents, significant interactions among members or between members and worker indicating in which episodes interaction took place:

5. Major obstacles, if any, to attaining goals during meeting:

6. Report of evaluative data collected during meeting:

7. Plans for next meeting:

Notes on contacts with individuals outside meeting:

8. Overall assessment of session

The major objectives of the session were accomplished *for* the following proportion of members

____ Completely	____ All
____ Almost completely	____ Most
____ Partially	____ About half
____ To a slight degree	____ A few
____ Not at all	____ None

SUMMARY

This chapter began with a general discussion of the current emphasis on accountability in social work. While some undesirable consequences of this emphasis were described, we favor the concept of the practitioner–researcher. In group work this requires the worker to be able, with the cooperation of the members, to assess changes in individuals, group conditions, and the environment of the group. The chapter, therefore, included a discussion of some of the major types of measures that the group worker should be able to employ to evaluate changes in each of these entities. In addition, some form of recording should be maintained for each group session. A sample recording form was presented.

GROUP WORK RECORDING EXERCISE

Goals

1. To understand the components of group work practice recordings.

2. To develop accuracy in recording group sessions.

Procedure

1. Trainees review and discuss Recording of Group Sessions in this chapter.

2. Trainees observe an example of a group session. This can be a role play, a tape, a film or a written, detailed account of a group work session. (For the latter purpose, the extended examples in Chapters 10-13 can be utilized.)

3. Each trainee completes the group work recording form presented in this chapter.

4. The teacher or trainer leads a discussion in the training group or class based on how each person has responded to each item on the form. Differences in responses are noted and discussed as a means of increasing members' skills in utilizing the form.

Chapter 9

THE GROUP AND ENDINGS

THE MEANING of the end of a group experience must be understood by workers so that they can be helpful as a great deal is determined at this stage. If the termination process is a successful one, members will be more likely to transfer the learning in the group to other life situations, to enter into other group experiences when the need arises, and to remember the group with positive feelings rather than with guilt or anger. Therefore, in this chapter we shall discuss the phenomona workers must understand and the tasks they must undertake in order to achieve the beneficial results of a "good" termination experience.

MEANINGS OF ENDINGS

In many ways all endings have some things in common. This is true whether the ending is of a relationship with a single person or a group; whether the ending is the termination of a relationship in which all parties simply separate or one in which someone has died. Some have even speculated on similarities with situations when one loses a treasured possession or even part of one's self as in surgery or disability. In all of these events, the person has invested energy, may have expressed affection, and has participated in an ongoing experience with the other person or object.

After the loss, the individual has the task of withdrawing this energy investment, of engaging in mourning for the lost person or object, and of establishing a new equilibrium in which the person, group, or object no longer plays the same role except in memory. From the earliest days of life, people must cope with the experience of loss. Young children who see their parents leave their field of vision are uncertain of the parent return until this has been repeated a number of times. When a parent leaves for work, this is experienced as a loss at least until the child understands the reasons for this absence. Playmates move away, teachers change, and sooner or later—often first with pets—the permanency of death must be dealt with.

Thus coping with loss is an essential part of life, perhaps one that creates some sense of tragedy, and life cannot be lived to its fullest until one comes to some terms with the inevitability of endings. The ability of the group worker to *understand* these issues and to use the ending of the group as an occasion to help the members add to *their understanding* is essential.

Somewhat different processes will take place, depending on the plan as to when the group will end. Some groups do not have a fixed time for ending. In these, various members may leave while the group goes on—either because they have accomplished their purposes or because they have given up hope of doing so. Some groups may end at the same time for all members when it is agreed that optimum benefits have been attained. Probably the majority of groups conducted by social workers have a fixed number of sessions whether these be short-term groups of a few months or long-term groups that last, for example, for a school year.

Unless there are strong reasons to the contrary, such as uncertainity as to group purpose or the complexities of the length of time it takes to achieve personality change, we prefer a time limit to groups—whether it is short or long term. This is because of our belief that time limits serve to mobilize the energy and the planning of activities by participants to achieve their goals—if the time limits are reasonable.[1] Other things being equal, we also favor a short period of time rather than a long one because of such ideas as those advanced by Reid and Epstein to the effect that people are most motivated to receive help when they experience disequilibrium in their lives and are most likely to terminate when equilibrium has been restored.[2]

Groups that have time limits, particularly short-term groups of eight to twelve sessions, start the termination process early, prehaps from their beginning. Members know the date of the last meeting, even if (as frequently happens) they deny this or try to negotiate an extension. Plans are made for activities with an awareness of the time frame available to the group. The depth of relationships is affected, also, by this awareness. Thus any discussions of relationships or choice of member goals are held with an implicit or explicit sense of the available time. Since the date of the ending is known in advance, members are not surprised when the worker raises issues around planning for the last sessions.

Groups which have no advance determination of the length and which are terminating because the goals have been attained pose a different issue.

[1]The author has always been interested in the ideas regarding the meaning of time in the helping process developed by the "functional" approach to social work. See Ruth Elizabeth Smalley, *Theory for Social Work Practice* (New York: Columbia University Press, 1967), pp. 142–51. Another approach to the time dimension may be found in Arnold P. Goldstein, Kenneth Heller, and Lee B. Sechrest, *Psychotherapy and the Psychology of Behavior Change* (New York: John Wiley, 1966), pp. 280–86.

[2]William Reid and Laura Epstein, *Task Centered Casework* (New York: Columbia University Press, 1977, p. 28.

Members are more likely to deny that they are ready for termination and they will raise questions as to why the worker has decided to terminate. They must adjust to an event whose timing was, at least initially, ambiguous or unknown.

As we have seen, there are differences between the termination of groups with established time periods and those in which the ending was determined later. Nevertheless, if the experiences have been positive and members have accomplished many of their goals, there is more in common in the way the worker facilitates the termination process in these two situations than there is with situations when the group was unsuccessful. Another dissimilar event is when termination was imposed by unanticipated circumstances such as the loss of the worker from the agency.

WORKER TASKS

For these reasons, we shall discuss the worker's tasks in groups when the group experience was generally viewed as a positive one and when all members terminate simultaneously. We shall return, at the end of the chapter, to a discussion of termination tasks under a variety of other circumstances. In the former circumstances the worker helps the members as follows:

- to evaluate the group in relationship to achievement of its goals
- to understand and cope with their feelings regarding termination
- to maintain the beneficial changes that have resulted from the group experience.
- to utilize the skills, attitudes, and knowledge gained through the group in an increasing variety of circumstances
- to seek out and utilize new services when this is appropriate.

There is no established order to any of these tasks. In each group the nature of the members' experiences will determine whether accomplishing one task will naturally lead to another. For example, in an evaluation of one group, as criticisms were offered, angry feelings were expressed. On the other hand, a discussion of new situations in which acquired skills will be appropriately used led to positive expressions. The worker, therefore, will usually plan with the members, for accomplishing each of these tasks in an order and in a way that makes sense to the group in question. Even after this process has begun, changes will take place in the termination plan because of unanticipated issues that arise. To help the reader apply the principles of termination planning, we have included a termination exercise at the end of this chapter.

In groups that have only met for a few months, a major emphasis on termination tasks will usually occur during the last two or three meetings. Long-term groups may devote part of several more sessions to termination issues.

EVALUATION

The last chapter was devoted to a presentation of many of the ways that changes in individuals, groups, and the environment can be measured. Of concern here is the way these or other instruments and procedures will be used by workers as part of the termination process. One aspect of this process is a decision as to which formal sources of information will be utilized in the group as part of termination. The evaluative instruments and design, for purposes of accountability, will already have been determined. The issue here is which findings will be examined *by the group members* and how this will take place.

Members' Evaluation of the Group

The worker should review the types of instruments that have been in use and their purposes. The members, on the basis of the issues they have decided are relevant for their termination concerns, will select, from the data available, the specific information to discuss. This discussion will emphasize the meaning this information has to the members and the reasons they perceive for their successes and failures in the group. These reasons are seldom produced by the questionnaires and instruments themselves.

Example. In an assertiveness training group the members discussed the changes in each member (on an assertiveness scale); all of these changes constituted an improvement but some gains were greater than others. One member with a small increment talked about the severe criticism he still receives from his employer when he asserts himself. Another member with a much greater gain spoke of the encouragement she had received from her friends as she became more assertive with her family.

An important part of the evaluative process is the free and unstructured discussion of their personal changes in which members are likely to engage. This includes things they liked and did not like about the group and changes in their environmental circumstances. Such discussion is invaluable to the worker as many dimensions of change can be identified that have not been included in any instrument and that can help the worker to plan for subsequent groups. The aspects of the experience that members believe caused their changes also will suggest potent aspects of the group experience that were not part of the worker's strategy.

A worker, for example, who attributed most of the members' changes to the kinds of techniques he used, such as role plays and demonstrations, was surprised to learn that the members thought many of their gains were due to his acceptance, liking, and concern for them. In a contrasting way, another worker attributed change to the supportive atmosphere of the group and was equally surprised to hear the members' asssertion that the most helpful thing to them was the specific advice they received as to how to train their children. There is no certain way of knowing whether the members' or the worker's perceptions of why changes took place were most correct but the ideas of the members should be seriously considered.

Similarly, when the members discuss what they liked and disliked about the group, they will frequently comment on dimensions that have not been formally measured and that may even have been unpredicted. Thus one group discussed at length an experience they had when a severe blizzard prevented their leaving the agency and they had to "camp out" there overnight: the things they learned about each other when discussion was unstructured; the small ways they helped each other with such problems as making plans for children and spouses; and the stronger identification they had with the group after the experience was over all demonstarted a great deal to the worker about the "causes" of the excellent outcomes of that group. While the worker cannot "program" blizzards, he did decide to consider a "marathon" session in similar groups in the future.

Members' Evaluation of the Worker

An important component to evaluation, not considered yet, is an evaluation of the worker. Workers should not wait until the termination of the group to ask for feedback from members on their activities and in long-term groups workers should ask for this several times. Most workers do not yet do this directly, but it is our conviction that this is a requirement for responsible practice and workers should be trained to include this with other evaluative activities. Asking for a personal evaluation is, of course, anxiety provoking for most, if not all, workers because of the desire to be regarded highly, a fear of negative criticism, and a concern that undesirable traits unknown even to the workers may be uncovered. Workers, however, who face these concerns and ask for an evaluation will demonstrate that they can take feedback in the same way as they expect members to. Workers also have an opportunity to model constructive ways of handling both criticism and praise.

The problem is how to ask for an evaluation by members. Ideally, the kind of trust that has built up between members and the worker will allow members to take responsibility for their critique and still be free to offer it sincerely. They can respond to written questions and discuss their answers openly. There will be times, however, even in effective groups, when the worker and the members will decide together that the most useful responses will be anonymous ones.

Some questions that workers can ask to receive feedback on their work are the following:

1. What are some of my actions you find most and least helpful?
2. What actions would you like me to take that are not being taken?
3. Are there personal qualities of mine you find helpful or not helpful (for example, ways of speaking, timing of interventions, sense of humor, ways of expressing self)?
4. How well do you think I understand what you are thinking and feeling? How do I communicate that?
5. How honest do you believe I am with you?
6. Do you experience me as supportive and caring?

An important thing for workers to remember is that members will find offering this type of feedback difficult. There are many social conventions against giving honest responses to these kinds of questions and this is compounded by the emotional meaning workers usually have for members. This makes it particularly difficult for members to express criticisms. Thus in such discussions the topic can subtly shift to a discussion of the group's program, the agency's inputs, or the general type of service offered. This shift can also be a response to a sense of the worker's discomfort. When the worker, however, clearly and honestly asks for evaluation, it is likely to be forthcoming.

UNDERSTAND AND COPE WITH FEELINGS

As indicated in the opening paragraphs of this chapter, people have many feelings with which they find it difficult to deal during endings. They must learn to handle these feelings for several reasons. One is that each time a person copes with feelings regarding endings, he or she will undoubtedly acquire strengths that will be useful in coping with the endings yet to come. Second, unresolved feelings about an experience such as group work can hinder the member's ability to remember and utilize the learning acquired through that experience.

All losses engender similar feelings although these feelings may vary in sequence and in intensity. Kübler-Ross, for example, in her seminal work on death and dying describes the sequence of reactions that she observed to occur when one learns of impending death.[3] We believe that these feelings are present to some degree whenever any ending is faced. The first response she notes is that of denial and this almost always occurs when the worker broaches the subject of the groups' ending. Members may not deny that the

[3]Elizabeth Kübler-Ross, *On Death and Dying* (New York: Macmillan, 1969).

group will end but they frequently do deny the feelings they have about this. They manifest this by continuing to engage in whatever activities were before them when the subject of termination was raised or they may state that they do not have feelings about the group's ending or that they have already dealt with these feelings. Another manifestation of such denial is seen in members who miss meetings after termination is first discussed or who diminish in their degree of group participation. Workers, particularly in short-term group or groups they deem less successful, may join in this denial and underestimate the meaning of the relationships, the activities, and the identification of members with the group.

In dealing with denial, workers can acknowledge to the members that endings are difficult and that feelings about them are also hard to express. They can ask the members to recall other endings of relationships and since those were more distant, members may be initially more able to express feelings experienced in those situations. Some workers have introduced a period in which members mill about the meeting room saying goodbye to other members as well as to the worker; a variation of this is to rotate around the group asking members to formulate a farewell statement. This type of experience elicits expressions of feelings on both verbal and nonverbal levels that can be explored.

Kübler-Ross describes another reaction, one which is also present in group terminations, that of anger. In groups this is often expressed at the agency which may have established time limits, at the group (and indirectly the worker) for not having accomplished more, and even at one's self for not having fully achieved one's goals. Anger can also be shown by members who become overly critical of the worker thus rejecting him or her before they are rejected. This emotion at termination is difficult for members and workers. Workers may feel guilt because of their sense of responsibility for what happened in the group; members will fear that positive aspects of the experience will be lost because of their anger. Nevertheless, a group that has encouraged an honest expression of feeling throughout its existence cannot do an "about face" at this point. The legitimacy of the feelings must be acknowledged through the worker admitting that imperfections of the group or one's self or both do make one angry. The important question is what the members will "do" with the anger. Ultimately, the anger must be channeled so that the member works to make future situations more responsive to the member's needs and the member more effective on his or her own behalf.

The third reaction described by Kübler-Ross is "bargaining." In groups, members who react this way seek to postpone the endings of the group or to create new experiences that may not be appropriate. In a sense, this may be one way the member channels anger and thus is a first step in coping effectively with it. The worker should continue to empathize with the members' desires to continue the group and the feelings that have elicited that solution. If the worker continues to be firm on plans for ending, however, more effective means of coping with anger over termination are likely to emerge.

Depression, according to Kübler-Ross, is another stage of this process. While we do not find that these stages appear discretely or consecutively in groups, depression often occurs after a phase of denial and bargaining. It is manifested in a lack of energy for the final activities of the group, a recounting of sad events or failures that occurred earlier, and even in direct emotional expression such as tears. We believe that this is a period of withdrawal of energy from the group and of mourning and is a psychological necessity. When it is not denied but is allowed full expression, it usually leads to a return of energy to perform the other tasks that are necessary for termination. The members invest energy in these tasks in a phase analogous to the one Kübler-Ross describes as "acceptance."

One way some members respond to the feelings of termination is through regression. They will behave in ways that they did earlier in the life of the group. Members in one group, for example, began to manifest relationship problems that had presumably been resolved. Members of a children's group increased their quarreling and cooperated less in activities than they had at the meeting before termination was discussed. While regression is a defense that some people use in times of stress, in groups it has the added function of demonstrating that members still need each other, the worker, and the group.

In a sense, this discussion of some of the feelings at termination suggest that they are all "negative" or "painful." If the group has been successful, there are also several positive feelings manifested. Members will experience pleasures at having attained their goals, mastered obstacles, and remained in the group through the difficulties. Members also inevitably experience some relief that the time investment and expense of attending meetings will end. They may feel some guilt for this latter emotion yet in the continuing spirit of disclosure they can also assert pleasure that these costs will cease.

As can be seen, the feelings toward endings are ambivalent ones and this typifies any change. During the group, members have hopefully come to understand ambivalence and this can be deepened as they explore their feelings toward termination. An ability to work through ambivalence is necessary during all transitions and this may be one of the most significant learnings that occur at the group's end.

Much of the "dual" nature of termination responses is reflected in Garland, Jones, and Kolodny's discussion of "flight" during the termination phase.[4] This can be a "nihilistic flight" or "destructive reaction to separation" such as "rejecting and rejection-provoking behaviors" or "positive flight" such as when "constructive moves are made toward 'self-

<hr>

[4]James A. Garland, Hubert E. Jones, and Ralph Kolodny, "A Model for Stages of Development in Social Work Groups," in *Explorations in Group Work*, ed. Saul Bernstein (Boston: Boston University School of Social Work, 1965), p. 44.

weaning' from the group." This latter "includes finding new groups, activities, work interests, friends, etc., outside the group while continuing as a member."

MAINTAIN CHANGES

The problem of helping the client to maintain changes after the end of the helping process is a general one. Research into all forms of change efforts shows that a significant proportion of the people participating in the effort do not maintain their changes. This has led to an increasing amount of attention to maintenance of change.[5] A major barrier to this is that members' ability to hold on to changes is not only a function of how the change was produced, as the strongest reverses often result from the negative impact of the environment. Friends and relatives may seek to reinforce older ways of behaving. Formal organizations such as schools and places of employment may punish the new behaviors. Even without these negative forces, the members may still be uncertain of acting in new ways.

The worker, therefore, as termination approaches, must apply techniques to help the members deal with those forces that can undo the beneficial effects of the group. Some of these have been discussed already but bear repetition here. One principle for accomplishing this is *overlearning*. This means that members have the opportunity to test out a number of times what they have learned before the group ends. If the termination plan includes a reduction of the frequency of meetings, members can assign themselves to a number of "trials" of new behaviors between these meetings.

Workers will also discuss the resistance members may meet in the environment and other members, familiar with each other's situations, can do the same. This has several effects: members will be less likely to become discouraged when "backsliding" takes place. They also should engage in problem solving as to how they will deal with these barriers. Such warnings are analogous to "paradoxical instructions," also. Some members have a tendency, for psychological reasons, to undermine their own progress, particularly if it has been recognized by others. It is harder to revert to this kind of negativism when both continued progress *as well as* regression are predicted.

Approaches to helping that involve work with representatives of all of the member's relevant systems are emphasized by "network" theorists who are most concerned about the kinds of environmental issues just discussed.[6] While there is much to commend total "network" approaches, research does not clearly indicate when they are required, especially if environmental issues have been extensively considered by group members.

[5]For a recent, extensive treatment of this topic see Arnold P. Goldstein and Frederick H. Kanfer, eds., *Maximizing Treatment Gains: Transfer Enhancement in Psychotherapy* (New York: Academic Press, 1979).

[6]R. V. Speck and C. L. Attneave, *Family Networks* (New York: Pantheon, 1973).

Some group members' problems are precisely that they do not have supportive networks that can be drawn on to help sustain changes. In these cases, the best way to help members maintain their gains is to facilitate their forming or joining support groups after the group work experience has ended. Sometimes the professionally led group itself will be continued without such leadership by the members for the same reasons. Some criticize these efforts on the grounds that group work has created a dependency on itself rather than on autonomy. We do not agree with this criticism. Most well-functioning people are able to draw on supportive and reinforcing networks consisting of family, peers, colleagues, or fellow members of church and other community groups. Many "graduates" of the group work experience do not have these social assets and there is nothing intrinsically demeaning for them in seeking support from self-help groups. Increasingly, group-based programs have responded to this principle.[7]

The concept underlying this section is that maintaining progress often depends on securing continuing reinforcement for it. Hopefully, this will come from the members' natural environment. They will often have to deliberately ask for reinforcement, however, even if this *is* a sad commentary on how unlikely we often are to express praise to each other. One of the final exercises in the group can be to help members role play ways of asking for recognition from significant others. The anxiety such requests often cause and the assumption that one is then devoid of humility can be overcome and can enable the members to make a small contribution to the creation of a society in which norms favoring positive statements properly outnumber those favoring negative ones.

UTILIZE SKILLS IN A VARIETY OF CIRCUMSTANCES

Helping the members to utilize what they have learned in the group in a variety of situations will also help them maintain their gains. This process of generalization begins within the group itself. Members who have relationship problems, for example, often begin to try out new ways of interacting with other group members. Nevertheless, the purpose of joining a group is not to learn to adapt to the group or even to learn how to secure changes in it but to acquire personal and social changes relevant to one's natural environment. Therefore, the worker must help the members to transfer what they have learned to appropriate situations in their lives.

There are several ways the worker can help the members in this regard. One way is to vary, even within the group, the contexts in which members use their skills. This can be done by taking trips with the group into en-

---

[7]Examples are the Synanon communities, the community-based programs developed by agencies using positive peer culture, and the types of services developed by Fairweather. For the latter, see George W. Fairweather and others, *Community Life for the Mentally Ill: An Alternative to Institutional Care* (Chicago: Aldine, 1969).

vironments, when this is possible, and when it is not, by simulating such environments through role plays and similar devices.

Example. In a group of retarded youths meeting under the auspices of a community mental health program, members had been learning the skill of asking for information and clarifying information that was not clear. During the final meetings of the group, the members took trips to a job program, a health service, a vocational school, and a department store. Before these trips, the group members discussed the types of information they would seek in each setting. Afterward, the members returned to their group meetings to discuss their experiences and to identify the common elements in their responses to each situation.

Since each environment in which a member uses a skill is in some respects unique, members must be able to solve the problems posed by these differences. Therefore, there is scarcely a group in which it is not appropriate to seek to enhance the members' problem-solving skills.

In addition, members must not only be able to "act"; they must also understand how to analyze situations and to explain why each situation calls for the solution that it does. Thus in some way all groups must seek to add to the members' understanding of human behavior. If members understand the principles that govern their actions, they will be able to apply these actions in the broadest range of circumstances. This ability to understand behavior has even broader ramifications, as Yalom points out:

> In part, however, explanation and clarification function as effective curative agents in their own right. Man has always abhorred uncertainty and through the ages has sought to order his universe by providing explanations, primarily religious or scientific. The explanation of a phenomenon. . . . Similarly with psychiatric patients: fear and anxiety which stem from uncertainty of the source, meaning, and seriousness of psychiatric symptoms may so compound the total dysphoria that effective exploration becomes vastly more difficult. Thus, didactic instruction, through its provision of structure and explanation, has intrinsic value and deserves a place in our repertoire of therapeutic instruments.[8]

The worker will utilize this principle of cognitive understanding throughout the group but the ending is a good time to reinforce it so as to prepare members to apply broadly what they have learned. There are a number of therapeutic systems we have described in this book that explicitly provide for teaching a causal framework to members; these include transactional anlysis, positive peer culture, and some approaches to behavior modification. In another sense, this is also true for ego psychological and other cognitively oriented systems whose goal is to enable the member to develop insight.

[8]Irvin D. Yalom, *The Theory and Practice of Group Psychotherapy*, 2nd ed. (New York: Basic Books, 1975), p. 11.

UTILIZE NEW SERVICES

Members will often seek out new services after the group ends as a logical sequel to their participation in the group. Thus in a group to help unwed mothers to make some decisions regarding raising their children or placing them for adoption, some members sought services to help them acquire child rearing skills; others wished services to help them resume their vocational and educational careers. In the last meetings of the group, the resources to meet these needs were discussed. The worker as well as members shared their knowledge of the agencies providing these services.

Giving knowledge about resources should be more than a simple presentation of information. In the group of unwed mothers just referred to, each member discussed her specific needs in relation to available services. She also was helped to present her expectations of the service, her fears regarding it, and any barriers she anticipated in its use. The members and worker presented their ideas as to the likelihood that these expectations would be met. Ways were also sought to alleviate anxiety about the service and to overcome the barriers. In some cases the worker and in other cases the "buddies" within the group, offered to provide support and additional information as the member coped with applying for and making use of the projected resource.

REDUCE COHESION

During the first phases of the group, the worker seeks to increase the cohesiveness of the group and this process is reversed during the termination phase. Members must be helped to become less attracted to the group and, when appropriate, more attracted to alternative relationships. The worker, therefore, also reverses the application of principles for attaining group cohesion. Instead of increasing the frequency with which members have contact with one another, this is reduced by having meetings less often and/or shorter. Some groups will taper off with a meeting every other week or once a month. The worker will place less emphasis on resolving conflicts within the group and will not call attention to commonalities of experiences or attitudes except as these relate to ways of coping with termination.

CEREMONIES

Transitions in social institutions are often marked with ceremonies. These include graduations, weddings, farewell parties, and even funerals. The function of these events is to demarcate clearly one status from another, to express aspirations, to give final rewards, to allow for the expression of sentiment, to provide group support for change, and to emphasize the positives even of sad occasions. The last meeting of the group, consequently, is often the occasion for a ceremony.

The elements that have been included in ceremonies when social work groups have ended include special refreshments, gift giving, "mock" diplomas, opportunities for members to say "last words," taking a group picture, short speeches by the worker, "rituals," or singing a beloved song together. All of these fulfill one or more of the functions just listed.

To be most meaningful, the ceremony should be planned by some or all of the group members together with the worker. This does not preclude some "surprise" elements, such as "diplomas," injected by the worker or a special planning committee. Members may also add spontaneously to these final events as the ceremony is in progress.

SPECIAL TERMINATION ISSUES

The discussion of termination presumed that the entire group ended; alternatively, one member may leave and the group still continues. This occurs in groups that meet indefinitely although members join for periods that coincide with their needs—so called *open-ended* groups. Another example of this is a time-limited group in which a member leaves for personal reasons such as a geographical move or even dissatisfaction with the group.

A modified termination process occurs, even when one member leaves. Unless this termination is appropriately responded to, the results can be negative for the same reasons as if the entire group ended without dealing with termination. This includes reinforcement of what the member has learned in the group, work with feelings about leaving, transfer of the learning to new situations, and movement toward new resources if this is necessary. For these reasons, the worker will encourage the member to attend at least two meetings after he or she decides to leave. The first of these sessions usually is devoted to feelings about leaving and the second to the reinforcement and transfer issues.

In addition to the value accruing to the member who leaves, there are benefits to all the other members. When a termination process does not occur, all members may worry about whether they are really valued by their peers and if their departure will be ignored. Members, moreover, need an opportunity to express their feelings of loss for the departing member. Finally, each member who leaves provides a preparation and a rehearsal for how other members will deal with their departures from the group.

A special case of the single person leaving is the departure of the worker, usually because he or she is also terminating from the agency. Members will often experience this as a rejection or as a punitive response to ways they have behaved in the group, even when they know rationally that this is not the case. Members, therefore, will need several sessions to discuss their reaction to the worker's leaving and at least some of these sessions should involve the new worker. This is because, even after the worker leaves, responses to that departure are likely to be discussed by the members. Depending on the nature of the group and the quality of the relationship with the worker, this ending will include an evaluation of the worker, expressions of appreciation, and even a ceremony.

Terminations are particularly difficult when the members and/or the worker view the group as unsuccessful in achieving its major objectives. Nevertheless, an absence of appropriate processes around that kind of termination can also compound the negative effects on the group by exaggerating them, by confusing responsibility, and by making it difficult for members to seek out group experiences that will be beneficial to them.

When the group is unsuccessful, members should still evaluate it so that specific reasons for failure are identified. Members can then seek group experiences hopefully devoid of those dimensions. Some reasons for failures that are frequently found are poor group composition, lack of readiness or commitment of members, lack of resources from the agency, negative responses from the environment, unrealistic or inappropriate goals, and poor leadership from the group worker. Reasons for lack of success are seldom any one of these singly and the task of the worker is to prevent a displacement of all the blame onto a single variable.

After discussing the issues just described, members will usually discover some positive elements that have been overlooked in the group and that can be reinforced. This will allow members, also, to express, without either guilt or overstatement, feelings regarding leaving individuals they have liked in the group as well as relief that the group has ended. Such an approach to ending even successful groups, allows for a rational approach to be taken to selecting alternative experiences that will obtain better outcomes for the members.

Sometimes, a group "peters out" with fewer and fewer members attending. In this case, the worker should ask the members to attend a formal ending to the group. This accomplishes all of the goals just described for unsuccessful groups; it is clear that the group has ended, feelings of members are responded to, reasons for failure of the group are clarified, and members are helped to make alternative plans. In some rare cases, the reasons for the group's failure are identified in ways that allow for these to be overcome and the group starts again with more likelihood of success.

SUMMARY

This chapter began with a discussion of the meaning of endings and an application of this to group situations. Specific tasks of the worker were described as these apply to the endings of relatively successful groups; these include dealing with feelings, evaluating the group, reinforcing gains, promoting transfer of learning, and making appropriate referrals to new resources. General issues in termination were also discussed as reducing cohesiveness and planning ceremonies. In conclusion, this chapter presented ideas on termination of individuals when the group continues as well as termination processes in unsuccessful groups.

TERMINATION EXERCISE

Goals

1. To learn to identify member responses to group termination.
2. To acquire skills in helping group members cope with termination.

Procedure

(This exercise is most effective when utilized with a training group that is actually terminating. Others must simulate this).

1. Participants review this chapter and discuss it.

2. Participants divide into four subgroups. Each subgroup is assigned a task as follows: Subgroup A plans an evaluation procedure for the entire group; this can apply to the group thus far, or if the group only convened for this exercise, for this session only. Subgroup B plans a procedure to help the group members to deal with feelings about termination. Subgroup C plans a procedure(s) to help the group to maintain and transfer something that the members have learned thus far. Subgroup D plans a ceremony for the group to utilize as a termination ceremony.

3. Each subgroup facilitates the group's participation in the procedures it has devised. The order can be determined by the trainer, by negotiation among the subgroups, or by the group as a whole.

4. This termination process is assessed utilizing the accompanying termination assessment form.

5. The group discusses how the termination process they have experienced might be used in some way with other groups as well as what modifications might be required with such groups.

TERMINATION ASSESSMENT FORM

Evaluating the Group Experience

1. Check whether the following dimensions were discussed.

    ____ Whether the activities were appropriate to goals.

    ____ Whether the interpersonal relationships in the group were conducive to attaining goals.

    ____ Whether the members' investment in the group was conducive to attaining goals.

    ____ The relationship of the worker's performance to goal attainment.

    ____ A summary of the individual member's goal attainments.

    ____ Relationship of agency conditions to goal attainment.

2. Discuss each of these dimensions of assessment in terms of the adequacy of the process.

Dealing with Feelings

3. Was denial of feelings about termination present and how was it dealt with?

4. Were there feelings of sadness and how were they dealt with?

5. Were there feelings of anger? At whom were they directed? How were these dealt with?

6. Were there feelings of pleasure regarding the ending of the group? How were these responded to?

7. If ambivalence was present, how was it dealt with?

Maintenance of Change

8. Check which of the following were employed.

    ____ Overlearning.

    ____ How to cope with a negative environment.

    ____ How to develop a supportive environment.

    ____ Other (specify).

9. Discuss how well each was employed and with what likely effects.

Generalization

10. Check which of the following were employed.

_____ Varying the context of the group experience.

_____ Enhancing understanding of general principles.

_____ Assignments to practice skills outside the group.

_____ Other (specify).

11. Discuss how well each was employed and with what likely effects.

Referral

12. Were suggestions made for future experiences that will be appropriate to the member's needs? (Specify.)

13. Were members helped to examine how they will apply for such experiences? (Specify.)

14. Were members helped to anticipate any barriers to the use of such experiences?

15. Were members offered any support from the worker or other group members in gaining access to such experience or overcoming barriers to their use?

PART THREE

Variations in Practice

INTRODUCTION

IN CHAPTER 2 we discussed the purposes assigned by agencies to the groups they serve. To assist in this analysis, we utilized a typology, which consisted of (1) anomie reduction; (2) role attainment; (3) social control; and (4) alternative role attainment. This typology was used to describe many of the group services available in social agencies. We emphasized that groups are often expected to fulfill several purposes and sometimes this helps the members and sometimes this confuses them, depending on whether or not the purposes are acceptable to the members and complement one another.

In Chapters 3 to 9 we presented general principles and procedures for working with groups. Since an entirely general discussion of group work principles was impossible, we illustrated some of the variations that can be found. To elaborate even more on these variations, we shall present four chapters in this part—each one devoted to one of the four categories in our typology. Since few, if any groups, have only one of the purposes we have identified, each chapter can be used to suggest group work approaches that can be drawn upon when that purpose, at least, is operative. When several purposes have emerged in a group, the worker will have to integrate suggested procedures in creative ways.

One advantage of the way we have organized these chapters is that we shall bring together in each chapter the group approaches that we believe are most effective for achieving the specified purpose. Since such approaches also vary depending on the phase of the group and other conditions, we shall incorporate this into each chapter's design. Thus each one shall have sections devoted to pregroup tasks, group formation tasks, goal pursuit tasks, and evaluation. As the reader shall see, these phases differ in relationship to the purpose of the group.

Each chapter will conclude with an extended practice example, chosen with the expectation that it will offer the reader additional insights into how groups with different purposes are conducted. Taken together, the examples should suggest some of the breadth and richness of practice that typifies group work today.

Chapter 10

WORKING WITH GROUPS TO REDUCE ANOMIE

IN THIS CHAPTER, we shall present ways of working with groups when the purpose of reducing anomie is at the forefront, such as when the worker wishes to help the members to determine their values, norms, and aspirations in situations where these are in flux, in conflict, or largely absent.

When we first conceptualized anomie reduction as one of the major functions of group service, we did not realize how pervasive this function was. In subsequent use of this material in teaching, the students were able to identify aspects of anomie reduction in their practice with all groups. This is probably because, as one writer states,

> All societal roles and practices are open to suspicion. Conventional sex roles are questioned for the limitations they place on individual expressiveness. The Anglo's domination of industry and education is questioned for racist practices and elitist control. Government and the courts are suspect. Formulas and principles of welfare and taxation are challenged. No longer are conventional marriages and single careers the norm; private medicine doesn't work; the environment is deteriorating at an unacceptable rate; and all hidden forms of influence, whether from the private sector or from the government, are being viewed for the limitations they pose to individual freedom and democratic values.[1]

No wonder that members of groups struggle with normative issues.

Beyond the fact that the material in this chapter pertains, to some degree, to all groups, as we indicated in Chapter 2, some groups are established primarily to resolve normative concerns. These groups are most likely to focus on people who, at a particular time, have become strongly aware, for political or social reasons, of their anomic state. As of this writing, related groups with which we have had contact have been devoted to men's, women's, homosexuals', youth's, and ethnic minority concerns. In addition,

---

[1]Samuel A. Culbert, "Consciousness-Raising: A Five Stage Model for Social and Organizational Change," in *The Planning of Change*, 3rd ed., eds. Warren G. Bennis and others (New York: Holt, Rinehart & Winston, 1976), p. 231.

some of the approaches used by these groups have been adapted for groups of the elderly, the handicapped, expectant fathers, employees, students, and the socially militant. Thus, for purposes of semantic simplicity, we shall use the phrase *anomie reduction group* to refer to groups specifically formed for this purpose as well as all groups that at some stages of their development focus on this purpose.

Many of the techniques used by such groups have come from "consciousness raising" and "values clarification" programs and, to a lesser degree, from the encounter movement. While we shall discuss a range of approaches to anomie reduction, we shall draw heavily from these programs.

In this, as well as the following chapters, we have organized our presentation around the basic tasks of work with groups, namely those occurring before the group meets (for example, selection of members, composition of the group), during group formation (for example, clarification of purpose, choice of strategy), when the group acts to attain its objectives (for example, choice of techniques and targets for change), and when the group is evaluated and terminated (for example, planning for next experiences, choice of evaluation instrument).

PREGROUP TASKS

As Culbert states, the people in a consciousness-raising group—and we believe in all anomie reduction groups—"should have a common relationship to the social system or structure serving as the focus of their discussion."[2] He gives, as an example of this, a group in which married women discussed their family roles. In this group all members were married and he argues that if the group included single women or men, this would have diffused its focus.

Workers, therefore, recruiting for such groups have a conception of the type of consciousness-raising purpose of the group and members are screened for their compatibility with this. We have found, beyond this compatibility, that heterogeneity in the way the members have defined their relationship to the role is valuable. Thus a group of men seeking to cope with changing masculine roles found it beneficial to enroll some members who were "gay" and some who were "straight." When members discussed their experiences as males at different stages of their lives, the similarities as well as differences between the "gay" and "straight" men helped each to clarify many of their conceptions of masculinity. Furthermore, this group was composed of men of different ages—the youngest being 19 and the oldest 50—and statuses—ranging from cook to college professor. Because of this compositional range, the similarities and differences in their experiences helped to illuminate many of the issues they discussed.

The fact that the men's group just described "worked" was, in part, due

[2]Ibid., p. 233. Because of the relevance of consciousness-raising activities for anomie reduction groups, we shall be making many references to the consciousness-raising experience.

to the fact that they broadly defined their consciousness-raising purpose as dealing with men's roles. Had they initially, or later, decided the primary focus was narrower (for example, the role of husband or of gay person), the most desirable composition would have been of persons with the same role.

When anomie reduction activities occur in groups primarily established for other purposes, how well they are handled will depend on the composition of the group. If the members seeking to clarify their roles and values share value and role concerns with some other members, these can be dealt with in the group—if opposition to such consideration is absent. Opposition may arise if the others find this process threatening or irrelevant.

Thus, in one social skills group of university students, a gay woman worked on some of her beliefs about her role because several other women in the group identified as lesbians and they were able to help her clarify some of her issues out of their experiences. The other members of the group, whose life styles were different, were not too naive, hostile, or uninterested to impede this process. On the other hand, a gay man in another group, when he dealt with analogous issues, had to respond to the curiosity of some members and the discomfort of others. The worker subsequently helped him to find another group that was more supportive as he dealt with his sexual orientation.

Anomie reduction activities are best conducted in groups containing between eight and twelve members. A smaller group, while providing for a great deal of intimacy, also is impeded when one or two members have to miss a meeting as a few absences in a group of this size are strongly felt. On the other hand, larger groups prevent members from receiving support from each other as they relate a general topic to individual experiences.

The anomie reduction group should begin with a clear idea as to the number of sessions it will hold. Two patterns are possible: either a short term or an indefinite term. The short-term (six to twelve sessions) experience is typical of a group whose focus is on a circumscribed role such as "working mother," "coming out gay," or "expectant father." The long, indefinite-term group is one in which the focus is so broad as to incorporate the whole range of men's or women's roles. In the latter type of group, the members should agree after the second or third meeting to evaluate how satisfactory the composition is, that is, whether they have sufficient compatibility, homogeneity, heterogeneity, and size for their purposes. When there are major problems in these aspects of composition, the worker should help the group to terminate and reform or seek changes in membership.

Group workers have organized and facilitated anomie reduction groups, particularly of the short term variety. Long-term groups frequently arise in the community out of the needs of their members or are recruited as part of the development of social movements. In the latter case, group workers are called on as consultants by all or some of the members. Long-term groups can also be the outgrowth of short-term, worker-led groups that decide to continue (on a leaderless basis) with occasional consultation. In that event, the group will have to chose members to fulfill coordinator and recorder functions and these should rotate so no one is overly burdened with these tasks or uses them to avoid a more intensive involvement in the group.

GROUP FORMATION TASKS

Some assessment and screening is usually accomplished prior to the beginning of the group. This process ascertains whether the person can function as a group member; that is, reveal aspects of self to others, engage in problem-solving efforts in a group, and accept help from others. The commitment of the individual to clarifying the role(s) relevant to the group's purpose is also examined as well as personal values in relationship to the role. This initial assessment is essential in determining whether the individuals have been appropriately referred to the group and how they will affect and be affected by its composition.

During group formation, the process of assessing the members' anomic concerns will continue. In this type of group, particularly, efforts to understand internal barriers to defining one's values and roles as well as barriers from the environment will be undertaken in the formation phase and will continue throughout the life of the group. The ability to look at both of these dimensions is important. Culbert found, in his examination of consciousness-raising groups, that the duality in assessment can be approached through a general discussion of what members feel is "off" in their interaction with some system. This discussion is facilitated by asking questions such as the following: "In what ways could this feeling be a clue that the system expects something from me that does not seem natural or consistent with my self-interests? In what ways could this feeling be a clue that something which seems natural enough to me is considered inappropriate or inadequate by the system?"[3]

Culbert further noted that many people are reluctant to identify the way the "system" has contributed to their problem and they will, consequently, blame themselves and their inadequacies for their role-related problems. He recommends that this issue be confronted and he suggests an exercise for this in which members relate instances "where they accepted the blame or responsibility for something that went wrong only to receive a later indication that they were not at fault."[4]

In our experience, the opposite is also found; in this case members project the blame onto the environment rather than seeing that they compounded their problems when they failed to take moral stands and avoided experiences that would help them make moral decisions.

Another major aspect of assessment in these types of groups is the type of personal identity the person has as well as the one he or she may be seeking.

[3]Ibid., p. 236.
[4]Ibid., p. 237.

These identity issues have often been suppressed or confused by environmental forces. To "uncover" identity processes, members will often relate their "life stories" with relationship to the role in question.

Example. In a men's consciousness-raising group, each member told how he had viewed himself at various stages of his life in regard to the concept of "maleness" and how this self-presentation was viewed by family, friends, and others. The men reflected on such issues as how they wanted to express emotions, how some of them wanted to engage in activities not usually defined as "masculine," and how they experienced friendships with other men. They asked each other questions that helped to open some long "forgotten" hopes and experiences. Because they shared a common cultural heritage, as men in our society, their questions to each other brought out highly relevant material.

The type of discussion just described adds to an assessment of how each member has made important role choices previously and whether such choices led to satisfaction or frustration. Value conflicts that still should be resolved can also be uncovered in this way. An examination of previous decision-making patterns illuminates the levels of self-awareness experienced by each member, his ability to engage in problem solving, and how he used or did not use relationships with others to work out problems relevant to his role. These dimensions can also be clarified as the members "process" whether and how they deal with such issues when they interact with each other. In such discussions, also, members will come to understand the kinds of role models they have or have not had and the types of models they still seek.

In addition to such people-oriented assessment, the members and the worker will engage in environment-oriented assessment to understand the nature of the anomie experienced by members and the environmental supports and changes required for clarifying one's norms and pursuing relevant goals. This is accomplished through looking at the kinds of norms present in the member's personal situations and whether they are ambiguous, unacceptable to the member, or conflicted. Examples include traditional norms in one's family or workplace that are not acceptable and normative conflicts in one's community, school, or peer group. The member may even report experiencing punishment in these systems for considering new role-related behaviors.

As the members begin to determine their values in anomie reduction groups, they will seek support from their environments. This requires the group to help the members determine which systems will be supportive, which can be changed to provide support, and whether the member can, with the help of other group members, even create new opportunity structures ranging from support groups to new conditions of employment.

During the group formation phase, in addition to assessment, the members will seek to clarify group purpose. This starts with a decision as to the way the roles to be discussed in the group will be defined. Thus, in a men's consciousness-raising group, a discussion took place on whether all issues of concern to the members as men would be discussed or whether some were beyond the purview of the group. This determination of the scope of the group will also help the members to review the appropriateness of any previous decisions such as the number of times the group will meet. Individual goals should also be defined at this stage so that their attainment can be measured and ultimately the effectiveness of the group evaluated. In a women's group, for example, one member developed the goal of making a decision as to what she thought should be her obligations in her marriage. Another member set as her goal a determination as to what kind of lesbian life style will fit her personality and her needs.

In the formation phase the members will also consider the general types of procedures they plan on using to achieve their goals even though their ideas on this may change as events unfold in the group. They can be told by the worker that the following are the most common types of procedures:

- exercises to help them become more aware of their own beliefs, wants, and preferred life styles
- experiences to help them develop their self-concepts
- problem-solving discussions, particularly around choices about which they are ambivalent
- group discussions in which each member shares current and developing beliefs with others so that members will have a number of models available to expand their basis for choice
- process-oriented discussions so that members may better see how they present themselves as well as how they use others for support or change
- discussions of their life situations so they may compare their perceptions of reality with perceptions held by others.

GOAL PURSUIT TASKS

The workers, in choosing techniques to help the members, will make decisions on targets to be affected by these interventions. For the person experiencing anomie, the internal target is most frequently an attitude. Workers, therefore, will draw on their knowledge about how attitudes are formed and how attitude conflicts are resolved. For example, we often modify our attitudes by our understanding of the world and how our behaviors affect it. The workers, therefore, will direct their attention to the kinds of cognitions that help to form attitudes. For example, one group, in which prejudice against racial minorities was an issue, examined information on the accomplishments of members of that minority group as well as the damage done to its members through lack of educational opportunity and exclusion from job markets.

Our attitudes are also linked to our emotions. In the group just mentioned, the members also feared members of the minority in question. The members, in their discussion of their experiences, were able to see the irrationality of these fears. This led to a willingness to meet with some people who were members of the minority group to learn more about their concerns and consequently to a further reduction in their fears.

In an anomie reduction group, the members, after they have clarified their attitudes and the forces that have produced them, will usually seek to change aspects of their environments that are in conflict with their new values or that hinder achievement of objectives based on such values. Members will decide to confront the actions of others who deny them opportunities to live according to their values; they will also seek to create opportunities for themselves or to challenge the ways they are prevented from gaining access to these opportunities. As an example, members of a gay group were more determined, after a consciousness-raising group experience than before, to challenge people who express stereotypes about gay persons and to demand their rights to hold jobs and secure promotions based on their skills rather than their sexual preferences.

Culbert presents a model for development of consciousness-raising groups that can be used to identify some of the major techniques used for anomie reduction. His first stage is incorporated in our discussion of group formation tasks in such groups, when members are helped to identify aspects of systems that are discrepant with their individual needs. Culbert's second stage is "understanding ourselves and the system."[5] In this phase, he recommends that members work to develop a better understanding of themselves, that is, "how we work and what we need" as well as of the systems with which they interact.

In the process of analysis of self and relevant systems, members sometimes tend to hold stereotyped perceptions or to make inferences from their existing picture of reality. The worker should seek to offset this limited way of thinking by asking members to examine their concrete experiences rather than their "pet theories." The members can discuss how such experiences relate to defects in their social situations as well as in incorrect or limited views of themselves. This process is enhanced when members ask themselves the following types of questions: If what I am feeling now (about my situation or my values or my needs) is an example of a more basic issue, what would that be? What is it about my qualities and the organizations, agencies, and other systems I have contact with that could have produced some of the conflicts I am experiencing?[6]

Members in the process of discussing such questions may discover both

[5]Ibid.
[6]These questions are similar to some posed by Culbert, *Consciousness-Raising*, p. 238.

similarities and differences among themselves. When only a few people identify a particular conflict, this may indicate that the issue is related to their needs and abilities; when a larger number of group members discover similarities, this will usually indicate dysfunctions in their environments.

One of the exercises that can be used to help members to gain a clearer idea of how their social behaviors indicate their needs is "Role Nominations." In this exercise members are given a list of various "roles," such as initiator, encourager, and dominator. The members check off the roles that have been enacted by each of the group members during group meetings. The "nominations" for each member are then tallied and a group discussion of the results is held.[7]

Another exercise for this purpose is "Adjectives." In this activity, members are asked to think of the person with whom they have the most satisfactory relationship and to write three adjectives to describe that person. Members then do the same for the person with whom they have the least satisfactory relationship. After this, the group worker explains that this can also tell a great deal about the values of the members. The members, usually in dyads, discuss what they have learned about themselves from this exercise.[8]

An understanding of relevant systems can be enhanced through answering questions such as the following:

1. What do you think your (boss, wife, teacher, and so on) expects of you and other people in the system?

2. How powerful is the person referred to in question 1 compared to others, including yourself?

3. How strongly does that person want to retain you as a member of the system?

4. Diagram the system in terms of its subsystems, for example, the people most closely allied to one another in the system; the people most antagonistic to one another.

In the third stage of a consciousness-raising group, Culbert states that the members should develop a better understanding of their relationship with the system. This should grow out of the previous stage when members increased their knowledge of both themselves and the system. He sees this understanding facilitated by responding to the following types of questions:[9]

---

[7]For details on this exercise, see J. William Pfeiffer and John E. Jones, eds., *A Handbook of Structured Experiences for Human Relations Training*, Vol. II, rev. (LaJolla, Calif.: University Associates, 1974), pp. 72–75. The reader can consult this series of annual handbooks for many other useful group exercises.

[8]For details on this exercise, see J. William Pfeiffer and John E. Jones, eds., *Handbook of Structured Experiences for Human Relations Training*, Vol. V (LaJolla, Calif.: University Associates, 1975), pp. 114–15.

[9]Culbert, *Consciousness-Raising*, pp. 239–41.

1. What are the goals we hold for our interactions with the system and what means do we use to attain them?
2. How do you think the system views you?
3. How do we influence the system and how does it influence us?

A major function of group discussion of these questions is to point out the assumptions members make in their answers. Sometimes this will require the group members to confront the individual regarding any resistance to examining such assumptions.

Example. In a men's consciousness-raising group, a member stated that his wife expected him to make the major family decisions; she became quite upset when he refused to do so. The members pointed out that there were a series of assumptions here about what his wife "really" wanted and why she became upset. One member stated that he had had a similar pattern and later found out that his wife feared that he planned on leaving her when he refused to continue making decisions; she actually resented his power but feared being left alone even more.

The fourth stage, according to Culbert, is one of "formulating alternatives."[10] The ability to do this should flow from a better understanding of member–system transactions and related assumptions. Specifically, "We do this by noting how assumptions which have been characterized by our relationship with the system are inconsistent with what we have learned about our own needs, interests and ideals."[11] These alternatives, logically, can include changes in the system or changes in our behavior with reference to the system. In the example of the husband who thought he made too many decisions, the alternatives he listed included (1) developing a different pattern of decision making in the system, such as working toward concensus on issues; (2) engaging in mutual problem solving; and (3) changing his relationship to the system by refusing to make decisions and explaining the role he would like to have in the family. Group members are helpful in this process because of their ability to suggest alternatives. They can also help members to analyze the consequences for themselves as well as others of carrying out each alternative.

The final stage of such a group is "affecting the lives of others."[12] Culbert makes the excellent point that effective consciousness-raising requires that the member secure the support of others outside of the group in this endeavor. This requires that these outside people, to some degree, have their "consciousness raised." Women in a consciousness-raising group will require that men see how they also are oppressed by stereotyped male roles; gay persons will require "straight" people to see the limitations in some definitions of that role (for example, narrow definitions of male and female "behaviors"); adolescents will require that relevant adults question "adult"

[10]Ibid., pp. 241–42.
[11]Ibid.
[12]Ibid., pp. 242–44.

roles that are too rigid and authoritarian or even too flexible and seductive. The same can be said of the "alter" group in relationship to any role that serves as the focus of consciousness-raising.

In this last stage of the consciousness-raising group, the members will help each other to plan how to receive the aforementioned support and change. This can often be initiated by what Culbert calls "friendly dialogue," which can even lead to others seeking support for a reexamination of their positions through forming their own groups. He also believes that, in this stage, members need support to work for long-term institutional changes in ways that guarantee the rights of others to do the same in their own interests.

EVALUATION

One of the major aspects of the evaluation of the effectiveness of an anomie reduction group is the determination of whether members have clarified values related to the role dealt with in the group. To effect this, members can decide the values around which they experience the most conflict. At early meetings they can rate how certain they are of their value stance and at subsequent points in the life of the group.

Example. On group devoted to helping adolescents with confusion on sexual issues developed questions such as the following:

Do you believe that adolescents of your age, if they have "mature feelings," should have sexual intercourse if they wish?

____ yes   ____ no

How certain are you of this belief?

____ Very certain

____ Somewhat certain

____ Slightly certain

____ Not certain at all

Members can also make ratings on additional scales to indicate how likely they are to declare their beliefs and act on them. Members can also indicate whether they have identified changes in themselves or their situation that they wish to make in order to actualize their values. Progress in accomplishing such changes can be charted using some of the types of measures described in Chapter 8.

On a group level, members can rate whether specific exercises, discussions, or meetings have helped with any of the preceding situations. The effectiveness of such events can also be assessed by using a value assessment instrument prior to and following the event.

AN EXAMPLE

A group of nine men came together through a series of mutual friends to examine aspects of the male role. They were dissatisfied with some of the ways they had been leading their lives and they attributed this to the changes taking place in sex roles in our society. They sought help from a local community mental health agency and were assigned a group worker from the staff of that agency to help facilitate their group. The following are excerpts from some meetings of the group.

First Meeting. The men began the meeting with a "round" in which each man spoke of his feelings about coming to the group. Some of these feelings included fears about confidentiality, eager anticipation about what the group could become, anxiety about being in a group composed only of men, and doubts about what such a group would accomplish. There was some "cross talk" but it was limited and guarded. The group worker spoke empathically about their feelings and acknowledged that these were realistic in a group such as this. He gave recognition to the members for taking the risk in coming and speaking openly about feelings.

Much of the first meeting was then spent on negotiation of group operating procedures such as meeting times, length of meetings, and rules about absences. The purposes of the group were also discussed, such as the idea that this was not a "therapy" group although the members expressed some ambiguity and confusion about the differences between this group and therapy. Some of the ideas around which there was a consensus were that this group was to help clarify what they wanted to be like as men; that they will have to discuss their relationships with women as well as other men; that this will entail self-disclosure; and that they wanted feedback from each other as well as an opportunity to compare experiences. It was also evident, by the end of the meeting, that a few of the men thought of themselves as "gay," several as "heterosexual," and at least two thought they might be "bisexual." Some others had lived their lives as heterosexuals but were not sure what their feelings were about other men as friends.

The men discussed how they would like to conduct their next meeting. The worker suggested that they spend some time telling about their lives so that they might get to know each other better. The worker asked at the end of the meeting how the members thought the meeting had gone and the members expressed positive reactions. He also asked if the members were committed to continuing the group and that also was strongly supported.

Second Meeting. At the second meeting, one of the men was not present and there was some speculation as to the meaning of his absence. The group again began with a "round." Several men spoke about how enthusiastic they were after the last meeting and how eager they were for this one. One member spoke of some anxiety about the variety of sexual orientations in the group.

There was little response to this and the worker indicated that this might be a "scary" topic and that the group should discuss this further when they were "ready."

The group spent the bulk of the meeting with two members telling their "stories." The first to speak, Bob, was 30 years old and a professional psychologist. He talked about his family composition as he was growing up and the sadness he still feels about the fact that his father died when he was an adolescent. He indicated that he was married and had recently become a father of a son and this had caused him to think a lot about himself and *his* father. He offered a number of recollections of his father—some were very positive, although he also spoke of situations when his father had been uncaring or even hostile to him. With some anxiety, he spoke about a homosexual "affair" he had had before he was married while he was a college student. He had, however, discussed this with his wife and had reached an agreement with her that he would seek no sexual experiences with either sex outside of marriage. This was said somewhat blandly and this was commented on by one of the members. Almost all of the members asked Bob questions about his life or briefly indicated that they had had similar experiences or feelings.

Sixth Meeting. By the sixth meeting, all of the members had told their "stories" and one member had dropped out explaining that he did not have time for the group although several members thought he was intimidated by the frank tone of the meetings. One of the members said he still was not sure what the other members thought "masculinity" meant. When others echoed this concern, the worker suggested several exercises that could help. The worker had brought a large pad of newsprint and he asked members to suggest adjectives that are often applied to men. The list that was generated included "strong," "unemotional," "aggressive," and "athletic." The worker asked the men to suggest adjectives that they thought applied to themselves whether or not these were on the first list. The new list included "tender," "artistic," "unsure," and "funny." A lengthy discussion then took place about the similarities and differences between the lists and the reasons for these.

Eighth Meeting. At the eighth meeting, one member, Jim, said that he had a serious problem and he wanted to know what the rest of the members thought about it. He had been having an "affair" with a woman that his wife did not know about. With the help of the worker and the members, he talked about some of his reasons for the affair; these included his desire to "still be free"; his belief that people should act on their feelings; and also dissatisfactions he had regarding his relationship with his wife. The other members asked Jim questions to clarify the situation such as his sources of dissatisfaction with his wife and his expectations regarding the woman with whom he was having this relationship. Ultimately, the discussion moved to consideration of ways he could change his relationship with his wife as well as the implications of carrying out various alternatives.

The worker asked the members to consider whether there were some general issues in Jim's situation that affected all of them. This led to a discussion of the values and consequences of monogamous relationships as well as those that were not.

During the discussion of Jim's problem, one member, Harold, became quite critical of the self-centered way he thought Jim was handling his life. This led to a hostile exchange between Jim and Harold and it was obvious to the worker that the members were fearful such anger could "bust-up" the group. The worker, therefore, supported a discussion of the members' feelings and values regarding conflict and expressions of anger. While time constraints prevented this discussion from continuing too long, the members agreed this was an important topic for them.

Analysis. In this sample of some of the issues in a men's group, many of the principles previously discussed are illustrated; these include the effects of the similarity in role concerns and small size on what became a very cohesive group. The group also began in a fairly typical way to become acquainted with each other and to share role concerns. The worker was supportive during the formation period through his use of empathic responses and his identification of issues for discussion. When necessary, he supplied programmatic experiences to facilitate group development. He was aware of process issues such as the conflict that arose between Jim and Harold and the fears generated by early disclosure of intimate material. He also was aware when one person's input showed concerns that were universally felt such as the constraints placed on individuals through their relationships. The group still had not progressed to the point that members could begin to emphasize alternatives in their goals for themselves and their "systems" and to work toward these but that clearly was the group phase they were approaching.

SUMMARY

In this chapter, we reviewed the nature of anomie reduction groups and described their similarity to groups referred to as consciousness-raising. We discussed the worker's tasks in preplanning such groups, including decisions on composition and specific definitions of purpose. The phase of group formation was then considered and we described the assessment issues that are most prevalent in anomie reduction groups. In discussing the phases when goal attainment is at the forefront, we used a paradigm developed by Culbert to conceptualize the phases present in consciousness-raising and, perhaps, all anomie reduction groups. Some issues in evaluation of anomie reduction groups were described followed by a brief case example of one such group.

Chapter 11

WORKING WITH GROUPS TO ENHANCE ROLE ATTAINMENT

THE ROLE ATTAINMENT purpose of groups is to help members to fulfill the requirements of roles that they aspire to or are already in. These roles might be those of student, parent, spouse, employee, friend, or retired person. Examples of groups related to anticipated roles are those for people approaching retirement or graduation or parenthood. Examples of groups for people already in roles and experiencing difficulties in fulfilling role requirements, because of personal behaviors, barriers present in the situation, or both, are those for school children with classroom difficulties, for parents with problems in raising their children, and for teenagers who do not have friends. Role attainment groups, therefore, may be thought of as prevention-oriented compared to other types of groups.

The role attainment purpose is sometimes the major one fulfilled by the group. To some degree, however, it is present in all groups. Therefore, the approaches to group work described in this chapter may be appropriately used whenever this issue predominates.

Several strategies are used in groups with role attainment purposes and they shall often be referred to in this chapter. These strategies are: social skills training, task-centered group work, and behavior modification in groups.[1] All these approaches have educational components, an emphasis on skill, and a concern with helping the member identify and contract for specific changes that will enhance personal functioning. Social skills training groups usually focus on specific components of social skills such as asser-

---

[1] An introductory discussion of these shall be presented in this chapter. For more detailed discussions of task-centered group work, see Charles D. Garvin, William Reid, and Laura Epstein, "A Task-Centered Approach," in *Theories of Social Work with Groups*, eds. Robert W. Roberts and Helen Northen (New York: Columbia University Press, 1976), pp. 238–67. For behavioral approaches to groups, see Sheldon Rose, *Group Therapy: A Behavioral Approach* (Englewood Cliffs, N.J.: Prentice-Hall, Inc., 1977). One detailed account of an aspect of social training skills is by Arthur J. Lange and Patricia Jakubowski, *Responsible Assertive Behavior* (Champaign, Ill.: Research Press, 1976).

tiveness, communication, and initiating and maintaining relationships. The techniques for training include presentation of models, discussion of principles, role playing, and homework assignments. Task-centered work involves helping members to select a task that, when carried out, will ameliorate a problem. Behavior modification in groups helps members to understand social-learning principles and to apply these in their lives. These social-learning principles include the modification of circumstances under which a behavior takes place or the likely consequences of behaving in specified ways—consequences that may be pleasant or aversive.

PREGROUP TASKS

One principle to follow in the composition of groups with a role attainment function is that members should have a similarity of relevant roles. This is because the strategy for work with such groups has a strong educational component and this can best be accomplished when members can be served by similar or common educational experiences, when they can accomplish tasks in the same sequence, or when the commonalities in members' roles facilitate the use of the group as a support system. There may also be common environmental barriers that can be overcome if the members of the group act together.

The worker, in assessing clients prior to the first meeting, will seek to learn the roles that are likely to be targetted by them as group members. This may require some prioritizing of their concerns prior to the beginning of the group. Thus an individual who sought help with parenting functions as well as assertiveness with her employer was asked to indicate which of these caused her the most concern. Since it was the parenting issue, she was invited to join a parents' skill-training group.

Prior to the first meeting, the worker should also assess the skills already possessed by the person in fulfilling the role, because while some homogeneity in this respect is not essential, it is desirable. Potential members also may vary in their skills and this can enrich the group. The group will have problems in establishing cohesiveness and developing a coherent program, however, if the differences are vast among members in the overall amount of skill. As an example, a member of one social skills group had always been very shy and had very few friends. Another member had many relationships but experienced considerable difficulty in handling conflicts that arose in them. The former person required elementary training in initiating and sustaining conversations while the latter did not—it was in later phases of relationships that his problems occurred.

Role attainment groups are usually time-limited, short-term groups that meet from ten to twenty sessions. Because they usually prepare members for specific roles, their content is focused and their educational approach often allows for something analogous to a "curriculum." This short-term framework can be made more feasible if members are prepared for the group prior to the first meeting. In task-centered groups, for example, the worker will help the members to define the problems that concerned them as well as the role to which the problems are related. Then the initial activity of the group will be to clarify and reaffirm the relevant roles as well as the problems to be resolved—although the latter are sometimes modified as members experience the reality of the group. If work of this sort is not done in advance, the short-term plan for the group is sometimes unrealistic.

Example. In the preparation of a group of young adults with problems in separating from their families, each prospective member was helped to clarify that he or she wished to work on the role of functioning as an independent adult. One member defined the problem as handling efforts of parents to impose their advice on him; another as establishing a separate residence against parental opposition; a third as helping the family to be less dependent on him for advice and direction. (This group provides the extended example used later in this chapter.)

In short-term groups, if the types of worker interventions are known in advance, these should also be explained to the members. In a task-centered group, members receive an explanation of the task concept. They are told that they will be helping each other to identify and work on tasks related to their problems. In assertiveness groups, members are often given "handouts" on the meaning of an assertive philosophy and are told about the sequence of activities (that is, learning about the meaning of assertion, assessing their own interactions, practicing, and then applying *new* ways of interacting.)

When the type of intervention to be used is known, this will also have an impact on how members will be selected for the group. Some people will be able to make use of planned formats while others will not. This issue can be assessed by noting carefully the response of the prospective member during the worker's explanation. The option is always available to the worker to modify the format. Also, initial interviews will have disclosed that for some members one format will be more useful and appropriate than another.

If the role attainment group is one with a fairly structured program, the group can accommodate a larger number of members than other groups. Some groups, devoted to parent training, for example, will enroll as many as fifteen to twenty members. The worker can still, when appropriate, subdivide the group into "buzz groups" for further discussion of selected topics. The larger group can also be used by people who are fairly adequate in their role functioning, such as many parents, college students, employees, and trainees. On the other hand, if the members of such a group are young or vulnerable in other ways, or the technology calls for discussion and feedback, a size of about seven to ten members will be best. An example of this was a group that we categorized as a role attainment group: a group of retarded young adults seeking to learn how to meet their sexual and affectional needs in socially acceptable ways. Even though a "training" format was used, the amount of personal support and problem solving required in the group necessitated a small group.

GROUP FORMATION TASKS

In the first stage of group development, even though the purposes and procedures to be used in the group have been discussed individually, they should be discussed again in the group-as-a-whole. Members who did not "hear" everything will then have another opportunity to understand and react to the plans for the group. It is also likely that when members actually see who is present and hear something of their "story," they will want to modify the concerns they intended to bring to the group. The opposite can also happen: members who were reluctant to discuss some aspects of their lives, at least initially, when confronted with the actual group composition may be more ready to do so because they feel that their similarity to other members reduces anxiety about reactions of other group members to their "deficiencies" or "weaknesses."

The amount of problem specification that takes place in a role attainment group will be related to the type of strategy the worker plans on using. If the group is similar to what Radin calls a "socioeducation" group[2] (for example, certain types of family life education), it may be sufficient for the worker to have an understanding of the major tasks called for by the role and to check this out with the group. Thus a worker in a parent education group will already have in mind the development of skills in discipline, self-care, preparation for schooling, and so on, and will ask the group members whether these are, in fact, on their "agenda." In contrast, in a task-oriented group, the worker will help the members to provide a fairly detailed description of their "problems" so that each member can be helped to develop tasks that are appropriate to their circumstances.

In behaviorally oriented, skill-training, and task-centered groups a further assessment of the members' role attainment concerns will take place so that interventions will be appropriate to these. In a behavioral group, this assessment will include a specification of: (1) the "antecedent conditions" of situations in which the member wishes to be able to act in a specified manner as well as (2) the types of consequences the member receives or will receive when he or she behaves appropriately or inappropriately. A considerable literature exists on ways members can help each other complete this type of behavioral analysis.[3] Because members share many similar experiences, they are often astute in suggesting antecedents and consequences to each other.

[2]Norma Radin, "Socioeducation Groups," in *Individual Change Through Small Groups*, eds. Paul Glasser, Rosemary Sarri, and Robert Vinter (New York: Free Press, 1974), pp. 89–104.

[3]See Rose, *Group Therapy*, pp. 26–40; H. Lawrence and M. Sundel, "Behavior Modification in Adult Groups," *Social Work* XVII (1972), 34–43.

The possibility of setting up role plays can also help members engage in this type of assessment in the group.

In task-centered groups, there is less emphasis on assessment; rather the members help each other devise tasks that will reduce problems. The process that most closely corresponds to assessment is that of designing a task that will be suitable for the person to accomplish, given his or her motivation, personal capacity, and the realities of the situation. After a task has been chosen, the members will—with the help of the worker—assist each other in assessing the kinds of barriers to accomplishing those tasks the members may encounter within themselves as well as in their environments.

Brim presents a framework that is useful in assessment relevant to role attainment. It can be used in a variety of social skill training situations Specifically, he states: "There are three things a person requires before he is able to perform satisfactorily in a role. He must know what is expected of him (both in behavior and in values), must be able to meet the role requirements, and must desire to practice the behavior and pursue the appropriate ends. It can be said that the purposes of socialization are to give a person knowledge, ability, and motivation."[4] This is summarized by Brim in a six-cell table as follows:[5]

	Behavior	Values
Knowledge	A	B
Ability	C	D
Motivation	E	F

In discussing this table, Brim explains that "Cells A and B indicate respectively that the individual knows what behavior is expected of him and what ends he should pursue; E and F indicate that the individual is motivated to behave in the appropriate ways and to pursue the designated values; C and D indicate that the individual is able to carry out the behavior and then hold appropriate values."[6] Some of the ways that the group and the worker can help assess the member relevant to Brim's formulation are now given.

Cell A. The member is asked to describe the behavior that he or she thinks is appropriate to the situation; alternatively, the members can be shown examples of appropriate and inappropriate behavior to see if they recognize what is called for in the situation.

Cell B. The member is asked what the goals or objectives of the behavior are.

Cell C. In cell C examinations are made of the member's ability to perform the behavior. This can be accomplished through the member either

---

[4]Orville G. Brim, Jr. and Stanton Wheeler, *Socialization After Childhood: Two Essays* (New York: John Wiley, 1966), p. 25.
[5]Ibid.
[6]Ibid., pp. 25–26.

describing to the group the ways he or she acted in the relevant life situation or role playing a simulated version of the situation as the other members and worker identify their degree of skill.

Cell D. As Brim indicates,[7] some people are "unable" to hold certain values because of "conflict within the personality." This is illustrated through the example of a son who did not pursue the value of going to college because he perceived this as placing him in competition with his father's record.[8] Group workers deal with many group members who have difficulties with holding desired values because of psychological and social conflicts. Often these must be resolved by the members before they can invest themselves in role attainment activities.

The assessment of the inability to hold particular values is a subtle process. The sign that this is present is often in the member's nonverbal cues. A member may proclaim commitment to a goal or a value while acting uncomfortable or showing inappropriate expressions of emotion. Other members may see, in the member's behavior in the group or outside of it, that the individual's commitments are lacking or in conflict.

Cells E and F. Members should examine whether there are any reinforcers in the member's natural environment for engaging in the appropriate behaviors or for proclaiming the goals and values that will support these behaviors.

This type of assessment (for example, Brim's framework) will help members and workers plan appropriate activities for role attainment. If the lacks, for example, are in values or motivation, the group's attention to increasing the members' abilities may be fruitless.

An analogous assessment of the environment must take place in role attainment groups. Members are unlikely to work very hard to adapt themselves to roles that there will be no opportunity for them to pursue. School children who perceive that their teachers will not give them the help they need; trainees in job programs who know about racial or sex discrimination or a recession in the relevant industry; elderly people who are aware their families do not wish them to be active in the community—these people will be frustrated by programs geared only to these behaviors and skills. These systems can be assessed by examining the experiences members and others have had with such environments. On occasion, also, members will be asked by the group to test out the kinds of opportunities available for group members from relevant systems.

In examining opportunity structures, members should perceive whether role steps are defined and properly paced. Earlier we referred to a group of retarded young adults who were helped with affectional and sexual

[7]Ibid., p. 26, footnote *.
[8]Ibid., p. 41.

behaviors. In addition to their learning how to deal with such situations, appropriate opportunities had to be permitted them, such as social occasions with the opposite sex, dating, and ultimately, for some, engagement and marriage. These "steps" were not defined by their parents and caregivers or graded in any way. Thus, some members were given too much responsibility for social contacts and others too little. The worker, with the help of group members, undertook an assessment of this and as a result, meetings were held with people in the environment who could bring about the necessary changes of clarifying and pacing such opportunities.

Based on these types of assessments, the worker and members will choose targets for the group's activities. As we discussed in reference to Brim's work, these targets may be any combination of members' behaviors, attitudes, and cognitions (knowledge) required for the roles the members seek to fulfill. Along with this, we have pointed out the futility of such role preparation when the environmental opportunities for role performance are limited. Thus associated aspects of the environment must also be targetted for change.

In a group of school children experiencing learning problems, the group worker and the members targetted the members' skill in paying attention to the teacher as well as the members' level of motivation for school success. In addition, the school was deficient in its opportunity structures in that remedial instruction to help these children "catch up" was lacking. The worker helped the members to compose a petition to their teacher and the principal in which this service was requested.

Also, during the formation period of the group, the members are helped to determine their role attainment goals. Almost always, in such groups, it is possible to attain a high level of precision in such formulations and this accomplishment, itself, goes a long way to enhancing the socialization processes in the group.

GOAL PURSUIT TASKS

One of the most frequently used procedures in role attainment groups is behavioral rehearsal. In this activity the worker helps the members to role play or in other ways simulate the behaviors they seek to possess. The following are some of the steps in this process:

1. The member, through role play or description, presents an example of the way the situation is customarily handled.

2. Members, with the help of the worker, suggest changes in the way the member acts. These changes are often guided by general principles that the group has learned. Examples of these from assertiveness training are "giving and receiving compliments," and "carrying on social conversations."[9]

---

[9]For exercises to teach these two skills, see Lange and Jakubowski, *Responsible Assertive Behavior*, pp. 74 and 77, respectively.

3. The member has an opportunity to clarify suggestions from the group and to plan how he or she will act.

4. A member of the group is chosen to play the "alter" in the role play and is briefed by the member who is learning the behavior.

5. The role play is enacted.

6. After the role play, members *first* state the positive aspects of the performance. Members then make suggestions for improvements.

7. The member should plan occasions outside the group to try out the behavior. At subsequent meetings, the member should report on this. Additional modifications and rehearsals may then be required.

Another major procedure in role attainment groups is modeling. A number of different people can model behaviors that the member desires to learn. Members who have successfully mastered the behavior can demonstrate it in role plays or can describe how they handled situations outside the group. The worker can also demonstrate behaviors. Members may select people outside of the group whose behavior they desire to emulate. Workers can also play tapes and films that present good examples of ways of handling situations relevant to the members' concerns.

In task-centered groups, any of the preceding procedures can be used to help in task accomplishment. The philosophy underlying task-centered work, however, calls for the maximum involvement of the group members in selecting their own tasks. The worker will illustrate the task concept by appropriate examples so that members will understand what is required. In our experience, the first selection of tasks proceeds slowly. The process, however, serves as a model for members who subsequently choose their tasks more quickly. In a homogeneous group, members may also select similar tasks and this is another reason for the acceleration in this process with time.

Rooney describes some innovative approaches for helping group members to define tasks as well as to accomplish them.[10] In working with a group of high school youths he proposed that members list on long sheets of paper their tasks as well as their progress on these tasks. These lists were then placed on the walls. He, as the worker, modeled this technique by creating his own list of tasks, such as activities he had promised to carry out to help the members achieve their goals. Members also formed a "buddy system" and worked in pairs to select means of overcoming barriers to task accomplishment.

During the task accomplishment phase, members are helped with their tasks as follows: they can rehearse them through group role plays or through verbally reviewing with other members how they plan to handle specific situations. They also secure support from other members for carrying out their tasks. This support can be supplied as members empathize with each other regarding their feelings about their tasks, as they reinforce one another

[10]Ronald Rooney, "Adolescent Groups in Public Schools," in *Task-Centered Practice*, eds. William J. Reid and Laura Epstein (New York: Columbia University Press, 1977), pp. 168–82.

through praise and recognition or even through awarding "tokens," and as they encourage one another to "keep on."

Problem-solving activities will also be used as members encounter problems in carrying out their tasks. The customary problem-solving phases of collecting information, identifying alternatives, evaluating alternatives, and carrying out the most desired alternative will, consequently, be used in such task situations.

"Coaching" is another approach that can be used to help members carry out tasks. It can also be used in analogous situations in other kinds of role attainment groups.[11] Coaching involves helping the member to create a series of intermediate goals, secure information from other members on task activities, obtain support when it is needed, ask for advice, and even request that the worker or other members be present when the member works on the task in the actual life situation.

In behavioral groups used for role attainment purposes, a major emphasis is placed, throughout the life of the group, on helping members to define precisely their problems in role attainment and to monitor changes through such measures as behavioral counts. Members are assisted in helping each other develop behavioral change plans through acquiring an understanding of social-learning theory. In adult and other literate groups, this can be done by assisting the members to read and understand texts designed for the lay person.[12]

As in task-centered groups, members of behavioral groups are often given homework assignments. These involve either monitoring behaviors or trying out approaches to behavioral change. To enhance this, workers can issue assignment forms to members to keep in individual notebooks. Assignments are recorded as well as the effects of carrying out the assignment. These personal accounts also can have the effect of reinforcing the members' participation in the program.

The worker will also train the members in a variety of behavioral change procedures. These include choosing appropriate schedules of reinforcement and reinforcers, as well as procedures for altering dysfunctional thought processes and communication patterns.[13]

The sequence of activities in social skills training groups has been fairly standardized but an increase in the training of workers as well as their willingness to incorporate other types of procedures has greatly expanded this field of practice. Initially these groups focused only on skills such as assertiveness, improved communication, or forming relationships. First sessions were spent describing and planning subsequent ones. A sequence of skills was taught through exercises and "homework" assignments. Opportunity was

---

[11] Anselem Strauss, "Coaching," in *Role Theory: Concepts and Research* (New York: John Wiley, 1966), pp. 350–53.

[12] See, for example, Wesley C. Becker, *Parents Are Teachers: A Child Management Program* (Champaign, Ill.: Research Press, 1971).

[13] See Rose, *Group Therapy*, pp. 86–102, for a discussion of these and other procedures.

provided for members to describe or enact experiences related to the skills and to engage in problem solving around problems. An assertiveness training group, for example, might offer exercises in the first meetings to teach members how to say "yes" and "no," how to initiate social conversations, how to identify personal rights, and how to assert these rights.[14]

Because of the problems some members have in learning and applying these types of skills, group workers have sought to understand how to overcome many obstacles, such as members' thought patterns that interfere with their ability to carry out desired behaviors. Members undergoing social skill training, therefore, should be taught how to recognize these patterns.[15] They include such statements people make to themselves as "one must have love all of the time from significant people," "one's life is bad when it does not go your way," "the solutions to life's problems should be found quickly," and "one cannot overcome the effects of past misfortunes."

When members find it difficult to apply some aspect of skill training to carry out a task, or to perform a behavioral assignment, the worker and members can ask about the person's thoughts under those circumstances. When these serve as barriers to success, the member can be taught to make other self statements that will facilitate forward movement. For example, Lange and Jakubowski present a list of self statements that can help a person deal better with anger such as "This is going to upset me but I know how to deal with it," or "Getting upset won't help."[16] While this approach may appear simplistic to some readers, the effectiveness of such techniques has been well documented.[17]

Similarly, people involved in role attainment experiences will often be hindered by their emotional responses. Most often these responses consist of anxiety in the face of trying out skills but they can also be excessive anger, jealousy, or sadness, the latter related to failures in carrying out tasks. Workers in such groups, therefore, must know how to respond empathically to such emotions and to help members to deal with them. Lange and Jakubowski, for example, describe several relaxation procedures that they recommended for use in assertiveness training groups.[18]

Because role attainment groups are so often oriented to educational procedures and task accomplishment, the worker should sometimes provide for a release of tension or a change of pace. Thus some of the "rounds" described in the previous chapter, in which members share their feelings at the

---

[14]For descriptions of these exercises, see Lange and Jakubowski, *Responsible Assertive Behavior*, pp. 69–113.

[15]Many workers draw on the techniques of Albert Ellis for such cognitive changes; see A. Ellis and R. A. Harper, *A New Guide to Rational Living* (Englewood Cliffs, N.J.: Prentice-Hall, Inc., 1975).

[16]R.W. Novaco, *Anger Control: The Development and Evaluation of an Experimental Treatment* (Lexington, Mass.: Heath, 1975), as quoted in Lange and Jakubowski, *Responsible Assertive Behavior*, pp. 150–51.

[17]Ibid.

[18]Lange and Jakubowski, *Responsible Assertive Behavior*, pp. 169–72.

moment, are appropriate. Members may also benefit from a "half-way-through" party or other social occasion. Rose, for example, described a social skill training group for fourth and fifth grade boys which met twice a week for half hour sessions for ten weeks.[19] At the first meeting members were given a cookie on entering and a token for sitting down. The children worked for tokens to be exchanged for such prizes as match box cars. When individual reinforcers were gradually withdrawn, group rewards included a field trip to the university to make a video tape and a picnic at the local park.

In the earlier days of group work, most workers were deployed in community centers and settlement houses. These agencies provided role attainment [that is, socialization] experiences through club activities and special interest groups (for example, arts and crafts, dramatics). These groups presumably attained their goals through the worker's facilitation of group development and group decision making and the selection of activities appropriate to the members' development tasks. While we are not offering in detail a discussion of group work in such situations, we believe that many of the procedures we have described throughout this book, and particularly in the Chapters on anomie reduction and role attainment, are useful to facilitate the members' role attainment in such groups.

EVALUATION

In behaviorally oriented groups, workers will help members to evaluate their success in role attainment through devices previously described, such as behavioral counts, self reports of coping with targetted situations, and reports by significant others. The latter can include behavioral checklists completed by teachers, employers, and parents. Rose, for example, has developed a children's behavior code that was employed by observers in the child's academic classrooom and gym class.[20] In one project Rose also used charts showing the number of behavioral assignments completed by each child.

Reid and his colleagues have developed a scale for evaluation of task-centered groups.[21] The problems on which members are working are listed and changes rated on a 10-point scale ranging from problem greatly aggravated to problem no longer present. The midpoint of the scale ("5") represents "no change"; smaller numbers represent degrees of problem aggravation and larger numbers represent degrees of problem alleviation. In the interest of reliability, workers secure these ratings from the client, a collateral person, and also make their own ratings.

[19]Sheldon D. Rose and Alison Roessle, "A Social Skill Training Group for Fourth and Fifth Grade Boys," *Behavior Group Therapy* 1, no. 5 (September 1979), 2–12.
[20]Ibid.
[21]See "Task-Centered Group Recording Guide III: Final Session," School of Social Service Administration, rev. (Chicago, Ill.: University of Chicago, 27 March 1977).

Lange and Jakubowski discuss a number of measures for evaluating assertiveness training that can also be used for a broad range of social skills training groups. One category of measurement is so-called "paper-and-pencil" measures. Examples of this are the College and Adult Self-Expression Scales[22] and the Gambrill-Richey Assertion Inventory.[23] Behavioral measures can also be used such as examining the behavior of members during role plays. The worker can create these although Lange and Jakubowski also cite some that have already been developed.[24] When such role plays are used, raters are trained to assign scores to the member along such dimensions as eye contact, length of conversation, loudness, and appropriateness of affect.

AN EXAMPLE

A group of three men and two women were organized into a group by a staff member of the counseling service of a university. All of these members had come to the agency asking for help with issues involving their emotional separation from their parents. The worker believed that a task-centered approach would help these members attain the role of an adult rather than a "child" in their "families of origin." Prior to this first meeting, the worker had ascertained that these clients wanted to work on this problem and that they were willing to join a task-centered group after this approach was explained to them. The following are excerpts from several group meetings.

First Meeting. At the meeting, the members introduced themselves by name and told a little about their courses of study, their "home" communities, and their families. The worker explained again what a task-centered group was and some further questions about this approach were raised and answered. The worker suggested that members tell each other about their family concerns. The first member to speak, Jack, described his parents and particularly his father as only being able to converse with him if they were offering him advice. Another man, Bill, described the pressures he received from his family to get married. Sally was about to graduate and wanted help to resist pressures from her parents to live with them when she returned to her home community. Phil, stated his problem as dealing with his family's expectancy that now that he was the first member of the family to go to college, he could solve *all* the outstanding problems in his family. The worker encouraged the members to ask each other questions so that they

[22]J. P. Galassi, J. C. Delo, M. D. Galassi, and S. Bastien, "The College Self-Expression Scale: A Measure of Assertiveness," *Behavior Therapy* 5 (1974), 165–71.

[23]Eileen D. Gambrill and Cheryl A. Richey, "An Assertion Inventory for Use in Assessment and Research," *Behavior Therapy* 6 (1975), 350–62.

[24]R. M. McFall and A. R. Marston, "An Experimental Investigation of Behavior Rehearsal in Assertion Training," *Journal of Abnormal Psychology* 76 (1970), 295–303.

could better understand each other's situations. This was done although members primarily sought out similarities and differences in each other's family situations. The worker ended the meeting by suggesting that the topic of the second meeting should be to identify change goals for each member.

Fourth Meeting. The two intermediary meetings were devoted to helping each member successfully list long- and short-term goals. The purpose of this fourth meeting was to help each member select task(s) that will help them reach their goal.

Jack, whose problem was his "advice-offering parents," volunteered to "go first." His short-term goal was to discuss this problem with his parents in such a way that they would understand the kind of relationship he wanted with them, which was one in which each party would both give and receive advice. This type of goal obviously led to a definition of his task as conducting such discussions with his parents.

In the process of helping Jack to develop this goal and task statement, the main problem the group experienced was the tendency of the group members to jump too quickly into making suggestions as to how Jack should solve his problem. The members also asked many questions of Jack that were not relevant to the purpose of defining goals and tasks. The worker used this situation to continue to educate group members about the model; in this case, he continued to define and illustrate what goal and task statements were. (In other task groups, the worker has role played this process with a co-worker to model it.)

The remainder of the meeting was spent on developing tasks for the other group members. The process did quicken as members learned more about the nature of such statements.

Sixth Meeting. At the previous meeting, Jack had discussed with group members the kinds of statements he will make to his parents. At this meeting, the worker suggested that he role play these. Two members of the group agreed to role play the parents; by this time, they heard enough from Jack that they thought they could do this realistically. The role play commenced and after about five minutes Jack seemed at a loss for words. The role play was stopped and the worker asked Jack to talk about his reactions. Jack indicated that he was feeling uncomfortable. After a little more reflection, he said that in some ways he was worried about how his "parents" were reacting. Sally wondered if he was concerned if his parents will still like him after this. Phil commented that perhaps he thought that his parents will begin to feel useless and old and that Jack would feel bad about being responsible for this. Jack said that both of these comments made sense. He wondered if the role players might have some feelings about what it was like to be his parents. A discussion then took place with the role players about their reactions. After this continued for a while, the worker asked if it was possible for Jack to ask for feedback from his actual parents on what they were feeling.

During this meeting, two other members asked for similar help with planning how to fulfill their tasks. Another two members briefly reported on their first steps in accomplishing their tasks and they were given support and encouragement from the other members.

Analysis. This example illustrates a number of processes typical of role attainment groups. The educational components are clear as members learn about tasks associated with attaining adult status in their families. Members also work at establishing clear goals related to their roles. Since all members experienced similar problems, they provided optimum levels of support and empathy to each other. The homogeneity of the group allowed members to work in unison at the various processes required by task-centered work. The group composition also provided many opportunities for members to experience vicariously the consequences of carrying out similar tasks.

SUMMARY

In this chapter we discussed the techniques and concepts that most pertain to role attainment groups. We noted that three approaches are frequently used in such groups: behavior modification, social skills training, and task-centered work. Pregroup tasks were discussed, such as group composition and member preparation. The ways that members are assessed in role attainment groups were portrayed as well as specific assessment issues when each of these major approaches is employed. The kinds of techniques workers use in the middle phase of the group were described, such as coaching, behavioral rehearsal, modeling, and reinforcement. The evaluation devices used by practitioners of these approaches were listed. The chapter concluded with a case example from a task-centered group.

Chapter 12

WORKING WITH GROUPS IN SOCIAL CONTROL SITUATIONS

IN THE TWO previous chapters, we presented some of the ways to work with groups whose members are in transition from one role to another or from one stage of a role to a later stage. As we stated previously, members of such groups are being helped with socialization tasks and, as such, are usually viewed as healthy, nondeviant, or prosocial members of the society. Their group activities are considered by many, including the members themselves, to be educational and voluntary. The group experience may be thought of as prevention in that the members are learning to cope with situations that often cause those who cannot to develop emotional illnesses or to act in an illegal or dysfunctional manner.

In this chapter and the next, we shall describe how group workers facilitate groups for members who are viewed by society in opposite ways to the ones to which we have just referred, perhaps because of a failure in such socialization. Thus the latter members are characterized as criminals or delinquents on the one hand or as mentally or emotionally ill on the other. The group is considered as "treatment" or "rehabilitation" more often than as education. The overall function is one of *resocialization*.

At times the members who are recruited for such groups do not yet share some or all of the goals that the agency has identified in offering such group services. Part of the group, or even the entire group, in fact may never move to this commonality of purpose with the agency. We have termed this phenomena as "working with groups in social control situations." The social control aspect is justified by the agency by the fact that the society, through legislative processes, has established the social control function and has created judicial and executive procedures to determine the individuals to whom it should apply. Thus people who break the law are placed on probation or sent by the courts to training schools or prisons. In an analogous manner, people who behave in bizarre ways or whose behavior is considered to be a danger to themselves or others can also, by judicial decree, be placed in mental hospitals or other psychiatric facilities.

We do *not* believe that social work as a professional activity is controlled solely by the social mission of correctional or psychiatric institutions. This is similar to the work of teachers, doctors, or psychiatrists in such settings who supply professional services to "inmates" or "patients" in the interests of their individual growth and health needs. Such services do, however, complement the social control functions of the agency by making it more likely that the participants will be able to meet their own needs in socially acceptable ways.

Working with groups in these types of social control situations is closely related to the type of work with groups that we have termed "alternative role attainment," which shall be discussed in the next chapter. Thus when the purpose of the group, as we conceive it, has been achieved and the members have identified the commonality between their desires and the goals of the agency, presumably they will seek help in attaining these mutually held objectives and the function of the group then becomes one of resocialization—for roles that are "alternativ·" in contrast to the previous ones. It is also possible that a "common ground" between the members' and the agency's purposes will not be found and members will resist participation in the group, even after an extended period. In these cases, there may be no viable group work purpose that can be achieved. There are many measures, however, which we shall discuss later in this chapter, that workers can take to avoid such an impasse.

Many ethical issues confront the workers in these situations. One is whether they should ever seek to impose changes on a member that the member has not chosen. This is not a simple matter because there is a very thin line between *coercing* a member and *urging* a member to consider alternative values and behaviors that the worker thinks will be beneficial. The complicating factor here is the power the agency wields contrasted with the power of the member—especially when the agency controls the clients' access to discharge from the agency, thus the clients' freedom. The worker is, in reality, as well as in the perception of the member, associated with such power. The clients' willingness to participate in the group, for example, may be used for or against them in a discharge proceeding.

In addition, the worker can be caught between two values: one is that of self-determination in which members choose their own goals. The other is the respect the worker holds for the worth of the individual—what the individual is and may become—and this latter may justify strong measures to involve the member in activities that the worker believes have the potential of enhancing or even saving the life of the individual.

There are no easy answers to such questions and all workers, especially in social control settings, must struggle with them every day. We believe that the workers must discuss their dilemmas in this regard with members, especially if they expect the members to reciprocate and share *their* conflicts. Also, worker honesty in this regard is a first step in helping members to protect themselves from improper pressures.

Another struggle for the workers is to avoid being inappropriately coopted by the agency, especially when the program is more custodial than therapeutic. For example, we interviewed some inmates of a federal prison regarding their experiences with social workers, including those facilitating inmate groups. One social worker was criticized by the inmates because they felt he had accepted the guards' attitude toward prisoners during a session. An example they gave was that when a prisoner spoke to this worker, during a session, of his desire for a pass to visit his seriously ill wife, the social worker was unreceptive and communicated his belief that prisoners were always trying to "con" the system and, therefore, the request was not merited.

Another type of ethical issue arises when the clients in a social control situation are diagnosed as psychotic or retarded or are not of legal age. We believe that in these situations, the worker must consult with the families of such members regarding goals when the members are incapable of taking responsibility for themselves. Efforts, however, must always be made to secure informed consent whenever this is even remotely possible. The worker might even consider establishing an advisory group of clients with whom to consult on procedures for protecting client rights in group situations.

As in the other chapters in this part, we call the reader's attention to the fact that some groups are established primarily to fulfill social control functions. These are most frequently found in correctional settings. On the other hand, many agencies form groups in which this represents one of several functions. An example of this is the use of groups in some school settings. A school, concerned about disruptive behavior (such as students ignoring teacher requests, committing vandalism or aggressive acts against other students), may form groups for stopping this behavior in addition to supporting the education of the members. The presence of such "mixed" goals can pose difficulties for the group in formulating purposes. Sensitive negotiation skills as well as clear and honest statements from the worker are essential in such situations.

The strategies for work in social control situations often have several components in common. They tend to involve a strong relationship between the way the worker is expected to facilitate the group and the treatment technology applied throughout the agency. Thus the approach employed by the group worker may be one aspect of a therapeutic milieu. An example of this is guided group interaction for delinquent adolescents in which the group, the educational program, the agency's routines are all used to reach the goal of creating a pro-social rather than delinquent subculture by changing the norms of the group.[1] Programs for adults such as Synanon and many drug treatment centers have analogous structures.

The reason for seeking a close correspondence between the approach to the group and the overall program of the agency, in social control situations, lies in creating optimum conditions for overcoming conflicts between member and agency goals. By definition, such conflicts exist and they are exacerbated when members see the agency as unconcerned, oppositional, or

---

[1]For a discussion of guided group interaction, see LaMar T. Empey and Maynard L. Erickson, *The Provo Experiment* (Lexington, Mass.: Lexington Books, 1972).

even punitive. When the overall concept of the agency is rehabilitative and the group is one instrument of this, a major barrier to attaining a member–worker contract is removed. Unfortunately, the number of such agencies, particularly in the correctional field, is not great. The major task of workers in such settings is to try, often with the help of members, to improve the responsiveness of the agency to member concerns.

Even in benign settings that have social control functions, members will often resist a reconsideration of their values and behaviors. The strategies employed by group workers in such situations involve the creation of a strong and supportive group in which members are aware of their caring for each other. In this climate the members will employ techniques with one another that are confrontive and direct. A great deal of controversy exists, however, among group workers regarding such interventions.

PREGROUP TASKS

A major factor in selecting members for and composing groups in social control situations is the nature of potential group members' existing group interactions. The interactional and social-psychological conception of deviance utilized in our approach to group work views the antisocial behavior of such people as maintained by their interactions with their families and their peer groups, particularly the latter.

This view requires the worker to examine the peer group interactions of potential group members. Frequently the worker will attempt to work with the peer group itself as a "natural" group. This is the approach taken in such services as street gang work with delinquent adolescents.[2] In residential institutions with delinquents, the group, for group work purposes, is often the living group such as the "cottage" because this is the place that delinquent norms may be maintained.

In any case, in a pregroup assessment the worker will seek to determine the members' subcultural identifications. Members will be asked about the groups they belong to and the activities of such groups. The kinds of behavior the members condone should be investigated. Particularly important to note are the possible conflicts among the members of such groups regarding their beliefs. This may indicate whether some motivation for change can come from such peer groups.

Motivation to either examine one's values and behaviors or change them is also assessed during pregroup interviews. Few potential members are likely to have strong motivation for change or, if they have, to admit it to people perceived to be in authority positions. Nevertheless, such motivation will make it more likely that the group will achieve the agency's objectives and the presence of it in some members will facilitate consideration of alternative lifestyles in the group. The worker can search this out by asking the potential

[2]Irving Spergel, *Street Gang Work* (Reading, Mass.: Addison-Wesley, 1966).

members about times they may have considered alternative goals, how they might now respond to new opportunities, and whether family members or other people in their social network are likely to support their entry into new roles.

A problem in group composition has been that the population in an organization such as a prison may not allow for much heterogeneity among members in life experiences, behaviors, and values. Members will, therefore, reinforce each other in their commitments to deviance. This does not preclude the use of groups, however. The worker can confront members about their adherence to such beliefs when the group has developed sufficiently to support members in dealing with such confrontation constructively. This type of confrontation, however, usually requires the members to be involved in other programs in the agency so that staff and participants in all programs can work together to promote a consideration of new roles.

Even under optimal conditions, however, the group composition will sometimes work against the achievement of the agency's objectives. A technique that workers have used to offset this is to "seed" the group with people who have been in the program long enough to have begun the process of personal change. Such "members" provide important models of how to overcome the pull of past social forces should members wish to do so.

Groups that seek to help members to consider alternatives in their lives as well as to attain related roles are usually not short-term groups but may involve members for many months. They may also be "open-ended" in that members "graduate" to new group experiences as they become ready to do so. It is also possible to have a planned sequence of groups—the first one to orient the members to the program and to promote a willingness to consider its values; the second to help members make appropriate choices regarding their careers and begin to pursue them; and the last either to facilitate termination from the program or to provide a supportive type of follow-up.

Members in many such programs are not prepared in any detail for the group. This is because of the importance of helping members to place most of their dependence on the group rather than on the worker. The group itself constitutes the strongest force for a reconsideration of norms. For this reason, also, such groups may not be as small as other social work groups and may have as many as ten to fifteen members. This allows for some members to be selected as models and for additional chances for heterogeneity and at the same time the group is not so large that a member becomes "lost."

GROUP FORMATION TASKS

In discussions of group development in this chapter we draw from the guided group interaction material, cited previously, as a model of how groups may develop in social control situations. Based on our reading and experience, we believe there are general elements of development in most groups of this sort.

As the reader will find in reviewing the literature cited here, there is considerable empirical support for this approach.

When a group is started in a social control situation, it is often hard work to overcome the initial distrust and hostility displayed by the members toward the worker and the agency and sometimes toward each other. Empey and Erickson describe a number of techniques used in the initial stages of a guided group interaction experience that have relevance for other social control situations as well.[3] They assume that members will behave in a manner that is "erratic and defensive" and, therefore, "the concern of a group leader should be with fostering interaction among group members and instilling some confidence that it might eventually be effective and rewarding."[4]

The recommended techniques are those, therefore, that will "foster and reward interaction" and that will teach members "that whatever interaction took place in a group and whatever progress was made, would depend on them, not just staff."[5] This is accomplished by showing sincere interest in what members say and by avoiding stereotyped responses often made by workers in these settings such as "the stern disciplinarian, the loving father, the kindly friend, or the all-wise doctor." In a sense, this requires the worker to behave even in a somewhat ambiguous manner which includes *not* declaring all of the rules and procedures to be followed in the group but casting these issues back to the members. This is in direct contrast to what workers do in role attainment groups.

In social control groups, the members usually seek formulas for the group and for their tenure in the agency. They will ask what they should be doing in the group and how this relates to their "stay" in the agency, particularly if it is a residential one and they have been committed there. Workers in guided group interaction programs are taught to redirect these questions back to the members for *their* ideas.

Another technique to encourage interaction and to set the stage for a willingness to use the group for problem solving is to ask the members to tell their "stories" (their histories) and to talk about their interests and their feelings about the program. This has the additional benefit of aiding the members in their efforts to find out from the group worker whether he or she will be understanding, supportive, and nonjudgmental.

The worker who is inexperienced in service to such groups will fear that the kinds of processes just described will continue indefinitely and that nothing worthwhile will be accomplished. The experience of such programs as guided group interaction is that members become bored with this activity and see that it, in itself, will not lead to discharge from the program. The members are then ready to consider using the group for problem-solving activity. The worker promotes this next phase by helping the members to reflect on what they have been doing and why their inputs have been shallow. While

[3]Empey and Erickson, *The Provo Experiment*, pp. 96–103.
[4]Ibid., p. 96.
[5]Ibid., pp. 103–35.

a change in the group may not happen quickly, such discussion does prepare members to invest their energy in seeking the commonality between their needs and the agency goals.

Workers will receive a good deal of information during this formation period, however, that will help them formulate an assessment of the members. Such procedures as the members telling their "stories" will give information about the kinds of norms they are committed to and how these norms relate to their present and past social relationships. Whether members experience conflict about their deviance can also be examined as well as their knowledge about role alternatives and opportunities available to them.

Attention must also be paid to an assessment of the social barriers faced by the members. These include the effects of racism as well as of "deviant labels" that may have been placed upon them. Means will have to be sought to cope with these when they are operative.

Helping members to choose new personal goals in social control oriented settings must often be paralleled by seeking changes at an agency level. Members who view the agency as unresponsive to their needs are unlikely to use the services of that agency to reexamine their own lives. The members have chosen their deviant careers in response to a lack of environmental opportunities and an unsympathetic environment, and an agency that recreates this will fail in accomplishing its purposes.

The assessment processes during this formation period must thus include an evaluation of agency conditions that are detrimental to group members. When this is done in good faith, it will encourage the members to look *also* within themselves for sources of their difficulties. The kinds of conditions that are frequently targetted in these circumstances are the resources the agency supplies the members (educational programs, recreation, physical facilities), the responsiveness of the staff to member concerns, the degree to which members can participate in agency decision making, the agency's procedures for disciplining members (use of punishment, arbitrary or excessive penalties, favoritism), and sexist and racist attitudes.

As implied by the preceding discussion, the development of the contract in social control situations is more problemmatic than in any of the others we have outlined. This is because it requires members to agree voluntarily to reconsider and then to change basic values. *This process only occurs when the agency is responsive to member concerns.* The intervention target thus must include the transactions occurring between the individual, the group, and the agency. After each participant in the interaction has made some changes, a contract for further client change becomes a realistic option.

GOAL PURSUIT TASKS

As we have stated, Empey and Erickson present a model for the development of guided group interaction groups that can be drawn on for other social control oriented groups. There are some distinguishing features of their type of treatment, however, that are not present in other programs, including the fact that when guided group interaction is used as the treatment approach, the setting is frequently residential. The Provo, Utah, program was an exception in that the participants were assigned on the basis of a judicial process but lived in the community and only spent part of each day at the program center. Program features included group meetings and a paid work program, school attendance, or both.

The Provo program, like others of its kind, employed little overall formal structure that could communicate to the boys that release from the program is simply a matter of conformity to the rules. The ambiguity created by this lack of structure, it was hypothesized, created anxiety that members turned to the group to relieve; it also elicited members' typical coping mechanisms and stimulated creativity in solving problems.

Because the boys were involved with each other outside of the group as well as in it, the group became the vehicle for dealing with many behaviors the boys observed and confronted in each other. The salience of the group was enhanced by granting it the power to help decide when each boy would be released. This was linked with whether the boy had worked on his problems in the group and this required that he be open and honest with other members.

Earlier in this chapter we described the formation period in such groups. This period ends as the members become frustrated with unproductive uses of the group and consider the possibility that they can use it for problem solving. Empey and Erickson refer to the next stage, then, as "stereotyped problem solving."[6] Members begin to raise concerns but are still well defended in the way that this is done. They ask the kinds of questions that they think they are expected to ask and they give answers of similar quality.

The group worker during this period must be very patient. Too early a confrontation will reinstitute the members' defensiveness and mistrust. On the other hand, the worker must be sensitive to genuine problem statements in contrast to the "role playing" of problem-solving processes members believe is of interest to the staff members.

The members' behavior during this period may appear, therefore, to be contradictory. Members are tentatively and ambivalently testing out the problem-solving potential of the group. Because this is a social control situation, steps in the direction of problem solving by some group members are seen by others as "giving in" to workers or currying favor with them and members will criticize each other for this. Thus, this phase is also marked by group conflict and the worker is in a more strategic position if he or she mediates it rather than bears the brunt of it.

Empey and Erickson note that this type of conflict is intensified in those institutional settings where members bring events that have occurred outside

[6]Ibid., p. 103.

of the group into it—members' antisocial acts, for example, which may have affected other group members. As they state:

> When a group encounters such problems, basic loyalties, basic beliefs, and commitments are subjected to strain. Boys are torn between their own self-interests and those of others. In a prison, a rule that is enforced by staff as well as offenders is that everyone should do his own "time," and not mess with the "time" of others. Some of the same behavior can be expected in a community program. The pressures against those who would assume a reformer's role is [sic] considerable. That is why group members at this stage of development cannot be expected to run much risk in dealing with the problems that emerge.[7]

The worker's role in responding to this type of situation must involve a recognition of how difficult a period this is for members. What is at stake here, when members begin to discuss each other's behavior, is their choice between antisocial and prosocial norms. As members wrestle with the issues of their evaluation of each other's behavior, they begin, as Empey and Erickson point out, to take responsibility for making judgments rather than being solely the targets of judgments made by "authority." This conflict also results in members directing hostility displaced from each other to the worker.

Empey and Erickson remind the reader that discussion of behavior in this phase introduces members to the "reformation role"; this begins to make the group a "medium for change" and is a modification of the traditional staff–client relationship. The overall dynamic, therefore, is still that of building an effective group rather than solving basic problems.[8]

The next phase in the group emerges as members begin to challenge some of each other's characteristic defenses. As Empey and Erickson wisely note, "Delinquents, like anyone else, do not enjoy a group in which daily interaction is characterized by perpetual tension, though they may not know what to do about it."[9] The alternative that the worker encourages is greater openness and honesty to "get beyond existing facades." The important ingredient here is a sense of timing. Too premature a pressure toward openness can coalesce the group around a strongly antisocial member as protection against the strong feelings that emerge.

If these issues are resolved to a sufficient degree, the phase that follows in the group is termed by Empey and Erickson "awareness of individual differences and alternatives." In this stage, members start to move away from stereotyped reactions to each other and beliefs regarding "individual differences and needs" emerge. This is accompanied by more openness regarding oneself and one's reactions to others in the group. Even this, however, is frightening, and so this phase is marked by reactions such as reaffirmation of the value of deviant behavior. This conflict can also be reflected in the emergence of subgroups that represent each point of view.

[7]Ibid., p. 104.
[8]Ibid., pp. 106–7.
[9]Ibid., p. 111.

Despite these continuing conflicts in the group, the presence of an increased number of members who are committed to openness allows for an investment in problem solving around current issues. The members who involve themselves this way will feel rewarded and the worker can help them to share their satisfactions with the others. This also is correlated with the group beginning to perceive each member as unique rather than as a stereotype.

Because of the openness of members that has surfaced, the worker will bring problems to the group that affect the members. This will include such day-to-day issues as nonattendance of members as well as problems that members are experiencing in other components of the agency's program such as its school or vocational facilities.

The next phase Empey and Erickson call "group awareness"[10] as its objectives are to increase the members' understanding of "group structure and process and to maximize group problem solving." The explanantion for this emphasis, is that since much of deviance is a *social* phenomena, an understanding of *social* processes is an important treatment goal.

The natural processes of the group support this phase in that members become concerned about the group as an entity. This interest is facilitated by the worker who actually, but in nontechnical terms, teaches about such group phenomena as unwritten norms, leadership, and sources of power in the group. This new "sophistication" will also contribute to the members' understanding the workers' actions and even criticizing them.

Thus in this phase, while members continue to solve individual and group problems, they will do so with a better understanding of the barriers to this process posed by group phenomena. This understanding also motivates the members to try to improve the operation of the group, such as by creating new group norms.

The final stage is termed "integration of group and program structure."[11] Empey and Erickson recognize that this phase might not be reached by many groups but when it does occur, members help to prepare new groups as well as take responsibility for the continuing development of the agency's services. In addition, members seek to extend the prosocial norms of the group into the other institutions of the community.

As an argument against the notion that the kind of group development described here is too idealistic a concept for "real" work with delinquents, Empey and Erickson cite research based on 1000 recorded group sessions representing 10 different groups. In this investigation it was found that "when groups remain closed, there was some rather clear-cut evidence that a developmental process does take place—a process in which therapist participation decreases, group-centered comments increase, greater member-risks occur in which candid and confrontive statements are made, and nontask-oriented comments decrease. The analysis revealed that this process is better described in terms of a developmental trend than in terms of sharply

[10]Ibid., pp. 119–25.
[11]Ibid., p. 134.

demarcated stages.''[12] In this discussion, the authors state that movement may include regressive shifts as well as forward ones. The worker under such circumstances must identify themes and directions rather than look for group changes that are without ambiguity or that cover all members at the same time.

The group phases just outlined fit partly into our concept of a social control function and partly into an alternative role attainment function. As we stated earlier, it is unlikely that a social worker will think of the former without the latter. In view of the back and forth movement of the group described by Empey and Erickson, at any given moment some members may be settling on efforts to change themselves while others are still considering whether or not to formulate such a contract between themselves and the group. The continued pull from antisocial peers as well as others keeps the social control function of the agency ever present as a force in the members' lives.

EVALUATION

In consonance with our concept of group work in social control situations as functioning to secure agreement among agency, group, and client on client goals, we have sought to identify ways of evaluating the attainment of such agreement. We reserve for the next chapter on "alternative role attainment" the issue of evaluating personal change in clients of psychiatric, correctional, and similar institutions with control functions *after* agreement about goals has been reached.

Because one of the first steps in fulfilling the function of groups in social control settings is to secure the commitment of the member to the group, this is a vital component for evaluation. Workers should carefully monitor such variables as meeting attendance, promptness in attending meetings, and the proportion of members who actively participate in meetings, even if such participation is hostile. We believe that the issue of contract is crucial in these groups, and workers, therefore, should monitor when each member has arrived at a contract regarding goals with the worker, group, and agency. This also implies that "behavioral agreement" with the contract should be examined. Workers can create simple log sheets in which deviations on the part of member (perhaps of the agency, too) from the contract are recorded and then examined by the worker to help determine the future of the group.

Most groups related to this function must also be concerned about the honesty and openness of members as this is essential to a viable contract. Workers can develop "climate" questionnaires to evaluate the attainment of this condition. These consist of questions in which members rate the trust

---

[12]Ibid.

they place in other members and the worker, the likelihood that the group will be helpful to them, the amount of support they feel from the group and the freedom they have to say what is actually "on their minds." Such questionnaires are usually completed anonymously. Because of members' fears about confidentiality, they may even request that a person whom they trust outside of the group tabulate and report on the findings.

AN EXAMPLE

An interesting example of a group that began with many social control functions and moved to a voluntary commitment to change on the part of the members was a group for husbands who physically abused their wives.[13] We have chosen this group as an example for two reasons: it illustrates the use of group work in an area that has not been adequately investigated before; it further shows that the ideas of Empey and Erickson on group development in a delinquency program have relevance for group development in groups serving a variety of deviant populations.

This group was a service of a program providing shelter to abused wives. While the men were not under court orders to participate in such a group, as the author states "it is clear that with the exception of one group member, the men did not initiate service." Many of the men were either under pressure from their wives to participate or were doing so as an effort to save their marriages. A long-term commitment to the group was not sought by the worker at first but simply an agreement to try it out.

First Meeting. At the first meeting of the group, the worker hoped to help the men "to be comfortable, to establish relationships, and to develop a therapeutic climate." This is similar to the beginnings of guided group interaction in which the first goal of the worker is to create a group support system rather than to challenge members' norms. The control function of the group, however, was not covert as the worker stated the goal of the group was to "discover why the men hit their wives and to stop this behavior." At the meeting the men blamed their wives for driving them to violence. The worker did not challenge this perception of the situation. The worker notes the important fact, nevertheless, that "In the sharing of information, identification with one another and acceptance by the leader, group cohesiveness began to develop." The increase in cohesiveness was attested to by the fact that the men asked for longer meetings and by their interactions outside of meetings.

Third Meeting. In the third session, the men continued to blame their wives for the violence. Their increase in positive feelings about the group were manifested in expressing liking for the worker who was differentiated

[13]Janet A. Geller, "Reaching the Battering Husband," *Social Work with Groups* 1, no. 1 (Spring, 1978), 27–38.

from "do-gooders." The idea that the group can be a vehicle for services was introduced as the worker discussed the availability of the agency's "hot-line." The men also began to consider some possibility of change when one member asked how many men had "Orders of Protection" against their wives. As in the guided group interaction group, these discussions still appeared to have a stereotyped and nonindividualized character.

Fourth Meeting. A step toward more analysis of their situations was taken at the fourth meeting when some men spoke of fears of the superiority of their wives in the face of their desire to still remain the "boss."

Fifth Meeting. It was not until the fifth session, however, that the men's violence was acknowledged by them as a problem. This led to the greater individualization stressed in the literature as some men talked about other manifestations of their violence (for example, anger at a dog and feelings of frustration at work). This led to some problem-solving discussions around alternatives to violence and yet, also consistent with the other material in this chapter, the problem solving had a stereotyped quality without full investment in it from the members (for example, a solution is that the men had to "look at themselves").

Sixth Meeting. By the sixth session, however, the problem-solving process seemed, at least to us, to be more genuine. The men took a firmer stand that wife battering was wrong. One member was even able to refrain from acting on a desire to hit his wife as he reflected on the group's response. This seems also to mark a movement toward seeing the group as a potent support system for achieving change.

Analysis. The group's next meetings were devoted to dealing with termination, planning a joint meeting with the wives, and planning a subsequent couple's group. We believe that the movement to a couple's group is analogous to the phase in guided group interaction termed "integration of group and program structure." Clearly, the men were beginning to cooperate with other "members" of the system toward the "growth" of the system (that is, the family).

SUMMARY

In this chapter we discussed the character of group work in social control situations. The function of the group when the social control function is dominant is to help the members seek out the common ground between their goals and those of the group and the agency—perhaps even of the larger environment. This is a difficult and sometimes long-term process in which the agency must also indicate a willingness to change itself so as to relate more to member needs. The major worker skills in this situation are those of mediating among member, group, and agency.

At times, however, members need a good deal of support to enter into this process as well as to increase their motivation to do so. This motivation is sometimes increased by workers through their use of confrontation, their support of inter-member confrontation, their reminders of the short and long-term consequences of behavior, and their heightening anxiety through the deliberate use of ambiguity.

A general model for the development of such groups and the workers' changing roles in different phases of the group was drawn from experiences with delinquents in a guided group interaction program. That program identified phases moving from the group-building efforts to stereotyped and, then, more individualized forms of problem solving. Research was cited as to the validity of this concept of group development as a general trend in groups but with backward as well as forward movement. This chapter concluded with an illustration of a group of battering husbands that moved through the phases predicted by the model.

Chapter 13

WORKING WITH GROUPS FOR ALTERNATIVE ROLE ATTAINMENT

IN CHAPTER 11 we discussed the use of groups to help members attain or perform better in their roles. We indicated that such people are usually defined as "normal" and their group activities have educational foci. There is another category of people who also seek to attain new roles or fulfill the requirements of existing roles; they, however, are currently performing in ways that are regarded by others as "sick" or "deviant." They have a double burden then: to overcome the forces that make it difficult to relinquish their previous positions as well as to acquire new behaviors, insights, and ways of coping with desired roles.

An example is that of patients in a mental hospital who have been diagnosed as schizophrenics. As they develop skills to cope with life stresses, they must also overcome forces in the family, the community, and the workplace that define them as "sick." An effective group program must be focused on both of these dimensions: the adaptation to new roles as well as the overcoming of conflicts between the new and the old. As we indicated previously, this is the reason for using the term "alternative role attainment."

There are major differences as well as similarities in the situations of the various types of people who fall within this aspect of group work. In very general terms, for example, a psychotic child or adult in a hospital, a prisoner in a training school or reformatory, and a client of a family counseling agency are faced with acquiring new roles while coping with the effects of the old ones. Nevertheless, the psychological and social dynamics in each case are quite different and the ways workers deal with such members will reflect this. Thus psychotic persons have few adaptive mechanisms; an outpatient client may employ approaches to cope with stress that maintain such stress; and prison inmates may "act out" many stresses rather than internalize them. Each of these "dynamics" call for different interventions with the individual as well as with the group. We shall comment on these in the course of this chapter.

Because of the extensive discussion of work in correctional and other social control settings in the last chapter. We shall give more weight in this one to psychologically oriented settings. We believe that some concerns and processes in a correctional setting and a psychological one are similar when the former is oriented to rehabilitation and once the social control issues have been, at least partially, resolved with members. This is also in recognition of the fact that it can be the operation of chance factors whether *some* people "end up" in prison or a mental hospital.

In discussing approaches to helping individuals in groups in this chapter, we shall cite five types. The first, referred to by Rose as a "minimal skill training group," involves training people in social skills that they may almost totally lack and that are necessary for any kind of functioning outside of a psychiatric or other institution. These are similar to the social skills training approaches described in Chapter 11 and yet are contrived so as to take into consideration the needs and abilities of very emotionally impaired persons. A second is the activity-oriented group for people less able to function in discussion groups. The third, typically considered to be "group psychotherapy," is for people who possess basic social skills and a considerable degree of reality testing and who are helped to overcome persistent patterns of responding to situations in self-defeating ways. The fourth is the transition group for people leaving such settings. The fifth, the so-called "patient government group," is designed to help people learn participatory democracy skills that exist (or should exist) in all communities. Such groups are formed in institutions to give patients a way of participating in making rules, planning programs, and solving organizational problems.

In all of these cases, however, work is required to alter environments that maintain people in "deviant" roles, although, in some, the individual and the group may be able to act more on their own behalf than others. In any case, individuals in these types of groups will experience conflict among the demands of differing systems and must be helped to cope with these conflicts so as to respond in functional ways.

PREGROUP TASKS

An assessment before the beginning of the group will include an identification of the roles with which the person seeks help. In a mental hospital or after-care program, those roles that are emphasized tend to be associated with peers, family, and employment. For people who are severely impaired, the roles may be even more fundamental such as "information seeker" (for example, asking directions), "consumer" (for example, how to make a purchase), or "initiator of relationships" (for example, making the acquaintance of someone else in class).

As the compositional principle often is to secure members who have similar levels of social functioning, this attribute must be assessed prior to starting the group. Some people in psychiatric settings have experienced a deterioration in their behavior and the worker may have to secure historical information from the prospective member as well as significant others. Such information includes the kinds of social interactions in which the client has engaged at different phases of his or her life and how well these were managed. For example, the worker will ask whether the individual has had friends during different periods, the kinds of activities engaged in with these friends, and whether they were of both sexes. This helps the worker to compose groups of people with similar skill levels, even if these skills are not manifested currently. The skill level of the group will also determine the kinds of techniques the worker employs in the group.

Goldstein, Sprafkin, and Gershaw have developed and tested skill survey instruments that can be used.[1] One version is for the staff to complete and the other is for clients. On the survey, the rater indicates the level of skill on a five-point scale ranging from "never good at using the skill" to "always good at using the skill." Thirty-six skills are listed such as "starting a conversation," "listening," "expressing anger," "apologizing," "following instructions," and "decision making."

If the worker seeks to develop a minimal skill training group, a specific number of sessions are usually planned. The number varies, however, based on the level of social competence of the members. Even within this type of planning, the worker can establish either a continuous training experience or divide it into segments with in-between periods when members work in the skills they have already developed without attempting new material. More research is needed on the effectiveness of such varying arrangements. Group psychotherapy experiences in which members are helped to develop insight into their behavior while also having an opportunity to try out new behaviors in the group can, in contrast, be at least a year in duration. Transition groups may meet only three to five times. Patient government groups are ongoing.

In any case, members should be prepared for the group experience. In one type of minimal skill training, "structured learning therapy," potential members are informed of the types of skills that may be taught in the group. The skill checklist developed by therapists using that approach can communicate to potential members what some of the purposes of the group may be.

Goldstein and his colleagues consider the possibility that the client may not be able to comprehend the checklist in which case it can be administered by the worker as a questionnaire. In any event, the worker should discuss the types of skills that may be taught, describe the procedures that will be used at meetings (to be presented later in this chapter), and contract with the individual regarding skills he or she is interested in pursuing. People invited to join the group are given a "trainee's notebook," which includes details re-

[1]Arnold P. Goldstein, Robert P. Sprafkin, and N. Jane Gershaw, *Skill Training for Community Living: Applying Structured Learning Therapy* (Elmsford, N.Y.: Pergamon Press, 1976), pp. 166–73.

garding meeting times and places, rules such as attendance and participation, and a description of the therapeutic procedures. The notebook includes pages for notes on each session as well as records of homework assignments and progress made on these.

In Chapter 3 we presented Yalom's procedure for preparing members for group psychotherapy. Some of the issues he clarifies for members are appropriate to any group experience. Several things he tells members, however, are unique to the group psychotherapy experience. One is his preparation of members for analysis of "process" by telling them that they must be "honest and direct with their feelings in the group at that moment, especially their feelings toward the other group members and the therapists.²" Frustration and confusion during the first dozen meetings are predicted. The difficulty many people have in expressing feelings in group psychotherapy sessions is described as well as "the tendencies of some to withdraw emotionally, to hide their feelings, to let others express feelings for them, to form concealing alliances with others."³

The long-term nature of group psychotherapy is also explained to members by Yalom as a product of changing behavior and attitudes that were created over many years. Rules are explained that may be required in group psychotherapy but not in other group experiences such as a requirement that members discuss in the group any experiences with other members outside the group. The members are told that such relationships may impede rather than enhance therapy because "friendships among certain group members may prevent them from speaking openly to one another in the group" because of loyalties that develop to those relationships.

Both minimal skill training and psychotherapy groups are usually small, consisting of five to seven members. The amount of individualization and support necessary for resocialization experiences requires this size. Activity-oriented and transition groups can sometimes be larger, depending on the nature of their program. Patient government groups may be large, depending on the number of units that must be represented.

GROUP FORMATION TASKS

After the initial assessment that occurs prior to the first group meeting, additional and often more complex assessments take place, which may continue throughout its life. In forming individualized goals during group formation, one of the first topics that must be attended to is the forces at play in each member's life that maintain dysfunctional patterns. This is because during the time the group meets, plans will have to be made to change these forces, to provide the member with better means of coping with them, or both. These

²Irving D. Yalom, *The Theory and Practice of Group Psychotherapy*, 2nd ed. (New York: Basic Books, 1975), p. 291.
³Ibid., p. 292.

forces include families and peer groups that reinforce antisocial patterns as well as social institutions such as schools and places of employment that do the same.

These interactions are assessed by asking members to describe reactions of significant others to their problems and actions. Because of the similarity that often exists in the members' circumstances, they can help each other to identify these reactions. Also the worker may have information from other sources in the agency regarding family, peer, and organizational responses that can be contributed to this analysis.

As members, in the beginning meetings of the group, clarify their goals for participation in the group and as they review situations that hinder their goal attainment, the worker and other members should note how the members indicate they cope with identified conflicts. Some members are able to engage actively in problem-solving and decision-making efforts while others deny conflicts, minimize them, or are overwhelmed by them. In such cases, the worker and others will help the members to remove such barriers to their effort to attain alternative, more functional roles.

Once the member has begun to accomplish tasks to attain his or her goals in view of forces promoting old roles and behaviors, the type of relevant assessment is similar to that conducted in role attainment groups. As we stated in Chapter 11, when the worker's interventions are composed of behavioral modification techniques, an assessment will specify the "antecedent conditions" of the member's behavior as well as the consequences of acting in functional or dysfunctional ways. This assessment should include information on the types of behaviors and attitudes also described in Chapter 11, that is, member's knowledge, ability, and motivation with regard to both behavior and attitudes.

The availability of opportunity structures is also as essential element of moving from dysfunctional to functional role performance and must also be ascertained. For example, people released from mental hospitals or other psychiatric rehabilitation programs must be able to find jobs, secure needed services, and obtain training. The group should examine whether these are available and open to the members who need them. Members can be coached on how to approach these resources and the group can plan group actions to make them more accessible. An assessment of such opportunities is, therefore, an integral requirement for group work services. The patient government group should be primarily devoted to improving the agency's or institution's opportunity structures.

The targets of group work intervention in alternative role attainment situations are thus similar to those we described previously for role attainment situations, namely the member's knowledge, skill, and motivation for performing designated roles. The essential difference, however, is that *the conflicts encountered in moving out of deviant positions must be addressed.*

The resocialization aspects of such groups have other effects on group processes during group formation. Some members may continue to respond with either resistance or ambivalence to the social control aspects of the agency. This can be manifested in some members opposing others in the group who wish to adapt in new ways. The entire group may also occasionally move into a resistive mode that is more typical of social control situations. This may be a response to either pressures from the environment or overwhelming anxiety about the changes taking place. Whitaker and Lieberman in their model of group psychotherapy, discussed in Chapter 5, present an analytical framework that is also pertinent to understanding the formation period of alternative role attainment groups.[4] To review briefly their formulation, they indicate that members will experience wishes regarding their personal outcomes that they term the "disturbing motive." While members may have different wishes, these become linked by the process of communication and association. In a similar fashion, some of the fears regarding these wishes also become linked and Whitaker and Lieberman term this the "reactive motive." These two motives form the "focal group conflict" for which, at any given time, the group seeks a solution. These solutions may either be facilitating or hindering.

During the formation period of alternative role attainment groups, members will wish that their relationships may become fulfilling, their activities less likely to get them into trouble, or their strivings met with success. This feeling of hopefulness can be shared by all group members. On the other hand, fears will also be felt—that the group will represent another promise that is broken, that the members and the worker are not sincere in their offers to help, that the hindering forces of the environment will be more powerful than the group, or that the members, themselves, will lack sufficient motivation or wisdom to help themselves.

Hindering solutions in this kind of conflict will include persistent efforts to test the group without really investing in it, a denial of the reality of the conflict taking place, a false sense of optimism in the face of problems, or a projection of the conflict onto others. Facilitating solutions should include the willingness to pursue the desired goals while still commiting oneself to overcoming barriers, and a commitment to both asking for help from others in this process as well as offering it. This can only be achieved, however, as the worker and the members engage in an examination of the focal conflicts in the formation period and the solutions proposed.

GOAL PURSUIT TASKS

Workers will combine sets of procedures so as to correspond to the unique requirements of each group. However, it is most feasible in this chapter to describe separately those procedures that pertain to minimal skill training, group psychotherapy, transitional, activity-oriented, and patient govern-

---

[4]Dorothy S. Whitaker and Morton S. Lieberman, *Psychotherapy Through the Group Process* (New York: Lieber-Atherton, Inc., 1965), pp. 14–40.

ment groups. When these are integrated it may be because members are able to use a set of techniques, after the group has been in existence for a while, that they were not ready for earlier or because the worker discovered gaps in skills that required departing from the planned approach.

Minimal Skill Training Groups

One model of a minimal skill approach is "structured learning therapy," developed by Goldstein and his colleagues.[5] This set of procedures was designed for people who function too poorly to be discharged from or remain out of mental hospitals. Under existing treatment programs such people sometimes spend years in psychiatric facilities during which they become even less able to function in the community.

Structured learning therapy, which has an impressive record of effectiveness,[6] combines elements of modeling, role playing, social reinforcement, and transfer of training techniques. The authors thoroughly examined the research related to each of these processes and developed a group training approach combining the most effective formats.

The modeling component includes securing the members' attention through physical and other arrangements that avoid distracting stimuli. Retention of the behaviors observed in the model is enhanced by helping the members to review the behaviors observed through learning a list of principles that are then demonstrated. The investigators assert that anxiety associated with the behaviors can also be reduced by having the models demonstrate a relaxed way of performing the skill.

The role-playing component is enhanced in the following ways: The members have a choice as to whether or not to take part in the role playing. They are asked to role play skills they had committed themselves to acquire. They are given an opportunity to improvise in the role plays. Finally, they are given verbal praise and other signs of approval for taking part.

The reinforcement principles that are part of structured learning therapy are: that reinforcement follows immediately after the desired behaviors, that reinforcement is contingent on the desired behaviors, and that reinforcement is on an intermittent schedule (that is, one that is randomly determined).

Transfer of training is enhanced by teaching members principles of behavior as well as providing models of the behavior. In addition, they are given opportunities to practice the behavior under varying circumstances, including "homework" assignments related to performing the behaviors that are to be learned.

Structured learning therapy sessions are held as often as three times a week. The setting for meetings is similar to a classroom in that members sit at tables placed at either end of the worker's table and perpendicular to it. This

[5]Goldstein, Sprafkin, and Gershaw, *Skill Training*.
[6]Ibid., pp. 126–45.

leaves space at the opposite end of the worker's table for role plays to take place. This physical arrangement, by communicating that members are learners, both encourages their receptivity to learning and generalizes to their involvement in later learning experiences.

After the initial meeting in which members become acquainted with each other and learn about the meeting format, the subsequent meetings have a basic similarity. They include a definition of the skill to be learned (for example, "starting a conversation") and the reasons for the skill. Members are given a "skill card" that outlines the "learning points" for that skill. The learning points, for example, for starting a conversation are:

1. Choose the right place and time.
2. Greet the other person.
3. Make small talk.
4. Judge if the other person is listening and wants to talk with you.
5. Open the main topic you want to talk about.[7]

After the learning points are reviewed, a demonstration tape of a role play is run. While the role play takes place, on a chart in front of the group the worker points to the learning points that are examplified by the action at that moment of the role play. Following this, the members discuss their reactions to the role play and this gives the worker additional opportunity to resolve ambiguities and to provide encouragement for the next step in which the members themselves role play the skill. When these "rehearsals" are over, the role players are given feedback by other members and by the worker. A format for providing such feedback is also supplied in the text that includes such points as asking the "co-actor" in the role play how he or she was made to feel; the "audience" is asked how well the learning points were followed; the "main actor" is asked for self-evaluation; and the worker provides appropriate feedback for all desired responses.[8]

The final phase of the meeting is devoted to determining homework assignments. Each group member is asked to try out the skill that was learned in the group in real life. Since the in-group role plays are based on people and incidents drawn from actual member experiences, in most cases the member is asked to carry out the assignment in the same situations. The member's notebook contains pages in which the homework assignment is noted, along with the member's description of what happens, and the member's evaluation of it. At the subsequent meeting, time is set aside, usually at the beginning, for discussion of these reports. Goldstein and co-workers note, however, that people who function very poorly will not be asked to do this much writing; presumably reports are oral.

The Goldstein, Sprafkin, and Gershaw text contains a good deal of in-oneself and others. The worker reinforces the existence of this norm through

---

[7]Ibid., p. 83.
[8]Ibid., pp. 50–51.

many other skills, including complex skills as well such as job seeking, handling both positive and negative marital interactions, and dealing with crisis situations.

Group Psychotherapy

Group psychotherapy for alternative role attainment is hard to specify because the procedures are seldom well spelled out and there is a lack of consensus on what the process is. There is also a great deal of variance in outcomes and the variables that account for this are not clear.[9] The group psychotherapy literature presents it as a long-term process in which people become aware of their dysfunctional interactional patterns through feedback from other group members and the worker. They are then able, in the group, to explore new ways of relating. This exploration is facilitated by forces present in such groups that are strengthened by worker activities.

One such force is a norm of openness in discussing one's feelings about one-self and others. The worker reinforces the existence of this norm through modeling it as well as encouraging it in others. The worker also helps members to understand the value of the norm as well as confronting the group when members act in violation of it. Another norm that the worker supports is that members should continually monitor the functioning of their group and should seek to identify and resolve group conditions that are antitherapeutic through problem-solving activity. These group conditions include the presence of antagonistic subgroups, the abuse of power by members, and group climates that inhibit the members' progress (for example, depressed or hostile emotional tone during a session).

The worker in a group psychotherapy situation also tries to maintain a "here and now" focus. This means that concerns of the members regarding events in their "outside" lives or in their past histories are related to patterns in the group that represent contemporary manifestations of these issues. The following are some examples of this from psychotherapy groups:

Example. A member in one group psychotherapy session said, "My mother always dominated me." In response, the worker questioned, "Do you see anyone else in the group that you have some of the same feelings about?" In another group, one member said "I wish that I could tell my wife when I want her help," to which the worker responded "Is there anyone in the group that you would like to ask for help?"

The value of such a "here and now" focus is to assist members in seeing how their current interactions are a continuation of patterns that have been

[9]For a recent compilation of such research, see Richard L. Bednar and Theodore J. Kaul, "Experiential Group Research: Current Perspectives," in *Handbook of Psychotherapy and Behavior Change: An Empirical Analysis*, 2nd ed., eds. Sol L. Garfield and Allen Bergin (New York: John Wiley, 1978).

dysfunctional in the past. Members can explore, as we have said, new ways of acting in the group as a safe environment for such testing. They should be helped by the members and the worker to try out this "interpersonal learning" in their other life roles. The worker's interventions for this purpose are not always as abrupt as the few examples just given. For some members, the worker will support a "there and then" focus so that the issue the member describes can be delineated clearly for both the member in question as well as for others.

In group psychotherapy, the worker will also use a number of procedures that are analogous to those used in individual psychotherapy. The difference for the skillful group worker is that it is not only the worker who utilizes the procedure. Members are also helped to use these processes appropriately with each other. One such procedure, for example, is interpretation. In discussing interpretation, some workers adopt a specific framework for making interpretations such as psychoanalytic theory in which an interpretation is defined as an action "through which the therapist makes material previously unconscious in the patient, conscious for him in a meaningful and affective way."[10] Some group therapists give a broader definition to interpretations as views of the causes of behavior that contrast (for whatever reason, including unconscious processes) with the views of those events already held by the member. The member is exposed to "cognitive dissonance" between old and new ideas that is then resolved by changing one's thoughts and/or behaviors.[11]

The skillful worker will not present interpretations to members and will limit such presentations among members until a good deal of preparation takes place. This preparation includes a slow and careful effort to help the member to see that the two events whose connection is to be asserted through an interpretation do exist independently (for example, anger toward mother and toward wife) and that manifestations of one are regularly associated with the other. Unless this slow process occurs, the member is likely to deny any but the most simple and obvious patterns. Psychologically oriented group members are often prone to make "quick" interpretations, often as a means of competing with each other and the worker. Once this kind of behavior is "processed," however, members, through their knowledge of each other, will develop and share many insights regarding each other's behavior.

Activity Groups

The third type of alternate role attainment group is an activity-oriented group. These groups are formed in residential institutions, communty-based

---

[10]Robert J. Lange, *The Technique of Psychoanalytic Psychotherapy* (New York: Jason Aronson, 1973), pp. 451–511.

[11]Leon Festinger, *A Theory of Cognitive Dissonance* (New York: Row, Peterson, 1957). For applications to a theory of interpretation, see Leon H. Levy, *Psychological Interpretation* (New York: Holt, Rinehart & Winston, 1963).

institutions, and halfway houses for both children and adults to help group members whose functioning cannot be enhanced on primarily a "verbal" level (that is, through discussion and problem solving). Such people are usually excluded from "group psychotherapy" such as that just outlined. These groups make use of a variety of program media to attain their goals.[12] The following are some examples of how such tools are used:

Arts and Crafts. Members are given opportunities to work with clay, paints, cloth and other materials. These media help them to express emotions, to communicate ideas to others, and to enhance their sense of creativity and individual accomplishment. Such projects may either be individual or may involve cooperation among group members depending on the effects that the worker desires to have on group and interpersonal processes.

Games and Sports. Members can be helped through games to assume roles related to their goals for being in the group (for example, leadership roles), to deal with interpersonal issues (for example, competition and cooperation), and to release tensions. These are obviously only a few of the benefits of this type of activity.

Cooking and Other Forms of Food Preparation. These activities often meet the needs of members to nurture and be nurtured. They can elicit concerns over these behaviors that are then "worked on" in the group.

Music and Dance. These activities are valuable in helping members with expressing emotions, with feelings of unity with others, and, in the case of dance, with feelings about body image and the development of a better sense of one's physical self.

Trips. Members can travel as a group to a variety of places that help them to learn skills and communicate concerns. Groups have gone to restaurants, stores, museums, amusement parks, and zoos, to name a few.

Dramatics. This activity ranges from the use of role plays to improvised as well as formal dramatic activities. Drama can help members to learn more about roles of concern to them, to communicate repressed ideas and feelings, and to practice new behaviors. Learning the actual skills involved in acting and producing a drama can also lead to a heightened sense of self-esteem.

Transition Groups

The next type of alternative role attainment group is the transitional group. Institutions will form groups for people who are about to be dis-

---

[12]Gertrude Wilson and Gladys Ryland, *Social Group Work Practice* (Boston, Mass.: Houghton-Mifflin, 1949).

charged to the community. Such groups focus particularly on helping members to cope with community and family forces that can pressure them to return to their dysfunctional ways of adapting. Of particular importance in these groups is helping members to explain their institutionalization or treatment in appropriate ways and times to others. The group will also help members to make specific plans for work and living arrangements and, less often, unfortunately, for social and supportive interactions.

The important consideration in planning such groups is to begin them sufficiently in advance of discharge so that they can fulfill their proper function. This will include the review of and in some cases the development of appropriate individual goals. The techniques used in such groups include rehearsal activities through role playing, homework assignments for members who have temporary "passes" into the community, educational programs, group trips, and opportunities for problem solving. Not the least of the sensitive tasks for such a group is to help members express and overcome ambivalence regarding leaving the institution. Members will, on the one hand, desire the autonomy, sense of accomplishment, freedom, and opportunity to develop themselves by a return to the community. On the other hand, they may be leaving a "safe"environment, one in which they can be relatively dependent and one in which less responsibility may have been expected of them because they were defined as "sick." It is rare for this ambivalence to be totally resolved, yet the balance must be tilted for any chance of a permanent return to the community.

Patient Government Groups

Group workers have facilitated groups of this sort for many years. They are usually established in institutions to help patients to participate in institutional decisions that affect them, including the rules of the institution as well as its programs. These groups are also sometimes used to mediate disputes between patients and staff and among patient groups.

Patient government groups are usually modeled on a legislative body. Members are elected by constituent groups such as wards or cottages. Within the group, members take responsibility for all the leadership positions. Ideally, the staff member functions as a facilitator and consultant to the group.

The major task required of the group worker is to train the members in skills required for their respective roles. This includes member skills in agenda planning, problem solving, decision making, and encouraging maximum participation of all "representatives." Problems in such groups arise when the decisions the group is permitted to make are not "real" and members lose interest in the group. It is also possible that the members of the group have been ill prepared to carry out their roles, thus creating strong feelings of frustration among members and staff alike. When properly charged and constituted, such groups can contribute to feelings of worth and power on the part of the members. When the groups are artificial, they can add instead to the feelings of unreality and impotence that already plague the members.

EVALUATION

Several measures that are intrinsic to structured learning therapy help workers to evaluate it. They may also be used for similar minimal skill training experiences. First, group members are required to keep a trainee's notebook that calls for a series of self-evaluations. These consist of a narrative report of what happened when members carried out their homework assignment, a listing of the "learning points" followed, and an overall rating of how well the skill was performed (excellent, good, fair, poor). Workers can examine the learning points followed and the ratings for evidence of group effectiveness. The narrative report can be used to substantiate the members' ratings as well as their claim to having followed specified learning points.

The schedule that we described earlier that is used to assess members' entering skills can also be used as an "after" measure by both members and staff. It can help workers to compare groups that have been more and less effective in order to determine with whom the training has worked best and for whom additional ways of helping should be devised.

Yalom, in his discussion of the need for the practitioner to evaluate the outcomes of group psychotherapy, suggests that the beginning group psychotherapist develop an understanding of the complexity of outcome evaluation by interviewing people who have terminated. He states: "It is a very valuable exercise for the student to attempt to evaluate the degree of change, the nature of change, the mechanisms whereby the group experience effected that change, and the contributing role of other factors in the patient's environment. The exercise becomes richer yet if the student has available a tape of the initial interview to which he and the patient can listen."[13]

Yalom criticizes approaches for evaluating member progress that depend on instruments that are not specific to the members' treatment goals. He concludes, "I can think of no alternative except a laborious individualized (idiographic) approach to outcome."[14] This can be "an individualized outcome scale for each patient." He also cites one writer who asked experienced clinicians to state "what type of changes would occur if the patient were to improve in therapy."[15] At the conclusion of treatment, each prediction is examined and rated for attainment. Yalom has used procedures of this sort and has based ratings on an examination of videotaped interviews held before and after group therapy. Yalom asserts that the changes in patients after group therapy may be of a different order than after individual therapy and that

---

[13]Yalom, *Group Psychotherapy*, p. 519.
[14]Ibid., p. 520.
[15]Ibid.

measures should be directed at the appropriate type of outcomes. These include interpersonal skills, reaching out to others when stressed, the ability to sustain relationships, and empathy skills.

In an analogous manner, workers should evaluate the outcomes of activity groups in terms compatible with the reasons the activity was chosen. If a game was used to help members to become less stressed in competitive situations, means should be devised to secure self-reports as well as observations of the members' responses to competition. If an art project is chosen to help members to become more comfortable with disclosure, the number of self-disclosure statements before and after the experience should be counted. If a musical session is held to increase group cohesiveness and member comfort, these variables should also be measured before and after the activity.

It is also important to plan a follow-up after members have completed a transition group. This can be accomplished by interviewing members after the group in reference to the purposes of the group. If the group was established to help members take steps to find employment, their employment plans should be examined both before and after the group. If members are to be helped to explain the facts of their treatment appropriately, they can be asked how they would handle this both before and after the group. Through such devices, the techniques used in such groups will be improved and our knowledge of the value of such experience enhanced. Patient government groups can be evaluated by assessing the quality of group decisions as well as member satisfaction with them. Leadership skills of members should also be assessed.

Since we stated that a unique aspect of all these groups is to help members reduce the conflict between old and new roles, this dimension should be examined. One way of doing this is to ask members when the group ends about some of their perceptions and attitudes regarding previous roles. Some examples of such questions are as follows:

1. Are there people who approved of the ways you acted before you entered the group, ways in which you no longer act? How do you feel about them now?

2. If you meet a person who tries to get you to [a "deviant" act] or makes you feel you want to do this, what would you do? How would you feel?

AN EXAMPLE

This example is from a transition group formed to help adolescents about to leave a residential treatment center.

First Meeting. As the meeting began, Tim said that John should tell the group what had happened to him on his last visit home. The worker asked

John if he wanted to do so and John said that he did. He had gone to his former school to apply for readmission. While he was there, a boy asked him where he had been for the past term. When he said he had been in a hospital, the boy responded that he hoped it was not one of those places for crazy kids. John was so upset after this conversation that he went home without registering for school. The worker said that he could see how difficult this was for John. He asked if any of the other members had had something like that happen to them. Rick said that when he was last home, several of his old friends seemed unwilling to talk to him when he approached them on the street. Tim added that when he was home and relatives were visiting his parents, they also seemed to avoid talking to him. The worker said that a number of the members had similar concerns about family and friends. He asked if any of the others had thought of ways of handling this.

Jack said he did not like to talk to anyone about "this place." Al said that he told people he was just away at school. He planned on telling the local school, when he returned home, that the school he had been going to had lost his records. Tim thought Al would be in for a lot of trouble if the school ever found out he was lying. Al responded by saying that it would be a lot better than people finding out where you had been. Rick thought, on the other hand, that it might be possible to explain things to people in a way they would understand. The worker summarized the ideas that had been presented and said that he recognized that John still did not have an answer as to what he could have done when he went to the school.

The worker said that he had some tape recordings of how members of groups like this one had talked to peers as well as relatives or people in school about where they had been. He asked if the boys would like to hear these so they could discuss some of the alternatives they could use. He added this might help John decide what he wanted to do. The members all agreed this was a good idea and the worker played the first tape in which a boy was talking to his friend "back home." He told his friend that he had been upset about a lot of things that had happened to him. He had gone to a special school where they help young people learn how to handle their problems without becoming so upset. The school employed doctors and social workers as well as teachers but this did not mean that you were "crazy."

John thought there were some ideas on this tape that he could use. He was not sure, however, about telling others about "seeing doctors." The worker asked the boys what they thought about this and there was a lot of discussion about doctors seeing you when you are sick and whether they were thought of as "sick."

The worker said that he could see that there was a lot more about this they wanted to discuss and perhaps they could go on with it at the next meeting as the time was up. He also had some more tapes they could hear and discuss.

Analysis. In the incident just described, we can see the conflicts the boys face in interactions between their "sick roles" and the roles they seek to assume when they leave the institution. The worker had not yet helped the boys to recognize this conflict, as such. He had, however, responded to their feelings so that they will be more able to deal with them. He also sought to increase their skill in overcoming obstacles to performing their new roles as well as their understanding of what had happened to them while in placement. The group was developing as a supportive and safe place to deal with these issues. Not the least of the facets of this experience was the fact that the worker saw the members as competent to cope with the difficult problems they faced. He used models in the form of tapes at this meeting but planned to move to such action-oriented approaches as role plays in which the members practiced ways of handling situations such as those described here.

SUMMARY

In this chapter, we presented the issues members confront in groups devoted to helping them move from "sick" or "deviant" roles into more functional ones. Of particular importance was the recognition of the kinds of conflicts encountered in this situation and the role of the group in helping members cope with such conflicts. In addition to discussing assessment issues and the ways in which groups are formed in the light of these, we discussed a range of types of groups fulfilling the purposes of alternative role attainment. These groups were categorized as those supplying minimal skill training, those devoted to group psychotherapy, those utilizing activity bases, those conducted at the point of transition to the community, and those involving patients in governance. The means of evaluating such groups were described and an example of a transitional group was presented.

An Epilogue

Chapter 14

THE FUTURE OF GROUP SERVICES IN SOCIAL WORK:
A Positive View

IN THIS BOOK we have sought to portray the past of group services in social work and at least one approach to the present. In this chapter, we shall use this material as a basis to forecast, hopefully in a not too utopian manner, what the future of such services may be. As we reviewed the material in the text, we detected cycles in the evolution of theory for group services—these cycles in their broadest form constitute movements toward and away from a unified approach to practice with groups. This is a dialectical process in which diversity arises within unity, which then leads to a new integration out of which diversity again arises. Our formulation is an optimistic one in that it views group work theory as evolving rather than simply repeating itself.

Specifically, as we saw in Chapter 1, group work arose as a unifying concept from a series of different ways of working with groups in such fields as education, recreation, social work, and psychotherapy. This unity was created by such founders as Coyle, Lindemann, Wilson, Ryland, and Kaiser, who focused on themes of the value of group participation for individual development, particularly for the ability of individuals to function as citizens of a democratic order. The methods they developed were aimed at the creation of well-functioning, eventually autonomous groups. The worker's actions were, therefore, supportive to the members on the one hand and, on the other, stimulated the members to interact with each other to plan appropriate activities so as to enhance the members' personal development and to resolve their individual and collective problems. This idea is still seen by some as the central one for social work with groups.[1]

As we have shown, group services spread to a variety of settings and were influenced by changes in the society, in the delivery of social services, in

---

[1]Norma C. Lang, "A Comparative Examination of Therapeutic Uses of Groups in Social Work and in Adjacent Human Service Professions: Part II—The Literature from 1969–1978," *Social Work with Groups* 2, no. 2 (Fall 1979), 197–220.

the philosophy of practice, in other human service professions, and in the social sciences. This led to a differentiation of group work approaches such as the development of what were called the social goals, remedial, and reciprocal models, each one claiming antecedents in what was seen as "traditional" practice. The word "traditional" is somewhat ironic here in that group services in social work are hardly ancient in their origins. In fact, we are opposed to the notion that there should only be *one* concept of group services in social work.

A still greater proliferation of ideas and models for group services was yet to come. Social workers either discovered the existence of or became more involved in gestalt therapy, guided group interaction, sensitivity training, values clarification, behavior modification, analytic group psychotherapy, bioenergetics, and still others. At least one writer views this as "hybrid practice."[2]

It is inevitable, therefore, with such a potpourri of techniques, that a period of attempts to create order, if not integration, among them has begun. Efforts to conceptualize better the group service field are occuring at a time when analogous work is being done to produce the same for *all* of social work practice. In a previous article, we concluded that integrative approaches can be categorized as coming from social systems, task, and social-psychological concepts.[3] In the years since that essay was printed, work for integration under those headings has been even more prolific. The fact that integration in the group service field is correlated with the wider effort is demonstrated by the fact that Roberts and Northen, when inviting authors to write for their volume asked the following questions:

> What are the linkages between work with groups and work with individuals? Are there criteria for defining when a client is best served by the group method, by casework, or by a combination of the two? If so, what is the empirical justification or theoretical rationales for such criteria?

> What if any behavioral science and practice theory concepts are shared with a major theoretical approach(es) to social casework? If such linkages exist, what additional concepts are involved in working with small groups and how compatible are they with the casework theory?[4]

Roberts and Northen were wise, we believe, in recognizing that efforts to conceptualize similarities and differences in group work practice models are not contrary to efforts to do the same for all of social work practice but complement it. We agree, therefore, with their statement that "existing theoretical models must be systematically defined, elaborated, and evaluated

[2]Ibid.

[3]Charles Garvin, "Education for Generalist Practice: A Comparative Analysis of Current Modalities," in *Teaching for Competence in the Delivery of Direct Services* (New York: Council on Social Work Education, 1976), pp. 18–30.

[4]Robert W. Roberts and Helen Northen, eds., *Theories of Social Work with Groups* (New York: Columbia University Press, 1976), p. xvii.

for logical consistence before valid integrated practice theories can be developed."[5] It is in that spirit that we offer this volume.

There are a number of ways to develop an integrated approach to group services; one is to identify common elements to all work with groups. We believe that we have furthered this work through our review of principles of preparing members for groups; composing groups; facilitating a group in the process of formation by helping it determine its goals and means of reaching them; offering appropriate change procedures for individuals, the group itself, and the group's environment; and, finally, evaluating and terminating the group experience.

An organization of knowledge about a field of practice also requires an account of practice differences necessary for enhancing effective service.[6] We believe that we have provided one analytic tool for describing this variation through our typology of purposes as anomie reduction, role attainment, social control, and alternative role attainment. We must state again that we do not believe that agencies plan for groups solely devoted to such purposes but rather agency circumstances provide for various combinations of these purposes and such a typology can help workers take these variations into consideration in determining their roles. This is also not to deny the fact that individuals, groups, and organizations are in constant, dynamic interaction with one another and this affects how purposes at any given moment will be construed.

Whether or not one or another way of conceptualizing similarities and differences in group service practices will become prevalent in this "integrating" period is difficult to predict. First, an integration of ideas will be dependent on agreement on basic value and philosophical controversies, primarily those that we described earlier as stemming from existential and positivist philosophies. We believe that these philosophical differences can be overcome as workers use scientific findings as predictive tools while seeking a commitment of members and themselves to *authentic* responses in the "here and now" and recognizing the potential impact of such responses on any predetermined goals.

The second factor in the choice of an integrated approach must be how that approach "holds up" in the light of research. We doubt that any "total" approach can or will be supported by a set of research findings. Rather, we believe that such an approach must be one that incorporates or allows for a maximum number of tested or testable practice propositions, where "tested or testable," include formal research, practitioner research, and accumulated practice wisdom. Many such propositions have been presented throughout

[5]Ibid., p. xi.

[6]There are other current efforts to fit variations in practice into an overall view of group service, notably the work of Lang. See Norma C. Lang, "A Broad Range Model of Practice with the Social Work Group," *Social Service Review* XLVI (1972), 76–89. Her current work, however, represents a school of thought that makes a distinction between the group in social work as an "authentic social reality in its own right" and the group therapies where, she believes, processes are manipulated for narrower ends. See Lang, "Comparative Examination."

this book, for example, evidence of the value of member preparation for groups, of techniques to enhance group cohesiveness, of social skills training for socialization purposes, and of short-term as compared to long-term groups for many classes of clients.

Finally, in thinking about the prevalence of one approach, we believe that it must include both general principles as well as variations for different clients, problems, cultures, purposes, and situations. The types of goals sought as well as the means to attain them are too diverse for any one set of techniques; the most that can be hoped for is that such sets of techniques will be related to a model of practice that can help workers to organize their activities while remaining open to creative responses.

In the preceding discussion, we did not intend to imply that competing models of group work practice will not continue to exist; we do intend to suggest that a model or models can emerge that for the current period represent prevailing approaches to group services in social work. Other ideas will serve to provide future challenges to any concensus that may arise and thus continue this dialectic process.

While we do not claim to have created a model that will become prevalent, we do have predictions as to some of its components, particularly its procedures. We shall discuss these first and shall conclude with some ideas on knowledge development activities that should help in the continued development of practice.

PROCEDURES

A number of practice procedures should be used in any approach to group work because they have attained a stage of procedural specificity and predictability of outcome. These have been described in this volume and include the following:

1. Preparation of members for the group experience.

2. Ways of deciding whom to invite to a group based on the knowledge of those people most likely to remain in a group, other things being equal. (We do not yet have any concensus as to who is best served in groups.)

3. Ways of determining group composition so as to increase interpersonal attraction among members.

4. Actions to enhance the process of group formation such as those to achieve concensus on group purpose, create operating procedures, determine initial group norms, and reduce approach–avoidance conflicts.

5. Ways of helping members determine individual goals and group goals and of mediating the process so as to relate individual and group goals.

6. Interventions aimed at helping members become more aware of their own needs and values and those of others so as to be most able to chose individual goals and means of attaining them.

7. Responses that create trusting relationships between worker and member and that, when modeled by members, create such relationships among themselves (for example, empathic responses).

8. Procedures to facilitate both individual and group problem-solving activities.

9. Strategies for effectively using the group as an educational medium.

10. Ways of choosing among nonverbal activities through predicting their effects on group processes.

11. Means of evaluating the group experience so as to provide useful feedback to members and the worker alike.

12. How to terminate the group experience so as to ensure the maximum transfer of learning from the group to the extra-group situation.

In addition to further refinements in these kinds of interventions and the development of other effective interventions that are generally useful, we also foresee developments that will enhance achieving the purposes that we categorized as anomie reduction, role attainment, and so on.

For anomie reduction experiences, we foresee that the many emerging approaches to value clarification and consciousness raising will be refined to the point that their effectiveness for different populations and under varying circumstances will be established. The importance of providing this type of service will be seen as a means of enhancing individual growth and social competence and as a major measure to prevent a sense of purposelessness and normative confusion that we believe leads to alienation from social institutions and resulting depression and frustration.

In addition to some of these approaches being offered in a variety of group service settings, when their preventive function is fully understood, group workers will provide them also in reference to the preventive aspects of community mental health programs. Group workers who work in community centers and settlement houses will also be more effectively employed when their preventive role is clearer and their practice more innovative. The anomie reduction function and related activities can lead to such a creative approach to the programs of such agencies.

Another set of preventive activities are those related to the role attainment function. Some of the most fully demonstrated and tested approaches to groups come under this heading, namely behavioral, task-centered, and social skills training. We anticipate that these types of services will continue to develop and will become widely available, not only in social welfare agencies, as such, but in a variety of educational institutions, such as colleges, high schools, vocational, and adult education programs. In these settings, individuals will use these services to supplement the educational components so that they can become socially competent in the fullest sense. The role attainment functions of "traditional" services in community-center-type agencies will also be clarified.

We expect that social systems' perspectives in social work will fully inform group workers so that they will not neglect the environmental conditions affecting such role attainment programs. As we have discussed in this book, people will only be frustrated if they are helped to prepare for roles that are denied them because of deficient opportunity structures and a lack of environmental supports. We have been mindful of the barriers to targetting aspects of the environment for change; resistance to change is often intrinsic to organizations and will not disappear. Our prediction, therefore, is that social workers with groups will be better trained to recognize the impact of environmental forces, will understand the potency of group forces working for change, and will acquire social change strategies that can be offered to group members, when needed.

With reference to groups in social control situations, our clearly utopian hope is that the need for such situations will diminish as our society better meets the needs of the people—for such things as employment, education, recreation, and other means of acquiring necessities and actualizing one's potential. To the degree that individuals are so thwarted in their growth that control mechanisms are required, we predict that the relevant institutions will become more humane in their operation and more responsive to the participation in policy making of their "clients." Participants will then be more likely to consider alternatives to deviance. Under such circumstances, and we believe only under these, should workers promote the powerful means of confrontation of deviant behavior that can be unleashed in groups.

Environmental forces that maintain deviance will be better understood. Out of this will grow a recognition that recidivism is a product of returning to an aversive environment even more than it is a product of an imperfect "treatment" technology. Our society will then create a full range of supportive institutions in the community in which group services play a major part. Most citizens are sustained by existing supportive social networks but for others these will have to be created, at least initially, by social welfare institutions.

Finally, under our heading of alternative role attainment, we described a number of group approaches that are effective, at least for some members, namely, minimal skills training groups, group psychotherapy, transition groups, patient government and activity groups. We believe that the populations for whom these and other approaches are effective will become better delineated. This will lead to modifications in existing practices as well as the creation of new ones. Not the least of these developments will be an understanding of the interrelationship of physiological, social, and psychological aspects of the person so that group services, for people such as those defined as mentally ill, will impact on all of these and thus attain greater effectiveness.

In all these types of services, we predict that there will be an emphasis on specificity of goals and on evaluation of effectiveness. Such a focus will primarily call for short-term and time-limited groups and these will be the most prevalent ones. People who require long-term group services will often be helped to develop self-help groups for which group workers will provide consultation and other forms of support.

KNOWLEDGE DEVELOPMENT

We anticipate that the number of research efforts relevant to group work practice will increase as well as conceptual essays and practice reports. The continued proliferation of such materials will require more substantial efforts than now exist to collate the relevant group work literature. There have been a number of reports that have organized the research relevant to group therapy[7] but we know of none since 1971 that has performed a similar service for group work (that is, work done by social workers or in social work settings).[8] We are overdue for an updating of this type of knowledge source and anticipate that this will soon be recognized and accomplished. The Roberts and Northen text was an effort to organize our understanding of approaches to theory but as theoretical work continues, it will have to be revised.

Some of the preceding types of organization of knowledge are necessary for identification of priorities for further knowledge development. Without such a comprehensive effort, our guess as to needs that will be identified and met is the following:

1. There have been developments in social psychology that have relevance for understanding group work processes. Examples of these are work on attribution theory, social exchange theory, group problem solving, and the interaction between group tasks and processes. We anticipate that some group work theorists will continue to suggest practice implications of these types of findings.

2. Research on processes in social work groups will increase. We admit that this is an optimistic prediction, as there have been very few recent doctoral dissertations in social work primarily devoted to analysis of group variables. Nevertheless, we believe that a recent increase in the amount of attention devoted to the use of groups in social work will again lead to research efforts. There are clearly many areas in which research is needed such as the effects of different approaches to group composition, of different strategies of intervention, of structured and/or time-limited as opposed to less structured groups, of different ways of facilitating transfer of learning, and of different worker styles. The effectiveness of various ways of resolving such group intervention issues as intra-group conflicts, scapegoating, poor

---

[7]For a recent one, see Richard L. Bednar and Theodore J. Kaul, "Experiential Group Research: Current Perspectives," in *Handbook of Psychotherapy and Behavior Change: An Empirical Analysis*, 2nd ed. (New York: John Wiley, 1978), pp. 769–816.

[8]One such effort is William Schwartz, "Neighborhood Centers and Group Work," in *Research in the Social Services: A Five Year Review*, ed. Harry S. Maas (New York: National Association of Social Workers, 1971), pp. 130–91.

morale, group isolates, indigenous leadership problems, completing tasks and assignments, and deviance should be examined.

3. As shown in the volume, a number of approaches in social work with groups are now being taught and are, in a sense, competitive. Many ideological statements are made about the comparative value of these approaches yet little is empirically known about how different they actually are in practice and what their differential effects are.[9] Research on this topic will be invaluable in better identifying both the existing approaches to practice as well as differences in outcomes among them.

4. Almost any type of research requires that what workers actually *do* be identified. This requires better typologies of worker strategies and techniques than now exist. Some of our conceptual efforts should be put into accomplishing this task.[10]

5. Since a major conceptual effort in social work today is the development of viable generalist models, we believe that work to conceptualize group work should be related to that task. We believe group work writers will be mindful of the broad effort and will continually seek to relate the two types of work.

We anticipate that the future of group service in social work is assured. There have been periods in our history when more attention was paid to groups by social workers than other periods. We are emerging from a time when attention to "generalist" approaches *to the exclusion* of the skills and knowledge required for specific applications such as with groups was occurring despite what we assume was widespread *practice* with groups. The recent emergence of a high-quality journal, *Social Work with Groups*, and such conferences devoted to group service as the one held in Cleveland, Ohio, in November 1979 and in Arlington, Texas, in November 1980 point to an inevitable growth period for this aspect of social work practice. It is to the anticipated products of this period that we truly dedicate this book.

[9]An exception is the work of Sallie Churchill in comparing students of the "treatment" and "reciprocal" models. See Sallie R. Churchill, "A Comparison of Two Models of Social Group Work: The Treatment and the Reciprocal Model," in *Individual Change Through Small Groups*, eds. Paul Glasser, Rosemary Sarri, and Robert Vinter (New York: Free Press, 1974), pp. 266–80.

[10]One of the early, yet still valid, efforts to categorize group work interventions may be found in "Seattle Atlantic Street Center Recording System," in *Effectiveness of Social Work with Acting-Out Youth, Third Year Progress Report, September 1964 to August 1965* (Seattle: Seattle Atlantic Street Center, 1965), mimeographed. We believe that updating this work will be a first step in developing a currently useful typology.

BIBLIOGRAPHY

BACK, K.W., *Beyond Words: The Story of Sensitivity Training and Encounter Movement*. New York: Russell Sage, 1972.

BALES, ROBERT F., *Interaction Process Analysis: A Method for the Study of Small Groups*. Reading, Mass.: Addison-Wesley, 1950.

BEDNAR, RICHARD L., and THEODORE J. KAUL, "Experiential Group Research: Current Perspectives," in *Handbook of Psychotherapy and Behavior Change: An Empirical Analysis* (2nd ed.), eds. Sol L. Garfield and Allen Bergin, pp. 769–816. New York: John Wiley, 1978.

BERNE, ERIC, *Transactional Analysis in Psychotherapy*. New York: Grove Press, 1961.

BERNSTEIN, DOUGLAS A., and THOMAS D. BORKOVEC, *Progressive Relaxation Training: A Manual For the Helping Professions*. Champaign, Ill.: Research Press, 1973.

BERNSTEIN, SAUL, ed., *Explorations in Group Work*. Boston: Boston University School of Social Work, 1965.

BERTCHER, HARVEY J., and FRANK MAPLE, "Elements and Issues in Group Composition," in *Individual Change Through Small Groups*, eds. Paul Glasser, Rosemary Sarri, and Robert Vinter, pp. 186–208. New York: Free Press, 1974.

BETTELHEIM, BRUNO, *A Home for the Heart*. New York: Knopf, 1974.

BION, W.R., *Experiences in Groups*. New York: Basic Books, 1959.

BRIM, ORVILLE G., SR., and STANTON WHEELER, *Socialization After Childhood: Two Essays*. New York: John Wiley, 1966.

CARTWRIGHT, DORWIN, and ALVIN ZANDER, eds., *Group Dynamics: Research and Theory* (3rd ed.). New York: Harper & Row, Pub., 1968.

CHURCHILL, SALLIE R., "Social Group Work: A Diagnostic Tool in Child Guidance," *American Journal of Orthopsychiatry*, 35 (April 1965), 581–88.

CLARK, FRANK W. and others, eds., *The Pursuit of Competence in Social Work*. San Francisco: Jossey-Bass, 1979.

CLOWARD, RICHARD A., and LLOYD E. OHLIN, *Delinquency and Opportunity*. Glencoe, Ill.: Free Press, 1969.

COMPTON, BEULAH R., and BURT GALOWAY, eds., *Social Work Processes* (rev. ed.). Homewood, Ill.: Dorsey Press, 1979.

COYLE, GRACE L., *Studies in Group Behavior*. New York: Harper & Row, Pub., 1937.

———. *Group Experience and Democratic Values*. New York: Women's Press, 1947.

———. *Group Work with American Youth*. New York: Harper & Row, Pub., 1948.

CROXTON, TOM A., "The Therapeutic Contract in Social Treatment," in *Individual Change Through Small Groups,* eds. Paul Glasser, Rosemary Sarri, and Robert Vinter, pp. 169–85. New York: Free Press, 1974.

CULBERT, SAMUEL A., "Consciousness Raising: A Five Stage Model for Social and Organizational Change," in *The Planning of Change* (3rd ed.), eds. Warren G. Bennis and others, pp. 231–45. New York: Holt, Rinehart & Winston, 1976.

DAVIS, ALLEN, "Settlements: History," in *Encyclopedia of Social Work* (vol. 2), pp. 1175–80. New York: National Association of Social Workers, 1971.

DEWEY, JOHN, *How We Think*. Lexington, Mass.: Heath, 1933.

ELLIS, A., and R.A. HARPER, *A New Guide to Rational Living*. Englewood Cliffs, N.J.: Prentice-Hall, Inc., 1975.

EMPEY, LaMAR T. and MAYNARD L. ERICKSON, *The Provo Experiment: Evaluating Community Control of Delinquency*. Lexington, Mass.: Heath, 1972.

FAIRWEATHER, GEORGE W., ed., *Social Psychology in Treating Mental Illness: An Experimental Approach*. New York: John Wiley, 1964.

FAIRWEATHER, GEORGE and others, *Community Life for the Mentally Ill: An Alternative to Institutional Care*. Chicago: Aldine, 1969.

FISCHER, JOEL, *Effective Casework Practice*. New York: McGraw-Hill, 1978.

FOLLETT, MARY PARKER, *The New State*, New York: Longmans, 1926.

GAMBRILL, EILEEN, and CHERYL A. RICHEY, "An Assertion Inventory for Use in Assessment and Research," *Behavior Therapy*, 6 (1975), 350–62.

GARFIELD, SOL L., and ALLEN BERGIN, eds., *Handbook of Psychotherapy and Behavior Change: An Empirical Analysis* (2nd ed.). New York: John Wiley, 1978.

GARVIN, CHARLES, "Group Process: Usage and Uses in Social Work Practice," in *Individual Change Through Small Groups*, eds. Paul Glasser, Rosemary Sarri, and Robert Vinter, pp. 209–32. New York: Free Press, 1974.

———. "Education for Generalist Practice: A Comparative Analysis of Current Modalities," in *Teaching for Competence in the Delivery of Direct Services*. New York: Council on Social Work Education, 1976.

GARVIN, CHARLES D., and PAUL H. GLASSER, "Social Group Work: The Preventative and Rehabilitative Approach," in *Individual Change Through Small Groups*, eds. Paul Glasser, Rosemary Sarri, and Robert Vinter, pp. 34–49. New York: Free Press, 1974.

GARVIN, CHARLES D., WILLIAM REID, and LAURA EPSTEIN, "A Task-Centered Approach," in *Theories of Social Work with Groups*, eds. Robert W. Roberts and Helen Northen, pp. 238–67. New York: Columbia University Press, 1976.

GELLER, JANET A., "Reaching the Battering Husband," *Social Work With Groups*, 1 (Spring 1978), 27–38.

GLASSER, PAUL H., and CHARLES D. GARVIN, "An Organizational Model," in *Theories of Social Work with Groups*, eds. Robert W. Roberts and Helen Northen, pp. 75–115. New York: Columbia University Press, 1976.

GLASSER, PAUL and others, "Group Work Intervention in the Social Environment," in *Individual Change Through Social Groups*, eds. Paul Glasser, Rosemary Sarri, and Robert Vinter, pp. 292–306. New York: Free Press, 1974.

GLASSER, PAUL, ROSEMARY SARRI, and ROBERT VINTER, eds., *Individual Change Through Small Groups*. New York: Free Press, 1974.

GOLDSTEIN, ARNOLD P., and FREDERICK H. KANFER, eds., *Maximizing Treatment Gains: Transfer Enhancement in Psychotherapy*. New York: Academic Press, 1979.

GOLDSTEIN, ARNOLD, KENNETH HELLER, and LEE SECHREST, *Psycho-*

therapy and the Psychology of Behavior Change. New York: John Wiley, 1966.

GOLDSTEIN, ARNOLD P., ROBERT P. SPRAFKIN, and N. JANE GERSHAW, *Skill Training for Community Living: Applying Structured Learning Therapy.* Elmsford, N.Y.: Pergamon Press, 1976.

GOTTMAN, D.M. and S.R. LEIBLUM, *How to Do Psychotherapy and How to Evaluate It.* New York: Holt, Rinehart & Winston, 1974.

HARTFORD, MARGARET E., *Working Papers Toward a Frame of Reference for Social Group Work.* New York: National Association of Social Workers, 1962.

———. *Groups in Social Work.* New York: Columbia University Press, 1972.

———. "Group Methods and Generic Practice," in *Theories of Social Work with Groups,* eds. Robert W. Roberts and Helen Northen, pp. 45–74. New York: Columbia University Press, 1976.

HARTMAN, ANN, "Anome and Social Casework," *Social Casework,* 50 (1969), 131–37.

HASENFELD, YEHESKEL, "Organizational Factors in Service to Groups," in *Individual Change Through Small Groups,* eds. Paul Glasser, Rosemary Sarri, and Robert Vinter, pp. 307–24. New York: Free Press, 1974.

HERSEN, M., and D.H. BARLOW, *Single Case Experimental Designs.* Elmsford, N.Y.: Pergamon Press, 1976.

HOWE, IRVING, *World of our Fathers.* New York: Simon & Schuster, 1976.

KAISER, CLARA A., *The Group Records of Four Clubs.* Cleveland: Western Reserve University, 1930.

KIRESUK, THOMAS J. and GEOFFREY GARWICK, "Basic Goal Attainment Procedures," in *Social Work Processes* (2nd ed.), eds. Beulah R. Compton and Burt Galaway. Homewood, Ill.: Dorsey Press, 1979.

KLEIN, ALAN F., *Society, Democracy, and the Group.* New York: Morrow, 1953.

———. *Effective Group Work.* New York: Association Press, 1972.

KONOPKA, GISELA, *Therapeutic Group Work with Children.* Minneapolis, Minn.: University of Minnesota Press, 1949.

———. *Social Group Work: A Helping Process* (2nd ed.). Englewood Cliffs, N.J.: Prentice-Hall, Inc., 1972.

KUBLER-ROSS, ELIZABETH, *On Death and Dying,* New York: Macmillan, 1964.

LANG, NORMA C., "A Broad Range Model of Practice with the Social Work Group," *Social Service Review,* 46 (1972), 76–89.

LANG, NORMA C., "A Comparative Examination of Therapeutic Uses of Groups in Social Work and in Adjacent Human Service Professions: Part II—The Literature from 1969–1978," *Social Work with Groups,* 2, no. 2 (Fall 1979), 197–220.

LANGE, ARTHUR J., and PATRICIA JAKUBOWSKI, *Responsible Assertive Behavior.* Champaign, Ill.: Research Press, 1976.

LAWRENCE, HARRY, and MARTIN SUNDEL, "Behavior Modification in Adult Groups," *Social Work,* 17 (1972), 34–43.

LIEBERMAN, MORTON A., "Group Methods," in *Helping People Change,* eds. Frederick A. Kanfer and Arnold P. Goldstein, pp. 433–486. New York: Pergamon Press, 1975.

LIEBERMAN, M.A., I. Yalom, and M. MILES, *Encounter Groups: First Facts.* New York: Basic Books, 1973.

LINDEMAN, EDUARD C., *The Community.* New York: Association Press, 1921.

LONDON, PERRY, *Behavior Control.* New York: Harper & Row, Pub., 1971.

MIDDLEMAN, RUTH R., and GALE GOLDBERG, *Social Service Delivery: A*

Structural Approach to Social Work Practice. New York: Columbia University Press, 1974.

MILLS, THEODORE M., *The Sociology of Small Groups*, Englewood Cliffs, N.J.: Prentice-Hall, Inc., 1967.

MORENO, J.L., *Psychodrama* (rev. ed.). Beacon, N.Y.: Beacon House, Inc., 1964.

MURPHY, MARJORIE, *The Social Group Work Method in Social Work Education*, New York: Council on Social Work Education, 1959.

NEWSTETTER, W.I., "What Is Social Group Work?" in *Proceedings of the National Conference on Social Work*, pp. 291–99. Chicago: University of Chicago Press, 1935.

NORTHEN, HELEN, *Social Work With Groups*. New York: Columbia University Press, 1969.

NORTHEN, HELEN, "Psychosocial Practice in Small Groups," in *Theories of Social Work With Groups*, eds. Robert W. Roberts and Helen Northen, pp. 116–52. New York: Columbia University Press, 1976.

PAPELL, CATHERINE P., and BEULAH ROTHMAN, "Social Group Work Models: Possession and Heritage," *Journal of Education for Social Work*, 2, no. 2 (Fall 1966), 66–77.

PARLOFF, MORRIS B., IRENE E. WASKOW, and BARRY E. WOLFE, "Research on Therapist Variables in Relationship to Process and Outcome," *Handbook of Psychotherapy and Behavior Change: An Empirical Analysis* (2nd ed.), eds. Sol L. Garfield and Allen Bergin, pp. 233–82. New York: John Wiley, 1978.

PERLS, FRITZ, R.F. HEFFERLINE, and PAUL GOODMAN, *Gestalt Therapy*. New York: Julian Press, 1951.

PFEIFFER, J. WILLIAM, and JOHN E. JONES, eds., *A Handbook of Structured Experiences for Human Relations Training*. LaJolla, Calif.: University Associates, 1974 [issued annually].

PINCUS, ALLEN, and ANNE MINAHAN, *Social Work Practice: Model and Method*. Itasca, Ill.: F.E. Peacock, 1973.

RATHUS, S.A., "A 30-Item Schedule for Assessing Assertive Behavior," *Behavior Research and Therapy* Vol. 11 (1973), 398–406.

REDL, FRITZ, and DAVID WINEMAN, *Controls From Within*. New York: Free Press, 1956.

REID, WILLIAM, and LAURA EPSTEIN, *Task-Centered Casework*. New York: Columbia University Press, 1972.

ROONEY, RONALD, "Adolescent Groups in Public Schools," in *Task-Centered Practice*, eds. William J. Reid and Laura Epstein, pp. 168–82. New York: Columbia Press, 1977.

ROSE, SHELDON, *Treating Children in Groups*. San Francisco: Jossey-Bass, 1972.

———. *Group Therapy: A Behavioral Approach*. Englewood Cliffs, N.J.: Prentice-Hall, Inc., 1977.

ROSE, S.D., J.J. GAYNER, and J.L. EDLESON, "Measuring Interpersonal Competence," *Social Work*, 22 (1977), 125–29.

SARRI, ROSEMARY, and MAEDA GALINSKY, "A Conceptual Framework for Group Development," in *Individual Change Through Small Groups*, eds. Paul Glasser, Rosemary Sarri, and Robert Vinter, pp. 71–88. New York: Free Press, 1974.

SCHOPLER, JANICE H., and MAEDA GALINSKY, "Goals in Social Group Work

Practice: Formulation, Implementation, and Evaluation," in *Individual Change Through Small Groups*, eds. Paul Glasser, Rosemary Sarri, and Robert Vintger, pp. 126–48. New York: Free Press, 1974.

SCHULMAN, EVALINE D., *Intervention in Human Services* (2nd ed.). St. Louis, Mo.: C.V. Mosby, 1978.

SCHUTZ, WILLIAM C., *FIRO: A Three Dimensional Theory of Interpersonal Orientations*. New York: Holt, Rinehart & Winston, 1958.

SCHWARTZ, WILLIAM, "The Social Worker in the Group," in *New Perspectives on Service to Groups*, pp. 7–29. New York: Columbia University Press, 1961.

———. "Social Group Work: The Interactionist Approach," *Encyclopedia of Social Work* (vol. 2), pp. 1252–63. New York: National Association of Social Workers, 1971.

———. "Neighborhood Centers and Group Work," in *Research in the Social Services: A Five Year Review*, ed. Henry S. Maas, pp. 130–91. New York: National Association of Social Workers, 1971.

———. "Between Client and System: The Mediating Function," in *Theories of Social Work with Groups*, eds. Robert W. Roberts and Helen Northen, pp. 171–97. New York: Columbia University Press, 1976.

SHAFFER, JOHN B.P., and DAVID GALINSKY, *Models of Group Therapy and Sensitivity Training*. Englewood Cliffs, N.J.: Prentice-Hall, Inc., 1974.

SHALINSKY, WILLIAM I., "The Effects of Group Composition on Aspects of Group Functioning" (unpublished DSW dissertation, Western Reserve University, 1967).

SHAW, MARVIN E., *Group Dynamics: The Psychology of Small Group Behavior*. New York: McGraw-Hill, 1976.

SHERMAN, T.M., and W.H. CORMIER, "The Use of Subjective Scales for Measuring Interpersonal Reactions," *Journal of Behavior Therapy and Experimental Psychology*, 3 (1972), 279–80.

SCHULMAN, LAWRENCE, "Scapegoats, Group Workers, and Pre-emptive Intervention," *Social Work*, 12, no. 2 (1967), 37–43.

SIMON, SIDNEY B., LELAND W. HOWE, and HOWARD KIRSCHENBAUM, *Values Clarification: A Handbook of Practical Strategies for Teachers and Students*. New York: Hart Publishing Co., Inc., 1972.

SIPORIN, MAX, *Introduction to Social Work Practice*. New York: Macmillan, 1975.

SLAVSON, S.R., *Creative Group Education*. New York: Association Press, 1937.

SMALLEY, RUTH E., *Theory for Social Work Practice*. New York: Columbia University Press, 1967.

SOMERS, MARY LOUISE, "Problem Solving in Small Groups," in *Theories of Social Work with Groups*, eds. Robert W. Roberts and Helen Northen, pp. 331–67. New York: Columbia University Press, 1976.

SPERGEL, IRVING, *Street Gang Work: Theory and Practice*. Reading, Mass.: Addison-Wesley, 1966.

THIBAUT, JOHN W., and HAROLD H. KELLEY, *The Social Psychology of Groups*. New York: John Wiley, 1959.

TRECKER, HARLEIGH B., ed., *Group Work: Foundations and Frontiers*. New York: Whiteside, Inc., 1955.

———. ed., *Group Work in the Psychiatric Setting*. New York: Whiteside, Inc., 1956.

TROPP, EMANUEL, "Social Group Work: The Developmental Approach," *Ency-*

clopedia of Social Work (vol. 2), pp. 1246–52. New York: National Association of Social Workers, 1971.

———. "Developmental Theory," in *Theories of Social Work with Groups*, eds. Robert W. Roberts and Helen Northen, pp. 198–237. New York: Columbia University Press, 1976.

TRAUX, C.B., R.R. CARKHUFF, and I. RODMAN, JR., "Relationships Between Therapist Offered Conditions and Patient Change in Group Psychotherapy," *Journal of Clinical Psychology*, 21 (1965), 327–29.

TRAUX, C.B., J. WITTMER, and D.G. WARGO, "Effects of the Therapeutic Conditions of Accurate Empathy, Non-possessive Warmth, and Genuineness on Hospitalized Mental Patients During Group Therapy," *Journal of Clinical Psychology*, 27 (1971), 137–42.

VINTER, ROBERT D., "Group Work: Perspectives and Prospects," in *Social Work With Small Groups*, pp. 128–49. New York: National Association of Social Workers, 1959.

———. "Analysis of Treatment Organizations," *Social Work* 8 (1963), 3–15.

———. "Social Group Work," in *Encyclopedia of Social Work*, pp. 715–24. New York: NASW, 1965.

———. "Program Activities: An Analysis of Their Effects on Participant Behavior," in *Individual Change Through Small Groups*, eds. Paul Glasser, Rosemary Sarri, and Robert Vinter, pp. 233–43. New York: Free Press, 1974.

———. "The Essential Components of Group Work Practice," in *Individual Change Through Small Groups*, eds. Paul Glasser, Rosemary Sarri, and Robert Vinter, pp. 9–33. New York: Free Press, 1974.

VORRATH, HARRY, and LARRY BRENDTRO, *Positive Peer Culture*. Chicago: Aldine, 1974.

WHITAKER, DOROTHY STOCK, and MORTON A. LIEBERMAN, *Psychotherapy Through the Group Process*. New York: Atherton Press, 1965.

WILLIAMSON, MARGARETTA, *The Social Worker in Group Work*. New York: Harper & Row, Pub., 1929.

WILSON, GERTRUDE, "From Practice to Theory: A Personalized History," in *Theories of Social Work with Groups*, eds. Robert W. Roberts and Helen Northen, pp. 1–44. New York: Columbia University Press, 1976.

WILSON, GERTRUDE, and GLADYS RYLAND, *Social Group Work Practice*, Boston, Mass.: Houghton-Mifflin, 1949.

WOLPE, JOSEPH, *The Practice of Behavior Therapy*, (2nd ed.). Elmsford, N.Y.: Pergamon Press, 1973.

YALOM, IRVIN D., *The Theory and Practice of Group Psychotherapy* (2nd ed.). New York: Basic Books, 1975.

INDEX